Today We Are Cooking...

Today We Are Cooking...

recipes that teach you to think like a chef

Tini Younger

PHOTOGRAPHS BY CAITLIN BENSEL

CLARKSON POTTER/
PUBLISHERS
NEW YORK

TO MY FAMILY FOR THEIR SUPPORT, Antoine for being my taste-tester, my mom for keeping me focused, my dad for working on all my home DIYs, Chef and Leia for being the prettiest models, and my twin girls, who were there with me through the whole cookbook process.

AND THE BIGGEST SHOUTOUT TO MY AUDIENCE, the people who watch and support me, and cook my recipes—without you, this book would not exist.

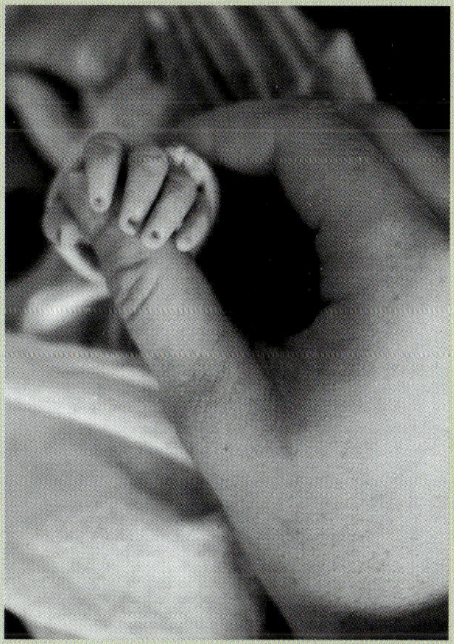

FOR ARYA

In memory of my sleeping angel Arya.
You and your twin sister grew inside of me while I was writing this book. As I progressed with the book, you and your sister progressed into two perfect little babies. This book, from start to finish, was something you, your sissy, and I got to do together—and I'll forever cherish that. We miss you every day.
To my beautiful angel Arya, we love you.

Contents

Foreword

From the moment I met Tini Younger, I knew she was special. She was a contender on *Next Level Chef,* a cooking competition I host with mentors Nyesha Arrington and Richard Blais. Chefs, home cooks, and social media creators work in three types of kitchens: a dream kitchen, a home kitchen, and a rough-and-tumble basement. The challenge is simple: Can you cook incredible food no matter the circumstances?

Watching Tini compete, I saw something you can't fake in the kitchen: passion, instinct, the hunger to learn the *right* way to do things. Yes, Tini is a TikTok star, but first and foremost, she is a great cook.

This cookbook reflects who Tini is as a chef: bold, creative, and deeply connected to the people she cooks for.

She has a real knack for flavor pairings, and her food is approachable without ever compromising. She invites you to get your hands dirty, trust your palate, and get comfortable in the kitchen

You'll find her personality all over these pages, from Tini's "tell it like it is" handwritten notes (don't f*ck up the roux!) to her sketches. She shows, step-by-step, that delicious, comforting food does not need to be intimidating—it needs to be honest and cooked with care. In these pages, she shares a repertoire of recipes you'll genuinely want to cook again and again.

Gordon Ramsay

Introduction
A NOTE FROM ME TO YOU

I had thirty seconds to choose a protein and I blindly grabbed something—it was cow tongue. "What the heck am I supposed to do with a cow tongue?" I thought. I was a contender on Gordon Ramsay's *Next Level Chef,* a competitive cooking television series that pairs contestants with a mentor, and mine was the chef and television personality Richard Blais. Chef Blais walked over to my chef's station and asked, "Have you ever cooked cow tongue?" My answer: uh, a hard no.

Yes, Chef Blais gave me some guidance, but there's no way I would have nailed that challenge and won praise from Chef Ramsay (he said, "It's an absolute delight"—I still get chills!) without discovering, a few years earlier, that I could understand culinary technique better than anything I'd ever done *in my life.*

So no, I'd never cooked cow tongue, but now it's actually one of my husband's favorite dishes. Once I learned how to cook at a basic level—what goes well together, how to make proteins tender, how to properly set up sauces and soups, layer flavors—my whole world got a little bigger and I could apply those techniques to most anything.

When it comes to food, I love to learn about it, make it, and *teach* it. And no, not just uncommon dishes like tongue. My favorite dishes, and the ones I share online, are the ones my husband, Antoine, and I love to eat—classic dishes, comfort foods, dips and wings for game night, cheesy pastas for cozy nights in—as does my online community.

Growing up, I wasn't the best student. I was always getting in trouble, and my grades weren't great. But then, when I got into a high school culinary trade program, my life changed. Something just clicked in the kitchen and my grades skyrocketed from C's and D's to A's and B's. I wanted to cook all the time, whether I was in class or not. I loved every part of it. I continued my education after graduating high school, attending culinary school and getting my degree. I worked super hard on the line in restaurants (sometimes I was the only woman in the kitchen!), and before I knew it, I was standing on Gordon Ramsay's stage and then cooking for millions online.

I never thought my life would pop off like it did. Getting in the kitchen changed everything. Now I want to help others gain their *own* confidence in the kitchen and feel just as passionate and excited about cooking—and making food for family and friends—as I am. Making food from scratch is my love language, and I am excited to share this collection of my favorite recipes that will help generations, young and old, learn to cook. Cooking is about focus—and pouring your heart into what you are doing. Relax and let me—and these recipes—be your guide. My ultimate goal: for you to gain a love for home-cooked meals like I do.

My name is Tineke, but most people call me Tini, pronounced "teeny" as in mar-TINI. I am small so people think I look young, but I studied for years in culinary school and worked in the restaurant industry, learning the techniques that make cooking accessible. I want to share these methods with you. My recipes are built on classic foundations, and if you follow my lead, you will be able to cook meals like a chef, too.

When I packed my bags for *Next Level Chef,* I crammed in three cookbooks: my treasured *Delicious Disney* cookbook (I love Disney!) plus two from culinary school. Those two books are thick, bulky, and definitely not fun. But they are loaded with information and have taught me a lot. Think of this book as a fun but practical take on a culinary textbook: It's cooking school done *my* way with fresh twists on basics—which you'll see are heavily influenced by my childhood in Maryland—and classics for a new generation. This is not a comprehensive culinary encyclopedia, but more like the best-of highlight reel, a crib sheet from someone you trust and who understands the average home cook.

I'm not fancy. I have a lot of training, but absolutely nothing about my teaching, my equipment, or my ingredients is out of reach for the everyday cook. If you are a beginner, fundamental recipes like Herb Butter Whole Roast Chicken (page 44) and Homemade Pasta Dough (page 103) will help you create a solid foundation, and you'll feel so proud after you've done it. You'll see "Learn It" on every recipe that lists the techniques you'll be using. These are essential concepts, like searing, braising, and broiling. You can read more about each one in my Technique Toolkit glossary (page 27). Once you nail these techniques, like searing a steak (see page 50), you'll start to see you can apply them to many different cuts of meats, even vegetables or tofu, and you won't need a recipe to follow. You'll *know* what to do. If you are more experienced, these essential recipes can be ones to build upon with my "Swap It" variations, which are spins and ways to level up a dish. Because I'm a chef, I think like one and have infused my technique-driven recipes with Tini's Tips, so by the time you've cooked your way through this book, you'll learn to think like one as well. I am a visual learner, so I've also loaded this book with how-to photos. I hope these, too, provide lots of clues for success. Regardless of your level of experience, you'll be cooking up killer recipes that your friends and family will love, and your confidence will grow and grow.

In these pages you'll find some of my OG favorites like Tini's Viral Mac and Cheese (page 89), Hot Sauce Buttermilk Fried Chicken (page 37), and my Banana Bread (page 238). These dishes have stood the test of time for a reason. But I'm also excited to share with you dozens of new, original elevated comfort food recipes, all of which have my special Tini spin, like my rich and spicy Coconut Curry Mussels (page 80) or my Creamy Grits with Sautéed Mushrooms and Butternut Squash (page 118). Basic does not equal bland in my book. As I do with my online cooking, I focus on flavors and prioritize fresh ingredients, but ones that are easily sourced. Using fresh produce, even things like herbs, can easily elevate a dish and add layers of flavor.

Because I get into making *everything* from scratch, I've included some project-style recipes that require a bigger commitment and are noted with a "Level Up" icon. That symbol is a heads-up that you will likely need to plan ahead: The recipe may require an overnight rise or special tools, and you should be prepared to follow multiple steps. If you don't feel confident in the kitchen, maybe try a few simpler recipes first.

And anyone who knows me won't be surprised that I've devoted an entire chapter to Game Day, which includes my famous Maryland Crab Dip (page 198). I end the book with my signature holiday and celebratory spreads, including Thanksgiving (think brined turkey with compound butter, page 211) and Christmas (always with traditional soft and Fluffy Milk Bread Buns, page 229).

My hope is that this book will become your go-to cooking guide, one that you'll reach for no matter the need. A book can't teach you *everything,* though. You will need to practice. If a dish doesn't turn out, try to figure out why. Take the time to see if you missed a step or ingredient in the recipe. If you are a beginner, I suggest following my recipes *exactly* the first time through. Then you can start going rogue and do your own thing. Like any new skill, you may pick it up quickly, or you may need to build to mastery a little more slowly. Give yourself space to learn and make mistakes.

Cooking is a basic life skill that I believe people are starting to lose, and no matter your age or skill level, I will be with you on your journey. I want to show you how easy it can be to make the most comforting, delicious foods.

You'll see just how *fun* cooking can be (and it's rewarding when people tell you how much they like your food!). To me, cooking is an art form that promotes creativity, with no hard-and-fast rules—and it's an emotional outlet, too. I'm not one for vocalizing my emotions, so I show my love through food. And for me, sharing these recipes with you is a true labor of love, and I hope you, too, can show your love by feeding someone, or yourself! So show me what you can make today!

Tini

Start Here

Tini's Top Tips for Thinking Like a Chef

- **Start by mastering knife skills.** This includes always having a sharp knife and keeping a wet rag or paper towel under your cutting board. No good chef uses a dull knife, ever.
- **Read *all the way* through a recipe.** You may think chefs don't use recipes, but I will tell you, they do—especially when making something new. Make sure you understand all the steps and techniques used (refer to my Technique Toolkit, page 27). Do you have the ingredients? Do you have enough time? It's important to say here that if you have never made the recipe and make a substitution or skip a step, it may not work. The recipes in this book are meant to be made as written. If you are an experienced cook, it's more than likely you'll know what you can sub or change.
- **Mise en place (you say it meez-ahn-PLAHS) is key.** Chef Anthony Bourdain called it "the religion of all good line cooks." It's a French term that means "to put in place." To me, it means getting your sh#% together before cooking—prepping the ingredients, gathering equipment, getting your head in the game.
- **Clean as you go.** It also helps your mindspace. If the chef de cuisine walked by your station, would they approve?
- **Taste as you go.** Don't wait until the dish is finished to make adjustments—it may be too late at that point.
- **Do not skimp on seasoning!** Chefs love salt. This piggybacks on "Taste as you go," but it deserves its own line. Salt is your best friend in the kitchen. If something doesn't taste just right, oftentimes it just needs a few pinches of salt (or for me, smoked paprika!).
- **Recipe timing is only a guideline!** Look for the visual clues a recipe provides and follow those. If it says "Broil until bubbly and a dark golden color, about 4 minutes" and after 4 minutes it's still pale, continue broiling, watching the dish *very* closely, checking it every minute or so. Everyone's equipment is different, so use your eyes and nose as a timer.

INGREDIENTS I LIVE BY

Like I said, I'm not fancy. I don't buy designer clothes—instead I invest my money in quality ingredients. I go to a butcher for my meat and a fishmonger for seafood. I used to buy my steak at Walmart, and if you do, I say great! It's still a whole food and not a processed one. And if you follow my recipe, it'll taste delicious. My advice: Buy the highest-quality ingredients you can afford—but don't feel pressure to break the bank!

Extra-virgin olive oil A favorite fat. Its fruity flavor enhances foods, and it has health benefits, too.

Unsalted butter Butter is fat and fat equals flavor. I used unsalted butter when developing these recipes so I could control the amount of salt in each dish.

Heavy cream, milk, and evaporated milk I'm a sucker for dairy. I love creamy things, so milk and cream are essential. Evaporated milk is handy to have on hand for added richness to soups and sauces.

Kosher salt, always I usually use Diamond Crystal, which is what you'll find in many restaurant kitchens. It's what I used to test all the recipes in this book. Whatever you do, *do not* use table salt in my mac and cheese or your rubs (or any of my recipes!). It'll make things *way* too salty.

Flaky salt I use it for finishing dishes. It looks pretty and adds more texture than kosher salt.

Freshly ground black pepper You'll never regret investing in a pepper mill for grinding fresh peppercorns. It's much more flavorful than pre-ground. You can also buy disposable pepper mills in the spice section of most grocery stores.

My go-to spices: smoked paprika, garlic powder, onion powder You'll find some combination of these three spices in most of my savory recipes. Buy small containers of spices more often to ensure freshness. Spices lose their potency over time.

Hot sauce I make homemade hot sauce (page 38), and I use store-bought, too, especially Frank's RedHot. It's essential for my Buffalo Wings (page 202), Buffalo Chicken Dip (page 201), and so much more!

Mustard It's a staple that I think of as my secret weapon—it can add a tangy, savory depth of flavor to dishes, but when it's used as a binder or emulsifier (one I use often), you may not even taste it. You should use it even if it doesn't seem important—if I call for it, there's a reason.

Old Bay Seasoning I'm from Maryland, what can I say? It's my favorite spice mix ever.

Fresh herbs I love them all—parsley, thyme, chives, rosemary, basil, tarragon, oregano, cilantro . . . most any herb you name. I use a combination in many recipes, and just like the name, they add freshness.

Alliums It's the group of vegetables that includes all those oniony-type things such as onions, shallots, garlic, leeks, and chives, which are one of the base flavors for many of my dishes. **A YELLOW ONION I, A SHALLOT J, BULB (ALSO CALLED A HEAD) OF GARLIC K, CLOVE OF GARLIC L, A LEEK M, AND A BUNCH OF CHIVES N.**

HERB PREP 101

When I call for a sprig of an herb, it is a single stem such as **A SPRIG OF ROSEMARY A**, or **A SPRIG OF BASIL B**. A bunch of herbs refers to a bundle, such as **A BUNCH OF THYME C**. I use lots of **FLAT-LEAF PARSLEY D**, too.

When a recipe calls for leaves, use your fingers to strip the leaves off the stems E.

When I call for chopped herbs, strip the leaves from the stem and chop them F.

I may call for coarsely chopped G or finely chopped H, depending on how they are used.

A Very Quick Review of Tools + Ingredients

ALL THE TOOLS IN MY KITCHEN

- **A** chef's knife
- **B** Tumbler rolling knife sharpener
- **C** cutting board
- **D** vegetable peeler
- **E** rubber spatula
- **F** offset spatula
- **G** frying spatula
- **H** fish spatula
- **I** tongs
- **J** spider
- **K** instant-read thermometer
- **L** candy thermometer
- **M** metal whisk
- **N** Microplane grater/zester
- **O** box grater
- **P** bench scraper
- **Q** ladle
- **R** measuring cups
- **S** spoons (wooden spoon, slotted spoon)
- **T** citrus squeezer
- **U** fine-mesh strainer
- **V** cheesecloth
- **W** 11 × 17-inch rimmed baking sheet
- **X** potato ricer
- **Y** Le Creuset Dutch oven
- **Z** nonstick frying pan (I like HexClad!)
- **AA** cast-iron frying pan
- **BB** mixing bowl
- **CC** parchment paper
- **DD** plastic wrap
- **EE** aluminum foil
- **FF** Tini's apron
- **GG** cleaning rag
- **HH** pastry brush
- **II** electric mixer or stand mixer
- **JJ** scale

W
P
T
D
F
V
R
O
E
S
H
I
HH
Q
B
N
K
L
TAYLOR
M
G
U
Y
X
GG
Microplane
LE CREUSET

LEMONS AND LIMES

I couldn't cook without them. I use the juice and zest (the grated rind) to add a hit of brightness to my dishes. For zest, I mostly use a Microplane to finely grate **B**. Avoid grating the white pith underneath the peel, though—it has a bitter flavor. And wash your fruit before zesting to remove any waxy coating.

Before juicing, rolling citrus fruit back and forth under your palm helps release the fruit's juices **C**. You'll also get more juice from room temperature fruit. Cut lemons and limes lengthwise to maximize the juice you get **D**.

HOW MUCH JUICE WILL I GET?

1 medium lemon =
3 tablespoons juice + 1 tablespoon zest **A**

1 medium lime =
2 tablespoons juice + 2 teaspoons zest **a**

A citrus press makes juicing easier **E**.

GARLIC

- Smashing a skin-on whole garlic clove with the side of a chef's knife or the bottom of a coffee mug makes it much easier to peel—the skin slips right off A B C.
- I mostly call for "finely grated" garlic, because for beginners, I find grating garlic on a Microplane D is preferable to mincing it. Of course, go ahead and mince the same amount of garlic in any recipe if you prefer.

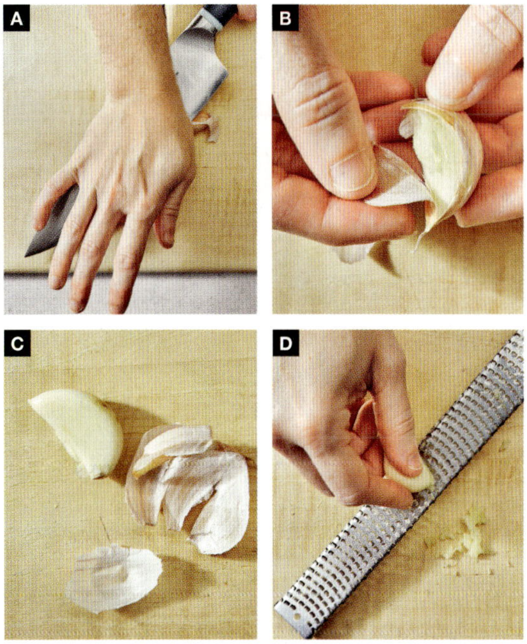

ONE THING: ROASTED GARLIC

I use roasted garlic *a lot!* Slowly cooking a head of garlic turns the sharp-tasting cloves into a smooth, sweet mellow paste. You'll find it in my mashed potatoes (page 218) and my tomato soup (page 145) and many more of my signature recipes. I also like it just smeared on crusty bread.

HOW TO ROAST GARLIC

Makes about ⅓ cup

2 heads of garlic

Extra-virgin olive oil, for drizzling

Kosher salt and freshly ground black pepper, for sprinkling

- Preheat the oven to 400°F. Cut the garlic heads in half crosswise A B. Drizzle the exposed cloves with olive oil and season lightly with salt and pepper. Wrap the garlic tightly in aluminum foil C and place directly on the center oven rack. Roast until fragrant and the cloves are tender, 45 minutes to 1 hour.
- Unwrap the foil packet and let the garlic cool slightly D. When cool enough to handle, squeeze the cloves from their skins and mash into a paste. Store in an airtight container in the refrigerator for up to 1 week.

Knife Skills

ONE KNIFE

- A chef's knife, with a long, broad 8- to 10-inch blade, can handle most kitchen cutting jobs.
- If you were to purchase one knife, this would be it.

bear claw →

KNIFE SAFETY

- Keeping your knives sharp is key. A dull knife is more dangerous than a sharp one.
- I use a Tumbler knife sharpener. I find it's easier to use than a whetstone, which many chefs use.
- Always place a wet towel or paper towel under your cutting board to keep it from slipping.

HOW TO PROPERLY HOLD A KNIFE

- I recommend looking online for knife tutorials. Buy a bag of potatoes and practice basic cutting motions along with a video, which should include a smooth rocking motion that is good to master.
- For a proper grip, hold the handle of the knife near to the blade (choke up on the handle) with the blade between your thumb and forefinger.
- To protect your fingertips, curve your fingers into a "bear claw" grip to hold the foods you are cutting.

HOW TO CUT AN ONION

- Cut an onion in half from root to tip, then cut a thin slice into the onion skin and peel it away **A**.
- Lay one half flat, secure it with your non-dominant hand, and make horizontal cuts across the onion leaving the root end intact **B**.
- Make vertical cuts across the onion, starting at the top end toward the root **C**.
- Make cuts perpendicular to the vertical cuts to create a dice **D**.

CUT SIZES

Dice

- Cut into uniform-size cubes; size of a dice can vary from fine to large.

Chop

- Cut into ¾-inch pieces.

Rough chop

- Cut into 1-inch or larger chunks or pieces.

CHIFFONADE BASIL LEAVES

- Stack the leaves **A**.
- Roll the leaves tightly **B**.
- Thinly slice crosswise **C**.
- Lightly toss to separate the ribbons **D**.

SUGAR
CORNMEAL
EGG NOODLES
ARBORIO
BAKING
BERTOLLI
SUSTAINABLY
VINEGAR AND OIL
SOUP AND SAUCE
OREO
Nature's Own
Honey Wheat
Honey Maid
Ziploc

Tini's Technique and Cooking Terms Toolkit

A GLOSSARY

For those new to cooking, this list will help you get fluent in kitchen-speak. For every recipe, under "Learn It," I've highlighted the techniques you'll be using to make that dish. Refer to this glossary when you want a better understanding of the terms you don't know. I want to teach you *why* you slowly add oil to emulsify it in a sauce and *why* you have to rest meat—I hope you're curious about these things. Commit to putting in the time and you'll be on your way to becoming a great, confident cook!

AL DENTE
A term used to describe food that is cooked until it still has a bite, or gives some resistance, as in pasta—cooked so it's tender yet firm. In Italian it means "to the tooth." It's how I cook the cavatappi for my viral mac and cheese (page 89)!

AROMATICS
Herbs and spices or something like a classic mirepoix (onions, carrots, and celery), used at the early stages of making a dish to build and enhance flavors.

BAKE
Using dry heat, usually in an oven at a temperature of 375°F or below, to cook food, often to keep it moist.

BASTE
Using a spoon or baster to pour juices, butter, or broth over meat to keep it moist. I like to baste with butter, as I do with my roast chicken (page 44), turkey (page 211), and steak (page 50).

BÉCHAMEL SAUCE
A classic white sauce made from a roux and milk and is the base for a mornay sauce, which I use in my mac and cheese (page 89)!

BLANCH
To quickly or partially cook food in boiling water (or hot fat or oil), then immediately cool it (called shocking) by plunging in ice water. Blanching can be used to loosen peels (as in peaches) or to preserve a food's color and texture (as in green beans).

BLOOM SPICES
To heat spices in fat or oil to make them fragrant and more flavorful. This is one of my favorite ways to intensify spices and add to a dish's complexity.

BRAISE
A two-step cooking method that includes searing a food, like chicken or beef, at high heat and then simmering it slowly in a liquid that partially covers it. Check out my short ribs (page 55) to see how this technique makes beef fall right off the bone.

BRINE
There are two types of brines used in this book. A dry brine is when you cover something in salt and refrigerate it, usually overnight, to give the salt rub time to draw out the moisture and allow the meat to reabsorb it for more flavor. It also helps create a crispy skin, like in my pulled pork (page 63). A wet brine is a solution of liquid, salt, and other seasonings used to infuse proteins; the high concentration of the salt breaks down the muscle fibers to make them more tender. I find it makes proteins especially flavorful and juicy, like in my baby back ribs (page 66).

BROIL
To use high, direct heat from above to form a crust or melt cheese. It's almost always the last step in cooking and is the closest you'll get to a salamander in a commercial kitchen. It's a great way to cook seafood as well, like in my bourbon-maple shrimp (page 79).

CARAMELIZE
To cook foods to brown the sugars, which enhances foods by adding a nutty or toasty flavor.

CARRYOVER COOKING
The term for cooking that happens after food has been taken out of the oven—internal temperatures of meat can rise 5 to 10 degrees from the residual heat.

CARVE
Hopefully this one is obvious! Carving is just cutting, as in making it easy to eat (see page 213 for how to properly carve a bird).

CHIFFONADE
To cut leaves, such as basil, or even bigger ones like collards, into pretty, thin ribbons by rolling up a leaf or stack of leaves and thinly slicing the roll (see page 25).

CHOP
To cut food, especially vegetables, into small pieces (see pages 24–25).

CURDLE
To separate milk, egg mixtures, or emulsions into curds (lumps), as in ricotta cheese (page 97). Curdling can be caused in liquids like sauces by high heat and is often unwanted!

CUT IN FAT
To blend fat, usually butter, into flour using a pastry blender, your hands, a food processor, or two forks to make crusts (page 251), biscuits (page 186), or other flaky baked goods.

DEEP-FRY
To fully submerge food in hot oil or fat to cook it. Check out my Hot Sauce Buttermilk Fried Chicken (page 37) to try it for yourself.

DEGLAZE
To add liquid, such as wine or stock, to a pan you just cooked in to release the brown bits (fond) on the bottom of the pan, usually to make a sauce.

DOUBLE BOILER
Two pots fitted together (or a bowl over a pot) used for indirect cooking; water gently simmers in the bottom vessel to warm the ingredients in the top one. It's a good way to melt chocolate (see page 243).

DREDGE
To lightly coat any food with dry ingredients like flour, cornmeal, or bread crumbs with seasoning. I almost always do it when frying. It helps make foods crispy, like my crunchy cornmeal-coated catfish (page 75).

DRY RUB
A mixture of dry seasonings applied to a food's surface, usually a protein, for added flavor, before cooking.

EMULSIFY
To force two usually unmixable liquids, such as water or vinegar and oil, to combine. There are certain ingredients, like an egg yolk, butter, or mustard that can bring unmixable liquids together. To practice emulsifying, make my hollandaise sauce (page 189). Vigorous stirring or shaking can also sometimes temporarily create an emulsion.

EN PAPILLOTE
A cooking method in which food is wrapped in parchment paper or foil and then heated—the steam that is created cooks the food.

FAT CAP
A white layer of fat, usually on the end of meat (which I like to render for flavor!) (see page 50).

FLAMBÉ
To pour alcohol on something and light it on fire. I'm obsessed with doing this, especially with bananas (see page 178).

FOLD
To gently incorporate two different ingredients together, for example egg whites or whipped cream, into dry ingredients. This technique is most often used when making a batter or desserts, like my chocolate mousse (page 234).

FOND
Yummy caramelized, browned bits that form on the bottom of a pan, usually released with a liquid, also called deglazing.

GARNISH
To make food look pretty with edible elements! I think of this as art with food, having fun with it, making it pleasing to the eye.

GLAZE
To brush or pour a thin glossy sauce or coating on sweet or savory foods.

(THE) HOLY TRINITY
A Cajun/Creole mirepoix made up of onions, green peppers, and celery (page 126 for its appearance in Cajun-Inspired Andouille and Rice).

INFUSE
To flavor a liquid by steeping it with ingredients, like herbs into oil.

INJECT
Using an injector to deeply penetrate meats with marinades or brines to add flavor and moisture, and/or to tenderize meat.

JULIENNE
A more cheffy way to cut things into even-size sticks. I rarely call for it, but when I do, like for the ginger in my Peach-Smothered Pork Chops (page 59), it looks really nice.

KNEAD
To work dough, by hand or with a mixer, to develop the gluten. If kneading by hand, push the dough ball forward with the heel of your hand, turn it a quarter turn, and repeat until it is soft, supple, and smooth. Make my Homemade Pasta Dough (page 103), and you'll definitely be kneading.

LEAVEN
To use a substance, either chemical, like baking soda or baking powder, or natural, like yeast, to make a batter or dough rise.

MACERATE
To soften foods, usually by using a liquid, or with fruit, sprinkling with sugar (and even salt). Macerating the apples in a pie gets the juices flowing (see page 251).

MAILLARD REACTION
Searing the meat before baking creates a browned surface in a chemical process called the Maillard reaction. I won't get into the science of it here (it involves proteins and glucose)—it's just a fun term to know because it's important to cooking, as it deepens the flavor of the dish and makes it look better.

MARINATE
To soak foods in a seasoned liquid, often acidic from citrus or vinegar, which can tenderize foods (especially meat by breaking down tough muscle fibers) and infuse them with flavor at the same time.

MINCE
To cut foods, such as onions, garlic, or ginger, into tiny pieces to break down their textures and infuse other foods with their flavors. Once you chop something, just keep going!

MIREPOIX (YOU SAY IT MEER-PWA)
A classic trinity of aromatics—onion, carrots, and celery—coarsely chopped and usually sautéed to add flavors to soups, sauces, and other foods.

MISE EN PLACE (YOU SAY IT MEEZ-AHN-PLAHS)
A French term for prepping your ingredients and equipment before cooking so that you have everything measured and at hand.

MORNAY SAUCE
A béchamel base sauce with grated cheese and seasonings added. This is the sauce I use for my mac and cheese (page 89).

PICKLE
To preserve foods in a vinegar brine or similar liquid. It always makes things a little sour and acidic, which I like. Try pickling butternut squash (page 164).

PLATE
To arrange food on a serving dish. Plating is important because we eat with our eyes first. I always want things to look good for aesthetic appeal—it makes people want to eat what I'm cooking.

POACH
To cook foods in a warm, simmering—not boiling—liquid. I mostly use this for fish (page 72), but it works great for chicken and eggs (page 190), too.

REDUCE
To cook a liquid, such as a sauce, down through evaporation, usually to concentrate it. For example, if you have 1 cup of sauce and the recipe says to reduce it by half, you will cook the liquid until ½ cup remains.

RENDER
To slowly heat meat to melt the fat from it. The rendered fat is then often used for cooking.

REST MEAT
Why rest? Because it allows meat to reabsorb juices and reach its final cooking temperature.

ROAST
To use high heat, usually in an oven at a temperature of 400°F or above, to cook foods and often to create a browned exterior and/or a crispy skin or crust.

ROUX
A mixture of equal parts fat and flour that is cooked together before adding a liquid; it is used to thicken sauces. I'm definitely a roux girl—I use them often.

SAUTÉ
To cook in a pan, usually stirring the food or flipping it in the pan. *Sauté* means "to jump" in French, which makes sense. If I said it to a French person, would they jump?

SEAR
To use a really hot pan and a small amount of fat to give food a browned crust.

SHALLOW-FRY
To partially submerge foods in hot oil to cook and create a crispy crust, like in my crave-worthy pork picatta (page 60).

SHOCK
To quickly cool blanched or partially cooked foods, usually in ice water, to prevent further cooking.

SIMMER
A slow, moist-heat cooking method. Liquids are heated until small, gentle bubbles appear (not boiling). Simmering foods in liquids can tenderize them, as well as develop their flavors, or even the liquid itself.

SLURRY
A mixture of cold liquid and raw starch, like cornstarch or flour, whisked together and used as a thickening agent, usually in sauces, soups, and stews.

STEAM
A moist-heat method of cooking food in which it sits above simmering or boiling water (usually in a basket or rack) in a tightly covered pot and the steam cooks it.

STIR-FRY
A dry-heat cooking method, similar to sautéing; foods are cooked quickly in a wok or high-sided skillet over high heat.

SWEAT
To cook foods in a pan over lower heat to soften them but not brown them.

TRUSS
To tie up meat using kitchen string or butcher's twine to help keep its shape and cook more evenly. My advice: Avoid using dental floss. It can give foods a weird flavor.

WHIP/WHISK
To beat something vigorously, like heavy cream, using a whisk or electric mixer to incorporate air. You'll get plenty of whipping time in making my favorite vanilla ice cream (page 257).

← you can test your oil by dropping in a few bread crumbs; if they sizzle, it's hot enough. you can also dip in a wooden skewer, the oil should bubble up around it if the oil's ready

your oil will start to shimmer and ripple like this when it's ready →

WHAT DOES "HEAT UNTIL SHIMMERING" MEAN?

You'll see me use this phrase over and over throughout the book. If you put food into oil that isn't hot enough, it won't cook properly; it could get soggy from absorbing oil and not develop a golden crust. If it's too hot, the food will burn. When your oil starts to shimmer or develop some ripples, it's the perfect temperature to start cooking.

Mastering Meat

Garlic and Herb Braised Chicken Thighs

WITH BABY POTATOES

Serves 4

- 2½ pounds bone-in, skin-on chicken thighs (6 to 8 thighs)
- 2 teaspoons kosher salt, plus more to taste
- ½ teaspoon freshly ground black pepper, plus more to taste
- ½ teaspoon garlic powder
- 1 tablespoon extra-virgin olive oil
- 1 medium yellow onion, thinly sliced
- 6 garlic cloves, thinly sliced
- 4 large sprigs thyme
- ¾ cup dry white wine, such as sauvignon blanc
- 1 tablespoon Dijon mustard
- 1 tablespoon all-purpose flour
- 1 cup homemade chicken stock (page 134) or store-bought
- 12 ounces small baby potatoes, halved
- 3 tablespoons minced parsley
- 2 tablespoons minced chives
- A loaf of crusty French bread, for serving

Braising is a kitchen workhorse that can be underrated. When was the last time you heard someone say "I'm going to go home and braise some chicken"? I make a lot of braised dishes during the colder seasons because they are so homey and comforting, and are usually an easy-ish one-pot meal. This herby chicken dish hugely benefits from braising. Browning the meat adds to the richness of the sauce. When you deglaze the pan with wine, which means adding liquid to release any cooked caramelized stuff on the bottom of the pan, you add to the complexity of flavors. (If you want to get fancy and use culinary terminology, those flavor-packed bits are called fond.) This dish may seem casual, but it tastes so good you could serve it at a dinner party. Make sure you have a loaf of crusty bread to soak up the savory wine sauce.

TINI'S TIPS

The technique of braising uses dry and wet heat. For this dish, browning the meat (dry heat), then cooking it only partially covered in liquid (wet heat), allows the skin to stay a bit crisp. Make sure you leave the chicken skin exposed, but completely submerge the potatoes for quicker cooking.

Look for the newest, smallest potatoes you can find, because they have thinner skins and are less starchy, so they will cook faster.

1. Brown the Chicken (This Gives It Lots of Flavor!)

- Preheat the oven to 375°F.
- Season the chicken with the salt, pepper, and garlic powder.
- In a large, straight-sided cast-iron skillet or Dutch oven over medium-high heat, add the olive oil and heat until it shimmers. Sear the chicken, skin-side down, until deeply browned and the chicken releases easily from the pan (don't move it around in the pan until you flip it), 6 to 8 minutes. Using tongs, turn and brown the other side, another 2 to 3 minutes. You may need to move the chicken pieces around in the pan for even browning, as some spots may be hotter than others. Transfer the chicken to a plate and pour off most of the fat into a heat-safe container (never put fat or grease down the sink!), leaving about 1 tablespoon in the pan.

2. Sauté the Aromatics

- Lower the heat to medium and add the onion, garlic, and thyme sprigs. Sauté until the onion is softened, about 5 minutes.

3. Deglaze the Pan

- Add the wine and bring it to a boil, stirring with a wooden spoon to scrape up any browned bits (the fond) from the bottom of the pan. Let the wine boil until it's reduced by half, about 2 minutes. Add the mustard, sprinkle with the flour, and stir to combine. Cook for a few minutes until the mixture becomes thickened and saucy.
- Stir in the chicken stock, add the potatoes, then return the chicken to the pan, skin-side up. Really nestle the chicken and potatoes into the liquid: The liquid should come halfway up the sides of the chicken, but the skin shouldn't be covered with liquid. Submerge the potatoes if you can.

4. Braise

- Bring the liquid to a boil. Transfer the pan to the oven and cook, uncovered, until the potatoes are fork-tender and an instant-read or meat thermometer inserted into the thickest part of the chicken thighs reads 165°F, 20 to 25 minutes. The chicken may be done before the potatoes, but it's okay to keep cooking until the potatoes are done. The liquid will keep the chicken moist.

5. Finish the Sauce

- Remove the pan from the oven, then cover the handle with a towel so you don't accidentally touch it and burn yourself (it's easy to forget how hot it is). Sprinkle with the parsley and chives. Taste a potato and season as needed. Serve in shallow bowls with plenty of sauce spooned over the chicken and with bread on the side.

SWAP IT

Change up the vegetables: Replace the potatoes with carrots cut into 1-inch pieces, and/or stir in greens like spinach or chard at the end of cooking.

A
B
C
D

Level Up

Hot Sauce Buttermilk Fried Chicken

Serves 4 to 6

MARINADE

- 2 cups buttermilk
- ¼ cup Tini's Homemade Hot Sauce (page 38) and/or ¼ cup pulp from it, or your favorite hot sauce
- ¼ cup pickle juice
- 1 tablespoon onion powder
- 1 tablespoon garlic powder
- 1 tablespoon chili powder
- 1 tablespoon smoked paprika
- 2 teaspoons cayenne pepper
- 2 teaspoons kosher salt
- 1 teaspoon freshly ground black pepper
- 3½ pounds bone-in, skin-on breasts, legs, wings, and/or drumsticks

DREDGING AND FRYING

- 2 to 3 quarts peanut oil, vegetable oil, or other neutral oil
- 2 cups all-purpose flour
- ¼ cup cornstarch
- 1 tablespoon onion powder
- 1 tablespoon garlic powder
- 1 tablespoon chili powder
- 1 tablespoon smoked paprika
- 2 teaspoons kosher salt
- 1 teaspoon cayenne pepper
- 1 teaspoon freshly ground black pepper

FINISHING AND SERVING

- Flaky salt

There are different kinds of frying, including pan-frying, shallow-frying, and deep-frying. We're going straight for the deep-fry here. There's no reason to wait. I'm here to show you how easy it is. Just follow my steps below and you're guaranteed the juiciest, crunchiest fried chicken. I add the chile pulp from my homemade hot sauce to the marinade for an extra kick. The cornstarch in the dredge absorbs liquid from the marinade, which turns into deliciously crispy, craggy bits when fried. My frying oil of choice is vegetable oil because it's easy to get and you can use it for a bunch of things. When frying for family or friends, do it on the spot so the chicken is nice and hot. (I kind of cheat because I have a heat lamp!) I serve this crispy chicken with whatever sides Antoine wants, usually my mac and cheese (page 89), braised collards (page 214), and a pasta salad. We're talking about everything he grew up with—a whole soul food spread.

1. Marinate the Chicken

- In a large bowl, whisk together the buttermilk, hot sauce and/or hot sauce pulp, pickle juice, onion powder, garlic powder, chili powder, smoked paprika, cayenne, kosher salt, and black pepper.
- Add the chicken pieces and toss to coat **A**. Cover and refrigerate for at least 2 hours and up to 24 hours for the best flavor. (If the bowl doesn't fit in your fridge, you can use a resealable plastic bag instead.)

2. Heat the Oil

- Pour 2 to 2½ quarts of the oil in a 6- to 7-quart pot or Dutch oven. You want at least 1½ to 2 inches of oil in the pot. Heat over high until the oil reaches 350°F on a candy thermometer.

3. Dredge the Chicken

- Meanwhile, in a wide, shallow bowl or dish, stir together the flour, cornstarch, onion powder, garlic powder, chili powder, smoked paprika, salt, cayenne, and black pepper.
- Fit two baking sheets with wire racks.
- Dredge the chicken pieces in the flour mixture using the wet hand/dry hand method **B**, placing the coated chicken on the rack until all pieces are dredged.

4. Fry It Up!

- Once the oil is ready **C**, using tongs or a fry spider, gently lower a piece of chicken into the oil **D**. Add as many as will fit without overcrowding. You want an inch or two between each piece or the chicken won't cook evenly.
- Fry the chicken until it turns a dark golden brown and the internal temperature is 155°F for a breast and 165°F for thighs and drumsticks when inserted with an instant-read or meat thermometer, 7 to 10 minutes, depending on the size of the pieces. Keep an eye on the oil temp and adjust the heat as needed to maintain it at 350°F.
- Transfer the cooked chicken to a clean rack to prevent it from getting soggy.
- Sprinkle with flaky salt and serve piping hot or at room temperature.

WET HAND/DRY HAND METHOD

When you lightly coat a food with a dry ingredient like flour or bread crumbs, called dredging, before frying, it adds flavor and helps form a crust. I use the wet hand/dry hand method when dredging marinated meats: With one hand (or tongs), remove the food, one piece at a time, from the marinade and let it drip into the bowl or bag—the hand you used is now your "wet hand." Set the chicken piece in the coating, and with your other hand (your "dry hand"), turn it several times to get the mixture all up in the creases. Place the coated chicken on the rack and repeat until all the pieces are dredged.

recipe continues ▸▸

TINI'S HOMEMADE HOT SAUCE

I like to use up whatever ingredients I can, so instead of tossing the chile pulp from my hot sauce, I add it to my fried chicken marinade (page 37). You can use the pulp alone or together with a quarter cup of hot sauce, depending on how spicy you like things.

Makes about ½ cup

⅓ cup water

⅓ cider vinegar

2 cups sliced fresh red Fresno chiles (about 8 large peppers) (see Cooking with Hot Peppers!), including the seeds and ribs

6 garlic cloves, coarsely chopped

2 teaspoons kosher salt, plus more to taste

1. Cook the Peppers

- In a small saucepan over medium heat, bring the water and vinegar to a boil. Add the chiles, garlic, and salt. Reduce the heat to low and gently simmer the peppers until they become tender, 10 to 15 minutes.

2. Blend the Sauce

- Transfer the mixture to a food processor or blender and blend until smooth, 2 to 3 minutes. Set a fine-mesh strainer over a spouted bowl or measuring cup and pour the mixture through. Save the pulp for the chicken marinade (page 37), if desired. Taste and add more salt if needed. Store in an airtight container in the refrigerator for up to 2 weeks.

COOKING WITH HOT PEPPERS!

Chile peppers vary in heat, which comes from an enzyme called capsaicin (cap-SAY-a-sin) that can irritate your skin and eyes. For this reason, wearing latex or rubber gloves is a good idea so that after you take them off, there is no residual capsaicin that can burn your eyes or faceif you touch them. (Of course, try not to touch your face while cooking!)

Removing the seeds and the white membranes from peppers can reduce the amount of heat added to a finished dish as well.

REMOVING THE RIBS AND SEED **A**
CHOPPING THE PEPPER **B**

FRY, BABY, FRY!

- Don't let deep-frying intimidate you. The "Oh, wow!" outcome is worth the effort.
- You don't need fancy equipment for frying. A large, high-sided pot or Dutch oven plus a spider or tongs and a slotted spoon work great.
- Use a high-smoking-point neutral oil such as vegetable, peanut, or canola.
- Temperature matters! Use a candy thermometer to maintain the ideal temperature for deep-frying, which is usually 350°F to 375°F. Too hot and your food may burn on the outside and not cook on the inside. If your oil isn't hot *enough,* food will absorb oil and become soggy.

- A candy thermometer, different from a meat thermometer, is heat resistant (it can stay in the oil) and has a wider range of temperatures (most meat thermometers only go to 200°F). They are available in both digital and analog. Keep a close eye on the oil, and raise or reduce the heat as needed throughout the cooking process to maintain the desired temp. When you first put food in to fry, you may notice the temp decrease. You can raise the heat until it reaches temp, then reduce it again. If your oil becomes too hot, you can add a cup or two of unheated oil to lower the temp. It's all part of the technique! Resist overcrowding the oil with too many pieces of food at once.
- If you don't have a thermometer, you can test the oil by dropping in a small piece of bread. The oil is warm enough if it sizzles and floats to the top. If it sinks and no bubbles form, the oil isn't hot enough. You can also test the oil temperature by dipping a dry chopstick into it. If bubbles continuously form around the chopstick, the oil is hot enough.
- Let the oil cool before disposing of it. You can also reuse your oil by filtering it through a fine-mesh strainer lined with cheesecloth and storing it in a jar (or the empty original oil container).

Level Up

Fried Curry Chicken Sandwiches

Makes 6 sandwiches

MARINADE

2 cups buttermilk (see page 185 for how to make your own)

½ cup unsweetened coconut milk

¼ cup red curry paste

2 tablespoons curry powder

1 tablespoon onion powder

1 tablespoon garlic powder

2 teaspoons freshly grated ginger

6 boneless, skinless chicken thighs, about 2 pounds

CURRY MAYO

¾ cup mayonnaise

5 teaspoons red curry paste

1 garlic clove, finely grated

DREDGING AND FRYING

2 to 3 quarts peanut oil, vegetable oil, or other neutral oil

2 cups all-purpose flour

¼ cup cornstarch

3 tablespoons curry powder

2 tablespoons onion powder

2 tablespoons garlic powder

¼ teaspoon kosher salt

Freshly ground black pepper

SERVING

6 soft buns

8 to 10 Quick Pickles slices (page 164) or store-bought

When Antoine hears oil sizzling in the kitchen, he knows something good is coming his way (he loves fried chicken sandwiches!). I start with a coconut-buttermilk marinade, which helps break down the meat's proteins to make it extra juicy and tender. Then I double up on the curry—a red chile curry paste and a powdered spice blend—to make sure the comforting, warm flavors come through nice and strong. Want to know the secret to my perfectly browned, crunchy coating? Cornstarch. It helps keep things light.

> **A TINI TIP**
>
> Take a taste of your marinade to see if you want additional spices. Pre-mixed curry powders vary depending on the blend and brand. If yours doesn't include cinnamon and cayenne, consider adding ½ teaspoon cinnamon and 1½ teaspoons cayenne.

1. Marinate the Chicken

- In a medium bowl, whisk together the buttermilk, coconut milk, curry paste, curry powder, onion powder, garlic powder, and ginger.
- Add the chicken thighs and toss to coat. Cover and refrigerate for at least 2 hours and up to 24 hours for the best flavor. (If the bowl doesn't fit in your fridge, you can use a resealable plastic bag instead.)

2. Whip Up the Curry Mayo

- Meanwhile, in a small bowl stir together the mayonnaise, curry paste, and garlic. Cover and refrigerate until ready to use.

3. Heat the Oil

- Pour the oil into a 6- to 7-quart pot or Dutch oven. You want at least 1½ to 2 inches of oil in the pot. Heat over high until the oil reaches 350°F on a candy thermometer.

4. Dredge the Chicken

- In a wide shallow bowl or dish, stir together the flour, cornstarch, curry powder, onion powder, garlic powder, salt, and a pinch of pepper.
- Fit two baking sheets with wire racks (if you have only one, try to put the raw chicken on one side of the rack, leaving the other side free for the fried chicken).
- Dredge each chicken piece in the flour mixture using the wet hand/dry hand method (see page 37), placing the coated chicken on the rack until all pieces are dredged.

5. Fry It Up!

- Once the oil is ready, using tongs or a fry spider, gently lower a piece of chicken into the oil. Add as many as will fit without overcrowding. You want an inch or two between each piece or the chicken won't cook evenly (see page 39 for more tips on frying).
- Fry the chicken until it turns a dark golden brown and the internal temperature reads 165°F when inserted with an instant-read or meat thermometer, 6 to 9 minutes. Keep an eye on the oil temp and monitor the heat as needed to maintain it at 350°F.
- Transfer the cooked chicken to a clean rack to prevent the chicken from getting soggy.

6. Toast the Buns and Serve

- Meanwhile, in a skillet or toaster, warm the buns and spread each with a tablespoon of the curry mayo.
- Put a piece of fried chicken on each of the bun bottoms, top the chicken with a dollop more of mayo and a few pickle slices. Add the top half of the bun and serve with any extra curry mayo on the side.

WHY MARINATE?

Marinating, or soaking something in a seasoned liquid, adds flavor, and to a certain extent can tenderize foods. Don't leave meat to marinate too long, though, as the acid in the mix can make it mushy. Generally, the heartier the meat—big cuts like pork shoulder—the better it does with a long marinate, and the smaller the cut, the shorter the marinating time. Chops and poultry require as little as 30 minutes to 2 hours. The acid in marinades will "cook" fish, so add them just before cooking for a hit of flavor.

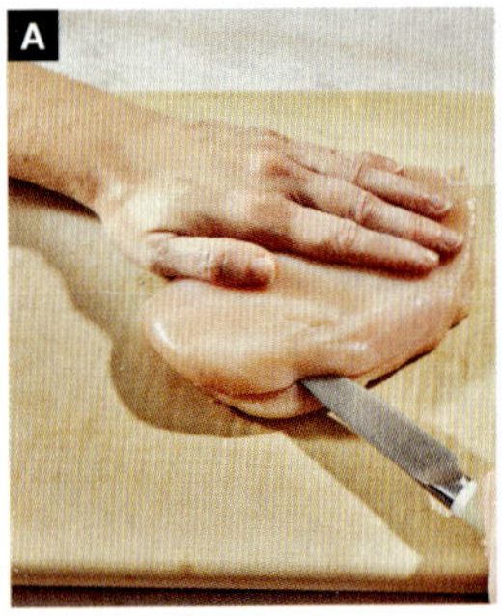
A

B

C

Whatever-You-Have Stuffed Chicken Breasts

Serves 4

FILLING

- 1¼ cups tightly packed spinach, chopped
- 1 cup whole milk ricotta cheese
- 1 ounce Parmesan cheese, finely grated (about ½ cup)
- ¼ cup oil-packed sun-dried tomatoes, drained and finely chopped
- ¼ cup finely chopped basil, plus four leaves for garnish
- 2 tablespoons finely chopped parsley
- 1 tablespoon extra-virgin olive oil
- 1 garlic clove, finely grated
- ¼ teaspoon onion powder
- ¼ teaspoon garlic powder
- ¼ teaspoon smoked paprika
- ¼ teaspoon kosher salt
- ⅛ teaspoon freshly ground black pepper

CHICKEN

- 4 (6- to 8-ounce) boneless, skinless chicken breasts
- 1 teaspoon kosher salt
- ½ teaspoon onion powder
- ½ teaspoon garlic powder
- ½ teaspoon freshly ground black pepper
- ¼ teaspoon smoked paprika
- 3 tablespoons extra-virgin olive oil

When I'm hungry, tired, and not wanting to cook because I've just come off a big job or have been traveling, I make this quick, cheap but still delicious meal. It's my version of a lazy dinner, and that's really big on the "my," because you can use whatever you have to stuff the chicken, which keeps things economical but interesting. I know chicken breasts may seem bland, which is why slicing them in half and filling them up makes them anything but. I particularly like a combo of ricotta and Parmesan with spinach and sun-dried tomatoes for a creamy, flavor-packed punch. Think of it as a choose-your-own-adventure. Try my version first to learn the technique, then freestyle it the next time (see Swap It below).

A TINI TIP

Searing the meat before baking creates a browned surface in a chemical process called the Maillard reaction, which deepens the flavor of the dish and makes it look better.

1. Get Ready

- Place a rack in the center of the oven and preheat to 375°F. Line a rimmed baking sheet with parchment paper or foil.

2. Make the Filling

- In a medium bowl, combine the spinach, ricotta, Parmesan, sun-dried tomatoes, chopped basil, parsley, olive oil, garlic, onion powder, garlic powder, smoked paprika, salt, and pepper. Stir well and set aside.

3. Prep the Chicken

- Place a chicken breast flat on a cutting board. Using a sharp, small knife, hold the breast steady with your palm and, starting at the thicker end, carefully insert the tip of the knife into the side, keeping it parallel to the board. Slice into the middle of the breast to create a deep, wide pocket, being careful not to cut all the way through **A**. Repeat with the remaining breasts.
- With clean hands, scoop up a quarter of the filling and form it into a long, oval shape. Open each chicken breast and insert the filling, spreading it with your fingers to evenly distribute it. Stuff in as much as you can—it's okay if some is peeking out **B**.
- Seal the cut sides of each breast with three toothpicks, inserted at an angle so they don't interfere with searing **C**.
- In a small bowl, stir together the salt, onion powder, garlic powder, pepper, and smoked paprika.
- Sprinkle the spice mix all over the chicken until it's fully coated.

4. Cook the Chicken (We Want It Nice and Golden Here)

- In a large ovenproof or cast-iron skillet over medium-high heat, add the olive oil and heat until it shimmers. Carefully place the chicken in the pan, keeping the toothpicks secure. Sear the chicken (don't move it around in the pan until you flip it) until deeply browned on both sides, 2 to 3 minutes per side. Using a spatula, transfer the chicken to the prepared baking sheet.
- Bake until the chicken is cooked through and registers 155°F on an instant-read thermometer, about 20 minutes. Let the chicken rest for 5 minutes before serving.

5. Chiffonade the Basil and Serve

- Chiffonade (see page 25) sounds fancy, but it's easy. While the chicken bakes, stack the remaining basil leaves on a cutting board and roll them up. Using a sharp knife, slice the roll into thin strips to make ribbons. Using your fingers, pull the strips apart.
- Spoon any sauces from the pan over the chicken before serving. Garnish with the basil ribbons and serve.

SWAP IT

Get creative with your fillings. Here are some of my favorite combos:

- Cream cheese, broccoli, cheddar, and onion
- Sautéed onion, shallot, and bell pepper with any cheese you'd like
- Switch out the spinach for other greens like kale or Swiss chard
- Stuff the breasts with leftover dips, like my Buffalo Chicken Dip (page 201)

Herb Butter Whole Roast Chicken

Serves 4

DRY BRINE

- 1 tablespoon kosher salt
- 1 tablespoon chopped rosemary
- 1 tablespoon chopped thyme
- 1 tablespoon chopped parsley
- ½ teaspoon freshly ground black pepper
- ½ teaspoon sugar
- 1 whole chicken (4 to 5 pounds)

HERB BUTTER

- 1 stick (8 tablespoons) unsalted butter, softened
- 4 garlic cloves, chopped
- 2 tablespoons extra-virgin olive oil
- 2 tablespoons chopped chives
- 2 tablespoons fresh rosemary leaves
- 2 tablespoons fresh thyme leaves
- 1 tablespoon fresh parsley leaves
- 1 tablespoon Dijon mustard
- 1 teaspoon smoked paprika
- ½ teaspoon freshly ground black pepper
- Zest of 1 lemon

Roasting a whole chicken was the first practical we did in culinary school—the equivalent of a first-term exam. We had four hours to make a whole spread, which was nothing compared to the speedy, competitive cooking I had to do on *Next Level Chef,* but still, it was challenging. Thankfully there's no rush for you. Give yourself time to learn this process. Dry brining the chicken overnight—rubbing the skin with a mixture of salt and, here, some herbs—makes the meat succulent and juicy, as does basting it during cooking. Once you get the technique of roasting chicken down, it's one of the easiest and most satisfying home-cooked meals you can make. It's easy on your budget, too—a whole bird costs around thirteen dollars and can feed a family of four. Save the carcass to use for chicken stock (page 134).

TINI'S TIPS

Bring the chicken to room temperature before smearing with the herb butter—condensation on a cold chicken will make it challenging.

I truss my bird, which means to tie it up, but it's not totally necessary. I find it helps for even cooking and keeps it together for a prettier presentation—otherwise your bird will splay. If you want to try something easier that doesn't require binding up the whole bird like I do in the instructions, just tie the legs together with butcher's twine and tuck the wings so they don't burn.

If you don't have a roasting rack, you can set your bird on five or six crumpled balls of aluminum foil to raise it.

1. Dry Brine the Chicken (Your Secret Weapon to a Juicy Bird!)

- In a small bowl, combine the salt, rosemary, thyme, parsley, pepper, and sugar and mix well with your fingers to combine.
- Place a wire rack in a roasting pan (the smaller the better to contain the juices when roasting) and put the chicken on top (see Tini's Tips). Remove and discard the neck and giblets if included and pat the chicken dry with paper towels. Using your fingers, rub the dry brine all over and inside the bird **A**. Place the chicken, uncovered, in the fridge, for at least 12 hours and up to 24 hours.
- When you're a couple hours out from roasting the chicken, take it out of the fridge to sit at room temperature for at least 90 minutes and up to 2 hours. There is no need to rinse off the brine.

2. Get Ready

- Preheat the oven to 400°F.

3. Make the Herb Butter

- In a food processor or blender, combine the butter, garlic, olive oil, chives, rosemary, thyme, parsley, mustard, smoked paprika, pepper, and lemon zest and pulse or run until well combined. You can also do this by hand and it'll be just fine. Mince everything up and stir it into the butter.
- With a rubber spatula or slightly damp hands, smear the butter all over the chicken and under the skin **B**. To do this, gently slide your fingers under the skin to loosen it from the meat, being careful not to rip it. Smear more butter all over the breast meat under the skin.

← carefully separate the skin from the meat so it doesn't rip

recipe and ingredients continue ▸▸

ROASTING

5 medium red potatoes, cut into halves

3 carrots, halved lengthwise

2 sweet onions, peeled and cut in half

2 tablespoons extra-virgin olive oil

Kosher salt and freshly ground black pepper

2 heads of garlic, cut in half

1 lemon, cut in half

2 sprigs rosemary

2 sprigs thyme

1 sprig parsley

1 cup homemade chicken stock (page 134) or store-bought

SPECIAL EQUIPMENT

Butcher's twine, instant-read thermometer

4. Prep Your Vegetables

- Remove the rack from the roasting pan you used for brining and add the potatoes, carrots, and onions. Drizzle with the olive oil and sprinkle generously with salt and pepper. Toss to coat.

5. Stuff and Truss the Chicken

- Place the chicken breast-side up on top of the vegetables and stuff it with the garlic heads, lemon halves, and sprigs of rosemary, thyme, and parsley **C**.
- Tuck the wings under the bird. Start with a piece of twine about 1½ times your arm's length. Start at the top of the bird and bring the twine down around the sides over the wings, cross the twine at the bottom, wrap it around each thigh, then up and around the ankles, cross the twine again to secure the feet, and tie it with a firm knot **D**. Cut off any excess string.

6. Roast and Baste the Chicken

- Pour the chicken stock into the pan and put your chicken in the oven. Then every 20 minutes, using a large spoon, pour the juices that have accumulated in the pan over your chicken. Continue to roast until the chicken is deeply golden brown all over and an instant-read thermometer registers 160°F when inserted in the center of a thigh, about 1 hour and 15 minutes. If the chicken's getting too dark while it's baking, tent the dark spots with small pieces of aluminum foil.

7. Rest and Serve (Don't Rush This Part—You Want Her to Be Juicy!)

- Let the chicken rest for 15 minutes before carving (see page 213). Serve the carved chicken on a platter with the roasted vegetables.

SWAP IT

Hot Honey Roast Chicken

Follow the procedure for the roast chicken, but skip stuffing the bird, nix the vegetables, and replace the herb dry brine with 2 tablespoons kosher salt, 1 packed tablespoon brown sugar, 1 teaspoon smoked paprika, and ½ teaspoon ancho chili powder. Replace the herb butter with a hot honey butter: In a medium bowl, combine 1 stick of very soft unsalted butter, ½ teaspoon black pepper, 1 teaspoon onion powder, 1 teaspoon garlic powder, 2 tablespoons Frank's RedHot or your favorite hot sauce, and ¼ cup honey and mix well.

CARRYOVER COOKING AND RESTING

You may notice in many of my recipes I tell you to stop cooking your meat before it reaches its final temperature. I do this because meat keeps cooking when you take it out of the oven—internal temperatures can rise 5 to 10 degrees from the residual heat, which is called carryover cooking. Allowing meat to rest for at least 10 minutes after cooking is key to a juicy finish. The extra time allows the meat to redistribute juices that have contracted during cooking, so they don't run out when you cut in.

Chimichurri-Marinated Flank Steak Tacos

WITH GRILLED CORN SALSA

Serves 4 to 6

CHIMICHURRI

- 1½ cups packed parsley, leaves and stems
- 1½ cups packed cilantro, leaves and stems
- 1 jalapeño, seeded if desired for less heat, minced
- 2 tablespoons chopped red onion
- 2 garlic cloves
- 2 tablespoons freshly squeezed lime juice, plus more to taste
- 2 teaspoons oregano leaves
- 1 teaspoon ground cumin
- ½ teaspoon smoked paprika
- ¼ teaspoon crushed red pepper flakes, plus more to taste
- ¼ teaspoon cayenne pepper
- ¾ cup extra-virgin olive oil
- 1 teaspoon kosher salt, plus more to taste
- ½ teaspoon freshly ground black pepper, plus more to taste

TACOS

- 1 flank steak (about 2 pounds)
- Flour or corn tortillas
- Grilled Corn Salsa (page 49)
- Cotija cheese
- Lime wedges, for serving

I grew up on ground beef tacos made from those grocery-store kits that had a packet of dry seasonings for taste. These fresh, flavor-packed tacos are *nothing* like those. I marinate the lean flank steak in my version of a chimichurri, which is an herby, tangy sauce from Argentina that is traditionally used as a topping for grilled meats. I swap lime juice for the vinegar and use tons of herbs for brightness. I save half the sauce for topping the tacos, too, which I know breaks tradition, but who says I'm good at following rules?

TINI'S TIPS

Cutting meat "against the grain" means to cut across its muscle fibers, which results in a more tender bite. If you cut with the grain, your meat will likely be tough and stringy. To find the "grain" on flank steak, simply cut across the long lines you see on the meat.

If you don't have a blender or food processor to make the marinade, you can finely chop everything by hand.

1. Make the Chimichurri

- In a food processor or blender, combine the parsley, cilantro, jalapeño, onion, garlic, lime juice, oregano, cumin, smoked paprika, red pepper flakes, cayenne, and olive oil. Pulse until everything is finely chopped. Season with the salt and pepper. Taste, and add more lime juice, red pepper flakes, salt, and/or black pepper if needed. You should get about 1 cup.

2. Marinate the Meat

- In a resealable bag, combine the steak with ½ cup of the chimichurri. Seal and rub the marinade into the meat. Let stand at room temperature for at least 30 minutes and up to 1 hour (rubbing occasionally), or refrigerate for up to 2 hours.

3. Heat the Grill

- Preheat your grill (or grill pan) to high (or to 425°F with a charcoal grill) with the lid closed.

4. Cook the Steak

- Remove the steak from the marinade and transfer it to a rimmed baking sheet. Using paper towels, blot the meat as dry as you can, scraping off any herbs to prevent them from burning. Drying the meat helps you get a better sear on the grill.
- Grill the steak until a nice char forms on both sides, 5 to 6 minutes per side. An instant-read thermometer inserted in the thickest part will read 130°F to 135°F for medium rare (or use the hand method, see page 49). Set aside to rest.

5. Heat the Tortillas

- While the meat is resting, line a large bowl or platter with a clean kitchen towel. Heat the tortillas on the grill or gas flame until lightly charred on both sides, 30 to 60 seconds per side. Transfer to the bowl and wrap them up in the towel to steam.

6. Slice the Steak and Serve

- Cut the steak across the grain **A**, then into smaller bite-size pieces. Divide the steak among the tortillas. Top with corn salsa, Cotija, and some of the remaining chimichurri. Serve immediately with lime wedges on the side.

← make sure to cut across the grain like this!

recipe continues ▸▸

GRILLED CORN SALSA

You can cook your corn in the husks—lots of people do—but you won't get much, if any, char on the corn. Instead, remove the husks and cook the corn over direct heat, turning occasionally for even charring. Be patient: Corn takes a surprisingly long time to cook on a grill.

Makes about 2½ cups

2 tablespoons freshly squeezed lime juice, plus more to taste

⅓ cup finely diced red onion

Kosher salt

3 ears of fresh corn, husks and silk removed

1 tablespoon extra-virgin olive oil, plus more for cooking the corn

Freshly ground black pepper

1 ripe Hass avocado, pitted, peeled, and diced

⅓ cup finely chopped cilantro

1 serrano or jalapeño, seeds removed for less heat if desired, minced

- Preheat your grill or grill pan to high.
- In a medium bowl, drizzle the lime juice over the onion and sprinkle with 1 teaspoon salt. Set aside to soften.
- Lightly brush the corn with olive oil and season with salt and pepper. Place the corn on the grill. Cook, covered (if using an outdoor grill), turning occasionally, until lightly charred and the color brightens, 8 to 10 minutes total.
- Remove the corn from the grill and let it stand until cool enough to handle. Remove the kernels from the cobs by holding the cob upright in a baking pan or large bowl and cutting downward with a knife (you should get about 2 cups).
- To the bowl with the onion, add the cut corn, avocado, cilantro, and serrano and stir to mix. Drizzle with the 1 tablespoon olive oil. Taste and adjust the seasoning with salt and lime juice. Serve immediately or refrigerate in an airtight container for up to 1 day.

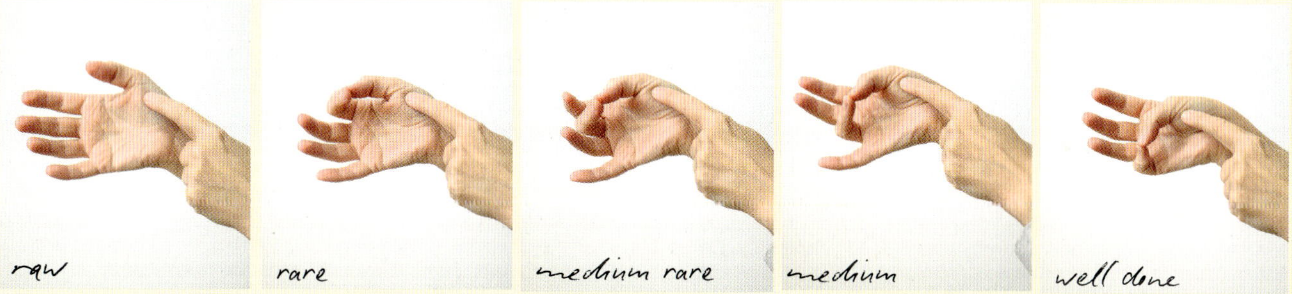

rare: 115°F to 120°F; after resting, 125°F

medium rare: 125°F to 130°F; after resting, 135°F

medium: 135°F to 140°F; after resting, 145°F

well done: 145°F to 150°F; after resting, 155°F

TEST MEAT LIKE A PRO

If you don't have a thermometer to check the temp of your steaks while cooking, use the hand method, which is what chefs often use.

To check for doneness, poke the meat, and then with your opposite hand, press your index finger to your thumb (as shown), and with your other index finger, the one that poked the meat, press the pad of skin right below your thumb (as shown). If the meat feels a similar "squishiness," it is likely rare.

If you press your middle finger to your thumb, the same area under your thumb should be a little firmer, which indicates medium rare. Repeat for your ring and pinky fingers, indicating medium and well done, respectively.

If you do this and also check the temperature with an instant-read thermometer, it can teach you what the doneness levels feel like. (See Carryover Cooking and Resting, page 46, to learn more about "after resting" temps.)

Seared Strip Steaks

WITH RED WINE REDUCTION

Serves 2 to 4

STEAK

- 2 NY strip steaks (each 1 pound and 1½ inches thick)
- Kosher salt and freshly ground black pepper
- 1 tablespoon vegetable oil or other neutral oil
- ½ stick (4 tablespoons) unsalted butter, cut into cubes
- 1 garlic clove, smashed and peeled (see page 23)
- 2 sprigs rosemary

RED WINE REDUCTION

- 1 small shallot, minced (about ¼ cup)
- 2 garlic cloves, finely grated
- 1 teaspoon extra-virgin olive oil
- 1½ teaspoons finely chopped rosemary
- 1½ teaspoons finely chopped thyme
- 1 cup red wine
- 1 tablespoon balsamic vinegar
- 1 teaspoon kosher salt
- ½ teaspoon freshly ground black pepper
- ¼ teaspoon sugar
- ½ stick (4 tablespoons) cold unsalted butter, cut into cubes
- 2 sprigs rosemary and/or thyme, for garnish (optional)

SPECIAL EQUIPMENT

Instant-read thermometer

I make steak at least once a week, and if we have leftovers, the next morning I make steak and eggs (fried over easy, always). As far as cuts go, a thick, juicy strip is my all-time favorite. The good amount of marbling means tender meat that still has good texture. I especially like a thick fat cap (the white layer of fat on the end of the meat), which I render down because fat equals flavor. No matter what type of steak you buy, a good sear is key. You want your pan smoking hot. While the steaks rest, I make a red wine and shallot reduction that becomes a rich, syrupy drizzle you may want to lick straight from the spoon because it's just that good.

TINI'S TIPS

When buying meat, look for steaks with a nice thick fat cap—or ask your butcher to cut them with one. I like to buy prime-grade meat because of the extra marbling, which makes the meat melt in your mouth (choice has less marbling). The price tag can be hefty, though, so get what you can.

Steak temperature is as important *before* cooking as during: Let your steaks come to room temp for a more even sear and cooking throughout. It's also the perfect time to do your mise.

1. Prep the Steaks

- Liberally season the steaks on both sides with the salt and pepper (I'm talking a few generous pinches of each) and let sit at room temp for 30 minutes or up to 1½ hours.

2. Sear the Steaks (It's All About the Crust!)

- Heat a pan, preferably cast-iron, over high heat, for at least 5 minutes. The pan should be ripping hot! Add the oil, then use tongs to hold the steaks fat-cap-side down in the pan **A** (if you can't hold two steaks at once, do this one at a time) until the fat renders (melts) and the edge of the steak turns a deep golden brown, about 3 minutes.
- Sear the steaks on both sides until they get a nice crust, 3 to 6 minutes per side, depending on the thickness and doneness **B**. Do not be tempted to turn the steaks earlier than 2 to 3 minutes. Let a beautiful dark brown crust develop **C**.

3. Baste the Steaks

- Flip the steak back to the side you seared first **D** and add the butter, garlic, and rosemary sprigs. Tilt the skillet 45 degrees up toward you so the butter forms a puddle while sizzling the garlic and rosemary. Using a soup spoon, quickly ladle the butter over the steaks in a repetitive, circular wrist motion until the steaks are cooked to the desired doneness, about 1 minute, or until an instant-read thermometer registers 115°F for rare, 125°F for medium rare, and 135°F for medium, keeping in mind the temperature of the steak in the pan will increase 5 to 10°F after it rests (see Test Meat Like a Pro, page 49).

4. Rest the Steaks (This Is SO Important!)

- Transfer the steaks to a plate and let them rest for 5 to 10 minutes while you make the sauce.

5. Make the Reduction

- In the same skillet you've cooked your steak, over medium heat, add the shallot, garlic, and olive oil. Cook until softened, 3 to 4 minutes.
- Add the rosemary and thyme and cook, stirring constantly, until the herbs are fragrant, about 30 seconds.
- Add the wine, vinegar, salt, pepper, and sugar and bring to a boil. Reduce the heat to medium-low and cook at a gentle simmer, until the liquid has thickened and reduced by about half (it'll almost be syrupy), 4 to 6 minutes.
- Remove from the heat, then add the butter, one cube at a time, whisking constantly to emulsify, until all the butter has melted and the sauce has become thick and glossy, about 2 minutes. It's important to move the pan completely away from the burner; otherwise the butter may "break" instead of emulsifying and you'll get an oily finish and not a creamy one.

6. Serve

- Thinly slice the rested steak against the grain, sprinkle with salt (I do this because the inside of the steak hasn't been seasoned—I learned this on *Next Level Chef*), and drizzle the sauce over the top. Garnish with the fresh herb sprigs, if desired. Serve immediately.

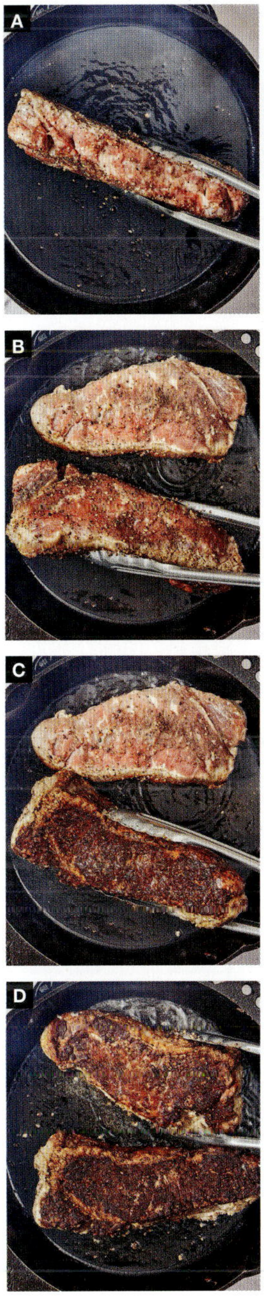

SWAP IT

Switch up the sauce you serve with your steaks. Try my chimichurri (page 47) or your favorite store-bought sauce.

Smash Burgers

WITH HOMEMADE AIOLI

Makes 4 burgers

BURGER PATTIES

- 1½ pounds (24 ounces) 85% lean ground beef, very cold
- 1 teaspoon vegetable oil or other neutral oil
- Kosher salt and freshly ground black pepper
- 8 slices sharp cheddar cheese

FINISHING AND SERVING

- 4 Homemade Brioche Buns (page 258) or store-bought
- ⅓ cup Homemade Aioli (page 54) or store-bought mayonnaise, plus more for serving
- 4 Bibb lettuce leaves
- 4 tomato slices
- Thinly sliced red onion
- Sliced pickles
- 4 slices cooked bacon

I don't like thick burgers because the meat just seems to fall apart. Enter the smash burger. The thin patties stay together nicely, *and* there's room to build up flavors and textures using lots of toppings (I pile 'em high, including two beef patties per roll!). Plus, I think it's really fun to smash things! Whatever you do, don't skimp on the seasonings here. It's key to the burger's crispy, flavorful crust. And if you're up for it, try making my homemade brioche buns. They turn out so perfectly, no one will believe you made them!

TINI'S TIPS

To get a classic "smashed" burger shape, use cold meat for easier handling. For the smashing, most any heavy item will do the job. I like using a cast-iron skillet. A metal spatula works too, and of course if you have a grill press, go for it.

A VERY hot pan is key to searing the meat, which gives the burger a crispy exterior while maintaining a juicy interior.

1. Smash Those Patties!

- Divide the meat into eight 3-ounce pieces and loosely form them into flat round balls. Place one flattened ball on a piece of parchment paper and top with a second sheet. Use the bottom of a skillet and "smash" into a thin patty 5½ inches in diameter (it should be ¼ inch thick or less) **A** **B**. Carefully transfer the patty to a parchment-lined baking sheet and continue to smash all the patties. Put them in the fridge.

2. Toast the Buns

- Split the buns in half and spread 1 teaspoon of aioli on each cut side. Heat a large skillet or griddle, preferably cast-iron, over medium-high heat. Working in batches if necessary, add the buns cut-side down and toast until golden brown, about 3 minutes. Set aside.

3. Cook the Burgers

- Using the same skillet or griddle, raise the heat to high and wait until the pan is smoking hot, at least 3 minutes. Add the oil, then working in batches if necessary, place as many patties as will fit in the pan. Sprinkle the patties generously with a pinch or two of salt and pepper—don't be shy. Using an offset spatula, press down on the patties. Cook until they are very well charred and crisp, about 2 minutes **C**. Flip, season again with another generous pinch of salt and pepper, put a slice of cheddar cheese on each patty, and cover with a lid until the cheese is melted, 1 to 2 minutes. Transfer to a plate and repeat until all the burgers are cooked.

4. Serve

- Serve the burgers, 2 patties per bun, layered with lettuce, tomato, onion, pickles, and bacon, with more aioli on the side.

SWAP IT

Maryland-Style Smash Burger

Instead of salt and pepper, season your burgers with Old Bay Seasoning.

Make it hot!

Add jalapeños and a drizzle of hot honey to your burgers.

A

B

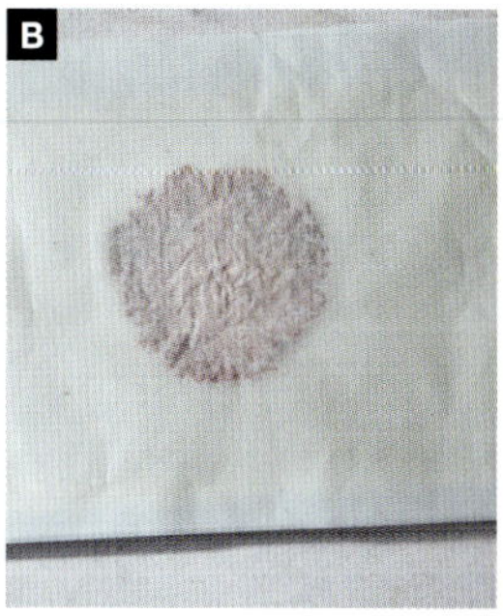

C

recipe continues ▸▸

HOMEMADE AIOLI

Aioli is a garlicky type of mayonnaise sauce that requires making an emulsion, turning oil into a thicker paste. The trick to forming an emulsion is to add the oil VERY slowly at the beginning, like a drop at a time. The more oil that is added, the faster you can add it! It's crazy, but it's true . . . start super-duper slowly, then as the emulsion forms, you can add it a bit faster. If it "breaks," gradually whisk in a teaspoon of warm water, and it should re-form.

Makes 1 cup

- **1 large egg yolk, at room temperature**
- **4 teaspoons lemon juice, plus more if needed**
- **¼ to ¾ teaspoon kosher salt**
- **1 cup safflower oil, vegetable oil, or other neutral oil**
- **1 garlic clove, finely grated**

- Set a large bowl on top of a wet washcloth to stabilize it **A**. Whisk together the egg yolk, lemon juice, and pinch of salt. Very, very gradually, a teaspoon at a time, whisk the oil into the egg yolk **B**, and keep whisking as the emulsion forms. The mixture will eventually start to thicken, which means the emulsion is stronger and you can add the oil in a thin stream (instead of drop by drop) until all of the oil is incorporated **C**.
- Stir in the garlic **D**. Season with more salt, a pinch at a time, up to ¾ teaspoon, and a bit of lemon juice if needed. Store in an airtight container in the refrigerator for up to 4 days.

I'm not kidding, go slowly here when adding the oil

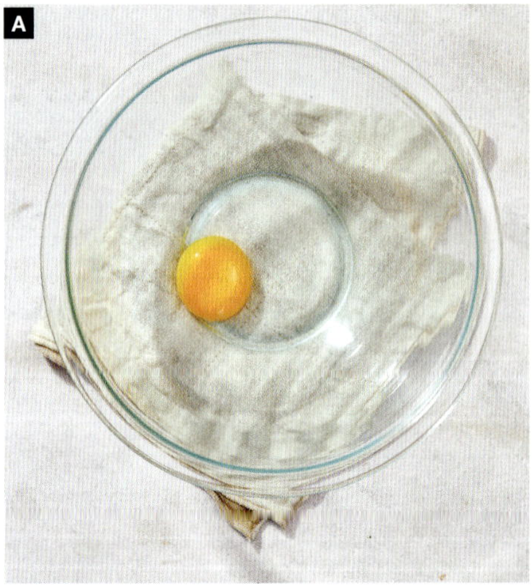

Wine-Braised Short Ribs

Serves 4

- 2 tablespoons kosher salt, plus more to taste
- 2 teaspoons freshly ground black pepper, plus more to taste
- 2 teaspoons garlic powder
- 4 to 4½ pounds bone-in English cut short ribs (6 to 8 ribs)
- 2 tablespoons extra-virgin olive oil
- 3 stalks celery, roughly chopped
- 2 large carrots, roughly chopped
- 1 large yellow onion, roughly chopped
- 1 tablespoon tomato paste
- ½ teaspoon smoked paprika
- 2 cups dry red wine
- 3 cups beef stock, plus more if needed
- 1 tablespoon Worcestershire sauce
- 1 head of garlic, halved crosswise
- 4 sprigs thyme
- 2 dried bay leaves
- 1 sprig rosemary
- 2 tablespoons cold unsalted butter, cut into cubes
- Mashed potatoes (page 218), for serving (optional)
- Finely chopped chives, for garnish

While I was in culinary school, I also worked in a restaurant, and they had the most delicious short ribs on their menu. My job was to reheat the cooked ribs and make the sauce. I wanted to make them at home, so I watched the prep team and then looked through my cooking school textbook for reference. Aha, they were braised. We had not learned that technique yet! It's easy, and foods cooked this way are somehow always deeply satisfying and cozy. Serve these ribs over my garlic mashed potatoes with plenty of the red wine sauce for the ultimate comfort meal. Leftovers make the best sandwiches.

TINI'S TIPS

You can opt for inexpensive dry red wine here, no need to get fancy. I usually use Dark Horse. If you don't want to use wine, you can substitute beef stock, pomegranate juice, or water mixed with a tablespoon or two of balsamic vinegar.

You'll commonly find two cuts of short ribs: English-style and flanken-style, also called Korean-style. English-style ribs, which are what you want for this recipe, are cut parallel to the bone and are usually 5 to 6 inches long. The meat tends to be thicker on this cut and is cooked low and slow, as opposed to flanken-style ribs, which are thinly cut (about a ½ inch or so) across the bone and are usually grilled or pan-fried. If you can't find bone-in English-style short ribs, you can sub in thickly cut boneless ones.

1. Get Ready

- Move a rack toward the bottom of the oven with enough space above it to fit a large pot and preheat to 350°F.
- In a small bowl, combine the salt, pepper, and garlic powder. Season the short ribs all over with the spice mixture, patting the ribs so the spices adhere.

2. Brown the Short Ribs

- In a large Dutch oven over medium-high heat, add the olive oil and heat until it shimmers. Working in batches if necessary, add the ribs.
- Sear the short ribs on all sides, using tongs to cook the short ends, too, until deeply browned all over, 16 to 20 minutes total **A**. Transfer the ribs to a plate and set aside.

3. Cook the Veggies

- To the same pot over medium heat, add the celery, carrots, and onion. Cook, stirring often, until the celery and carrots are softened and the onion is translucent, 8 to 10 minutes.
- Add the tomato paste and smoked paprika. Stir well to evenly coat the veggies, and cook until the paprika is fragrant, about 1 minute.

4. Add the Liquids and Herbs

- Raise the heat to high and pour in the wine **B**. Bring it to a boil and stir well to deglaze the pot, scraping up any browned bits that may have accumulated on the bottom.

recipe continues ▸▸

A

B

- Add the beef stock, Worcestershire sauce, garlic, thyme, bay leaves, and rosemary. Return the short ribs to the pot, meat-side down (the liquid should almost fully cover the ribs—if not, add more stock or water) and cover. Transfer to the oven.

5. Braise

- Cook the short ribs until the meat is completely tender and nearly falling off the bone, 2½ to 3 hours **C**.

6. Make the Sauce

- When the ribs are done cooking, using tongs, carefully transfer them from the pot to a large plate and cover with foil to keep warm.
- Set a fine-mesh strainer over a large measuring cup or bowl and carefully pour or ladle the contents of the pot through the strainer **D**.
- Discard the solids, pour the liquid back into the pot, and bring it to a simmer over medium-high heat **E**.
- Continue to cook the liquid until it has thickened, is a deep, dark brown, and has reduced by about half, about 15 to 30 minutes, depending on how much liquid you started with. Taste the sauce and season with salt and pepper. If it's too salty, add more beef stock, up to 1 cup, and reduce a little more as needed.
- Remove from the heat and whisk in the butter, 1 cube at a time, until the sauce is glossy **F**.

7. Garnish and Serve

- If serving with mashed potatoes, spoon the potatoes onto individual dining plates or a serving platter, top with the short ribs, spoon the sauce over the ribs and potatoes, and garnish with chives.

SWAP IT

Turn leftovers into a short rib ragù to serve over pasta (or polenta): In a medium pot over medium heat, combine 1 (28-ounce) can crushed tomatoes (preferably fire-roasted), 1½ cups leftover short rib braising sauce, and ¾ pound chopped short rib meat. Cover with a lid and cook for 8 minutes. Remove the lid and add 1 sprig rosemary, 2 sprigs thyme, 1 tablespoon balsamic vinegar, and ½ teaspoon freshly ground black pepper. Simmer uncovered, until the sauce reduces a tiny bit and thickens slightly. Remove the rosemary and thyme stems, and season to taste. Serve over pasta or polenta.

Peach-Smothered Pork Chops

Serves 4

- 4 ripe peaches (about 1½ pounds)
- 2-inch piece of ginger, peeled
- ¼ cup all-purpose flour
- 1½ teaspoons kosher salt
- 1 teaspoon chili powder
- ½ teaspoon garlic powder
- ¼ teaspoon freshly ground black pepper
- ¼ teaspoon smoked paprika
- 4 bone-in loin (or center-cut) pork chops (about 1 inch thick)
- 2 tablespoons extra-virgin olive oil
- 2 tablespoons unsalted butter
- 2 large shallots, thinly sliced
- 3 garlic cloves, finely grated
- ¾ cup homemade chicken stock (page 134) or store-bought
- 2 tablespoons packed light brown sugar
- 1 tablespoon cider vinegar
- 2 sprigs rosemary

When I was growing up, my dad made the pork chops in our house—and he cooked them dry. I was not a fan. It seems a lot of people encounter dry chops. If you are one of them, I created this recipe to change your mind. It certainly did mine. Since I live in Georgia, peaches in season are plentiful, and smothering pork with them makes the meat next-level. The savory, fatty chop is perfectly balanced by the sweetness of the fruit and the acidity of the sauce. A hint of ginger and rosemary round out this sweet-tart one-pan meal. You could serve it with a side of creamy grits (page 118), too, for an even more Southern spin.

1. Blanch the Peaches

- Cut a small x in the bottom (or non-stem side) of each peach. Bring a pot of water to a boil and fill a bowl with ice and water. Add the peaches to the boiling water and cook until the skin starts to peel back from the flesh, 1 to 2 minutes. Transfer the peaches to the ice bath and let them cool for 2 minutes.
- Remove the peaches and peel. Cut the peaches into quarters and place in a small bowl. Discard the pits.

2. Get a Little Cheffy and Julienne the Ginger

- Thinly slice the piece of ginger, then stack a couple of the slices and cut into thin strips like matchsticks **A**. Set aside.

3. Dredge the Pork

- In a shallow bowl or dish, stir together the flour, salt, chili powder, garlic powder, black pepper, and smoked paprika. Fully coat, or dredge, the pork chops with the seasoning and put them on a plate or baking sheet.

4. Brown the Pork

- In a large skillet over high heat, add the olive oil and heat until it shimmers. Add the seasoned chops, and cook until golden brown on both sides, about 3 minutes per side. (They won't be cooked all the way through yet.) Using tongs, hold each piece on its side to render and brown the fat cap. Transfer the browned pork chops to a clean plate.

5. Sauté the Peaches and Aromatics

- To the same pan, add the butter and cook over medium heat until it melts. Add the peaches and cook until they begin to caramelize, 3 to 5 minutes. Remove four of the nicest pieces and set them aside for garnish. To the pan, add the shallots, garlic, and ginger. Cook until the shallots are translucent, about 3 minutes.

6. Make the Sauce and Cook the Chops

- Stir in the chicken stock, brown sugar, and vinegar and bring to a boil, scraping up any browned bits from the bottom of the pan.
- Return the pork chops to the pan, snugging them in as much as you can, along with the rosemary sprigs. Bring the liquid to a boil. Cover and reduce the heat to medium. Simmer until the pork chops are cooked through (an instant-read thermometer inserted in the thickest part of the meat next to the bone should read about 140°F), mashing some peaches into the liquid as it cooks to help thicken the juices, 4 to 6 minutes.
- Serve from the pan, topped with the pretty sautéed peaches you set aside. If you prefer to plate the chops, top each one with a couple spoonfuls of sauce and a peach quarter.

5 Level Up

Crispy Pork Parmesan Piccata

Serves 4

CHOPS

- 4 small boneless pork loin chops (about 1½ pounds total)
- Kosher salt and freshly ground black pepper
- ½ cup all-purpose flour
- 2 large eggs
- 1½ cups panko
- 1 tablespoon dried oregano
- 2 cups neutral oil, such as canola or vegetable, plus more for frying
- 4 to 6 ounces fresh mozzarella cheese, thinly sliced

SAUCE

- 3 tablespoons unsalted butter
- 1 tablespoon extra-virgin olive oil
- ¾ cup halved grape tomatoes
- 3 tablespoons capers, drained and rinsed
- 2 garlic cloves, thinly sliced
- 2 teaspoons all-purpose flour
- ½ cup dry white wine
- 2 tablespoons freshly squeezed lemon juice
- 2 tablespoons finely chopped parsley

ARUGULA

- 1 tablespoon freshly squeezed lemon juice
- 1 tablespoon extra-virgin olive oil
- 2½ cups baby arugula
- ¼ cup parsley leaves
- 1 ounce Parmesan cheese

If pork piccata and chicken Parmesan had a baby, this would be it. Perfectly crispy, golden-fried pork cutlets are topped with creamy, melted mozzarella plus the tastiest tomatoes, garlic, and capers doused in a buttery white wine sauce. Plus, there's my nod to another cutlet queen, Milanese: the lightly dressed peppery arugula on the side it's frequently served with. Dinner is guaranteed to be an eleven out of ten.

TINI'S TIPS

To test your oil, add a pinch of bread crumbs—if they sizzle immediately and turn golden brown, the oil is ready.

Use any heavy instrument you have to pound the pork chops: a meat mallet, heavy-bottomed skillet, or rolling pin.

If you prefer not to use wine, substitute chicken broth.

1. Get Ready

- Preheat the oven to 375°F. Line two rimmed baking sheets with wire racks.

2. Pound the Pork

- Place the pork chops, one at a time, on a cutting board lined with plastic wrap, then cover with another piece of plastic. Using a heavy skillet, pound each chop **A** to an even thickness, about ¼ inch **B**. Season both sides with salt and pepper.

3. Dredge and Bread the Pork

- Put the flour in a shallow dish; crack the eggs into a second dish and whisk; combine the panko and oregano in a third dish. Stir a big pinch of salt into each dish.
- Dredge a pork chop in the flour, tapping off any excess, then dip it into the egg, allowing the excess to drip back into the dish. Lay the chop in the panko, and turn to fully coat the entire piece, pressing to help the crumbs thoroughly adhere. Transfer to the wire rack on the baking sheet. Repeat with the remaining chops.

4. Shallow-Fry the Pork

- In a large, heavy-bottomed skillet, preferably cast-iron, over medium heat, pour in about ½ inch of the oil and heat until it shimmers. You can raise the heat if the oil is taking a while to heat up, but lower it before frying.
- Working in two batches, carefully lower the pork chops into the hot oil. Cook, flipping once, until golden brown, 2 to 3 minutes per side **C**. Transfer the chops to the clean rack, sprinkle with a pinch of salt, then lay the mozzarella slices evenly over the top.

5. Make the Piccata Sauce

- Discard the oil from the skillet into a heat-safe container. Add 1 tablespoon of the butter and melt it over medium heat. Add the olive oil, then the tomatoes, capers, and garlic. Cook, stirring occasionally, until the tomatoes begin to soften and the garlic turns golden, about 2 minutes. Add the flour and cook for 30 seconds. Whisk in the wine and bring to a boil. Add the lemon juice and the remaining 2 tablespoons butter, stirring until the sauce thickens slightly, about 30 seconds. Remove from the heat and stir in the parsley and another pinch of black pepper **D**.

6. Finish and Serve

- Transfer the fried pork chops to the oven and bake just until the mozzarella melts, 4 to 5 minutes.
- Meanwhile, in a medium bowl, whisk together the lemon juice and olive oil. Add the arugula and parsley leaves, and using a vegetable peeler, shave the Parmesan cheese over the greens. Toss to coat; season to taste with salt and pepper.
- Transfer the pork chops to plates and drizzle the sauce over the top. Serve with the arugula salad on the side.

SWAP IT

Switch out the pork chops with pounded chicken breasts or thighs or thin cuts of white fish, such as tilapia.

A

B

C

D

Level Up

Oven-Cooked BBQ Pulled Pork

WITH SPICY SLAW

Makes 12 to 15 sandwiches

SMOKY BRINE

- ¼ cup pure maple syrup or honey
- 2 tablespoons sherry vinegar
- 2 tablespoons cider vinegar
- 1 tablespoon liquid smoke (use your favorite wood flavor)
- 2 teaspoons smoked paprika
- 2 teaspoons kosher salt
- 1 boneless pork butt (about 6½ pounds)

DRY RUB

- ¼ cup packed light brown sugar
- 2 tablespoons smoked paprika
- 2 tablespoons onion powder
- 1 tablespoon garlic powder
- 2 teaspoons cayenne pepper
- 2 teaspoons freshly ground black pepper
- 1 teaspoon dry ground mustard powder
- 1 teaspoon kosher salt
- 1 teaspoon crushed red pepper flakes

APPLE CIDER GLAZE

- ½ cup cider vinegar
- ½ cup orange juice
- ¼ cup light brown sugar
- 2 tablespoons liquid smoke

If you're a BBQ fan like me, I promise, this juicy, flavorful, succulent pork is worth the effort. For a long time I lived in an apartment, and I didn't have a backyard, which meant I couldn't have a smoker. I can't live without barbecue, though, so I came up with an indoor method that gives big pork butts a smoky depth of flavor—enter the injector. I also use this method with my turkey, and I swear, it's a game changer. Also, basting with my apple cider glaze helps you achieve a crispy "bark," that deliciously dark, crusty, chewy rind on the pork. Heads up, though: It does take *hours.* But it's worth it. The yield is large, so you can easily freeze the meat for any time you are craving that summer BBQ vibe. Or just throw a big party!

TINI'S TIPS

No ifs, ands, or butts: A Boston pork butt, which is fatty and marbled, is the best cut for pulled pork. Funny enough, a Boston pork butt is actually part of a pig's shoulder. It's the upper part, as opposed to a picnic pork shoulder, which is below the butt and usually sold bone-in and skin on. You may need to preorder a pork butt during busy holiday weekends.

Because the bottom of the pan tends to turn dark with stubborn stains from the drippings, an extra-large disposable foil pan works great for cooking this pork.

1. Get Ready

- The day before you want to serve, place a roasting rack inside a large, heavy metal roasting pan that will fit in your fridge. You can also use a disposable foil pan. Set aside.

2. Make the Smoky Brine

- In a small bowl, whisk together the maple syrup, sherry vinegar, cider vinegar, liquid smoke, smoked paprika, and salt.
- Place the pork butt on the rack inside the pan fat-side up. Using a meat injector, press the smoky brine deep into the center of the pork butt, inserting the needle at several different points **A**. Rub the meat all over with your hands to help evenly distribute the brine (don't worry if some of it spills out—this will help the dry rub stick to the meat).

3. Make the Dry Rub

- In a medium bowl, stir together the brown sugar, smoked paprika, onion powder, garlic powder, cayenne pepper, black pepper, ground mustard, salt, and red pepper flakes. Reserve 2 tablespoons of the rub in a separate bowl for the homemade BBQ sauce (page 65).
- Cover the entire outside of the pork with the remaining spice rub **B**. Using your hands, massage it into any folds, getting the rub all up in there **C**. Refrigerate the pork in the pan, uncovered, overnight.
- If you are making the BBQ sauce and the Spicy Slaw rather than using store-bought (go for it if you have time), you can make them now so they're ready.

recipe and ingredients continue ▸▸

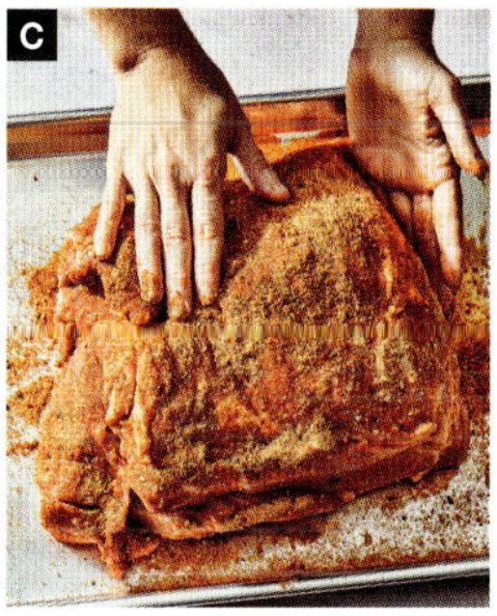

FINISHING AND SERVING

- 2 cups Tini's Homemade BBQ Sauce (page 65) or other favorite BBQ sauce, warmed
- 12 to 15 burger buns or Homemade Brioche Buns (page 258)
- 1½ cups Spicy Slaw (page 65)

SPECIAL EQUIPMENT

Heavy metal roasting pan fitted with a roasting rack or a disposable foil pan, meat injector (preferably stainless-steel with a long, open-tip needle), baster (optional), instant-read thermometer

4. The Next Day, Cook the Pork

- Remove the pork in the pan from the refrigerator and let sit at room temperature for 1 hour.

5. Make the Apple Cider Glaze

- In a medium bowl, combine the cider vinegar, orange juice, brown sugar, and liquid smoke. Set aside.
- Move a rack so it's as close to the bottom of the oven as you can get it and take out the others (or move them high enough so the pork will fit under them). Preheat your oven to 325°F.
- Cover the pork, still fat-side up on the roasting rack in the pan, tightly with aluminum foil. Transfer the pan to the oven and cook until the pork is mostly tender (a knife inserted deep into the pork will meet just a little resistance), 4 to 4½ hours. The pork should release some drippings into the bottom of the pan, but if it hasn't after an hour or two, add a generous splash (½ cup or more) of water to the bottom of the pan.

6. Baste and Glaze

- After 4 to 4½ hours, unwrap the meat and pour the apple cider glaze over the top. Return the pork to the oven, uncovered, and cook for another 1 to 1½ hours, basting the meat with the pan juices every 15 minutes or so. When the pork is done, the skin, or "bark," will be deeply browned and crispy and the meat will be falling apart when pierced with a fork (it will reach 195°F to 205°F on an instant-read thermometer).

7. Broil (You're Almost There!)

- Remove the pork from the oven. Move a rack 8 inches from the broiler (or more if needed for your pan to fit) and preheat it to high. Using a basting brush, cover the pork with about 1 cup of BBQ sauce. Broil until the coating bubbles and forms a glaze, 5 to 8 minutes. Keep a close eye on the pork so it doesn't burn.

8. Rest and Pull

- Remove the pork from the oven and let it rest for at least 15 minutes, then use two forks (or meat claws) to "pull" the pork, shredding it into bite-size pieces and discarding any large pieces of fat **D**.

9. Serve

- For each sandwich, pile the shredded meat on a bottom bun, spoon on a tablespoon or two of BBQ sauce, and top with a large scoop of spicy slaw and a top bun.

SWAP IT

Use leftover pulled pork for more than just sandwiches: Fill tacos or quesadillas, top your favorite pizza with it, add it to a stir-fry, or use it in chili (page 205).

TINI'S HOMEMADE BBQ SAUCE

Makes about 2 cups

1 cup ketchup

⅓ cup cider vinegar

¼ cup packed light brown sugar

2 tablespoons honey

2 tablespoons Tini's Homemade Hot Sauce (page 38) or store-bought

2 tablespoons reserved dry rub (page 63)

1 tablespoon Worcestershire sauce

1 tablespoon liquid smoke

1 tablespoon smoked paprika

- In a medium saucepan over medium heat, combine the ketchup, vinegar, brown sugar, honey, hot sauce, reserved rub, Worcestershire sauce, liquid smoke, and smoked paprika.
- Bring the mixture to a slow boil, then reduce the heat to medium-low and simmer, stirring occasionally, until the sauce thickens a "Tini" bit, 10 to 15 minutes. Store in an airtight container in the refrigerator for up to 2 weeks.

SWAP IT

Switch up your sauce to fit the season:

- In colder months, add a splash each of maple syrup and bourbon to your sauce.
- For spring and summer, stir in some citrus juice (orange and lemon) and add a spoonful of mustard for a tangy Carolina-style sauce.

SPICY SLAW

Makes 1 quart

½ cup mayonnaise

2 to 4 tablespoons Tini's Homemade Hot Sauce (page 38) or store-bought

1 tablespoon cider vinegar

1½ teaspoons sugar

¼ teaspoon kosher salt, plus more to taste

⅛ teaspoon freshly ground pepper, plus more to taste

1 (12-ounce) bag pre-cut coleslaw mix or 6 cups shredded cabbage

- In a large bowl, stir together the mayonnaise, hot sauce (start with 2 tablespoons), vinegar, sugar, salt, and pepper until well combined. Taste and add more hot sauce if desired.
- Fold in the slaw mix until everything is well coated. Cover and refrigerate until you are ready to serve; the flavors develop as the slaw sits. Before serving, toss again and taste. Season with more salt and pepper to taste. Store in an airtight container in the refrigerator for up to 3 days.

Baby Back Ribs

WITH BLACKBERRY BBQ SAUCE

Serves 4 to 6

BRINE

3 cups orange juice

⅓ cup cider vinegar

3 tablespoons kosher salt

2 racks of baby back ribs (about 3 pounds each, membrane removed) (see Tini's Tips)

DRY RUB

¼ cup packed dark brown sugar

2 tablespoons smoked paprika

1 tablespoon kosher salt

1 tablespoon garlic powder

1 tablespoon onion powder

1 teaspoon freshly ground black pepper

1 teaspoon chili powder

1 teaspoon ground cumin

1 teaspoon dry ground mustard powder

1 teaspoon cayenne pepper

BLACKBERRY BBQ SAUCE

12 ounces fresh blackberries

2 cups of Tini's Homemade BBQ Sauce (page 65) or your favorite BBQ sauce

I didn't always have a grill, so I perfected the process of cooking ribs indoors. I tenderize the meat overnight in a citrus brine, cover them with a flavorful dry rub, slow roast them, and finally brush them with my sweet and savory blackberry BBQ sauce for a final touch. There are a few steps, but I'm telling you, these babies fall off the bone.

TINI'S TIPS

A rack of ribs has a thin layer of connective tissue, called a silverskin or membrane, on the bone side that can make the ribs tough or chewy if you don't remove it. To do so, flip the rack so the bone side is facing up, and using a blunt knife or your fingers, slide under the thin, silvery membrane at one end and gently loosen it from the bone. Once you have enough to grip, use a paper towel to help you hold it tightly and slowly peel it off (it's like peeling a sticker off glass). If you're lucky, you'll get it in one piece. If it tears, just work it up again from another spot until it's all removed **A**.

While you may find other cuts of pork ribs available, I highly recommend baby back for their tender meat.

If you do have a grill, instead of oven-roasting the ribs, you can barbecue them for an extra-smoky flavor. Cook them slowly over a low charcoal fire or low setting on a gas grill, or if you do oven-roast them, instead of broiling them in the oven (step 6), baste the ribs with sauce over a hot coal fire or a high setting on a gas grill.

1. Brine the Ribs

- In a large roasting pan, add the orange juice, vinegar, and salt. Whisk until the salt dissolves, then add the ribs, meat-side down. Soak a few paper towels in the brine, then drape them over the top of the ribs. Cover the roasting pan tightly with plastic wrap and refrigerate for at least 8 hours and up to 24 hours.

2. Get Ready

- When you are ready to roast the ribs, take them out of the fridge and preheat the oven to 275°F.

3. Make the Rub

- In a small bowl, combine the brown sugar, smoked paprika, salt, garlic powder, onion powder, black pepper, chili powder, cumin, ground mustard, and cayenne.
- Remove the ribs from the brine and discard the liquid. Pat the ribs dry and season them all over with the rub. Place the ribs, meat-side down, in the roasting pan.

4. Roast the Ribs Low and Slow

- Cover the pan tightly with aluminum foil and slow roast until the meat is tender and nearly falling apart, about 3 hours.

5. Make the Blackberry BBQ Sauce

- Meanwhile, in a food processor or blender, puree the blackberries until smooth. With a fine-mesh strainer set over a small saucepan, strain the blackberry puree, pushing the liquid through with a rubber spatula. You should have about ¾ cup of liquid in the pan. Discard the pulp and seeds.
- Set the saucepan with the puree over medium heat, and pour in the BBQ sauce and cook, whisking often, until the sauce is reduced by nearly a quarter, about 20 minutes.

6. Sauce the Ribs and Broil

- When the ribs are tender, remove them from the oven. Discard the foil and any liquid in the pan.
- Move a rack 8 inches from the broiler (or more if needed for your pan to fit) and preheat to high.
- Brush the bony side of the ribs with about a ½ cup of the sauce, then flip the racks over and brush the meat side with another ½ cup of sauce.
- Broil the ribs, meat-side up, in the pan until the sauce is slightly caramelized and you see some char spots, 3 to 5 minutes. Keep an eye on them so they don't burn.

7. Cut and Serve

- Cut the racks into individual ribs or larger sections and serve with the remaining sauce on the side.

Success with Seafood

Honey-Lemon Salmon en Papillote

Serves 4

- 1 stick (8 tablespoons) unsalted butter
- ¼ cup honey
- 1 lemon, zested and juiced
- 5 garlic cloves, finely grated
- 2 tablespoons chopped dill, plus a few sprigs for garnish
- 1½ teaspoons Old Bay Seasoning
- Kosher salt and freshly ground black pepper
- 1 skinless center-cut salmon fillet (1½ pounds)
- 1 lemon, thinly sliced

Antoine likes fish way more than I do, so he makes most of the fish in our house. I often sit on the couch, which faces our kitchen, and talk him through how to make it—cooking fish is just *that* easy. The method I use here, cooking the salmon in parchment, steams it, which keeps the fish flaky and moist. This is called en papillote, the French way of saying "wrapped in a paper pouch and cooked," or to me, it means "pretty easy." This is really a no-recipe recipe because you can fold up anything into the packet with the salmon: herbs, vegetables, even fruit. I like honey and lemon because it's a natural combo—the sweetness is balanced by the acidity of the citrus—and a little bit of Old Bay. I like to cook the salmon as one big fillet with a really big sheet of parchment because it's less work (remember, I'm also sitting on the couch!), but you can get fancy and cut the fillets into single servings and make individual pouches if you like.

A TINI TIP

Buy a skinless center-cut fillet to ensure even cooking. Salmon skin turns rubbery when steamed, so no need to keep it. Ask your fishmonger to skin it. Or, to do it yourself, first place the fillet skin-side down on a cutting board. Slide a sharp chef's knife between the skin and flesh, then angle the knife down toward the skin and gently move the knife back and forth like a saw, as close as you can to the skin, to cut the flesh off **A**.

1. Get Ready

- Preheat the oven to 375°F.

2. Make Your Sauce

- In a small saucepan over medium heat, stir together the butter, honey, lemon zest and juice, garlic, 1 tablespoon of the dill, the Old Bay, ¼ teaspoon salt, and 2 generous pinches of pepper until the butter is melted.

3. Prep the Salmon

- Pat the fish dry with a paper towel.
- Place a large piece of parchment paper on a rimmed baking sheet (the paper should be at least double the width of your baking sheet). Lay the slices of lemon in a fanned pattern the size of your fillet in the center of the parchment paper, then place the salmon, with the nice side facing down, on top of the lemons **B**. Brush the salmon with a quarter of the butter mixture **C**, gently flip the fillet, and brush the other side (the nice side) with another quarter of the butter (the pretty side should be facing up with the lemons underneath).
- Make a salmon packet by bringing two sides of the parchment together and folding them in, then bring the other two sides together and fold them together, rolling them down a few times to seal. You want to make sure your packet is well sealed **D**.
- Turn the packet over on the sheet tray so the lemons are on top and the folded seam is tray-side down.

4. Cook the Salmon

- Bake until the salmon easily flakes with a fork and the internal temperature reads 145°F with an instant-read thermometer, 20 to 25 minutes, depending on the thickness of your fillet.

5. Plate and Serve

- Place your parchment pack on a serving platter, folded-side up/lemon-side down, and open the pack. Using a large offset spatula, gently slide the fish and lemons (the lemons should be underneath the fish) onto the platter. Pour the remaining half of the butter mixture over the salmon and sprinkle with a pinch or two of salt and pepper and the remaining 1 tablespoon dill. Garnish with the dill sprigs. Serve immediately.

A

B

C

D

5 Level Up

Brothy Poached Cod

WITH HERB OIL

Serves 4
(Makes about ½ cup herb oil)

HERB OIL

- Fennel fronds
- 1 tablespoon kosher salt
- ½ cup unpacked basil leaves
- ½ cup unpacked chives
- ¾ cup neutral oil, such as canola or vegetable

FISH

- 2 tablespoons unsalted butter
- 1 tablespoon neutral oil, such as canola or vegetable
- 1 large fennel bulb
- 1 medium leek, white and light green parts, finely chopped (1½ cups)
- 1 medium sweet onion, finely chopped
- 1 medium yellow summer squash, finely chopped
- 12 garlic cloves, thinly sliced
- 1 Fresno chile, minced
- 3¼ teaspoons kosher salt, plus more to taste
- 1 teaspoon lemon pepper seasoning, plus more for serving, if desired
- 1 lemon, rind removed with a vegetable peeler (avoid the white pith), juiced (2 tablespoons juice, plus more to taste)
- 2 sprigs basil
- 2 (8-ounce) bottles clam juice
- 3 cups dry white wine
- 2 cups water
- 4 (6-ounce) skinless cod fillets (each ¾ to 1 inch thick)

SPECIAL EQUIPMENT

- Cheesecloth

If you want to cook fish, poaching is one of the simplest, no-fail ways to do it. It's a basic technique that uses moist heat (you cook the fish in a warm, simmering—not boiling—liquid), which almost guarantees a perfectly cooked fillet. Poaching is really good for delicately flavored foods like fish and chicken, which you can enhance by adding herbs, vegetables, and seasonings to the poaching liquid. Here, cooking the cod fillets in a fennel-and-basil-infused broth subtly flavors the mild fish (if you need to convert a non-fish-lover, cod is a great place to start!). Heads up, though, this is a pretty cheffy recipe and will likely make you appreciate all that goes into a restaurant dish. There are lots of people in a professional kitchen contributing to one dish (this is a good recipe to cook with a friend—give them some things to dice!). Sharpen your knife, slide into the prep, and think of it as earning your stripes in the kitchen. The grind for this perfectly cooked, herby fish is worth it.

TINI'S TIPS

Upcycle the leftover herb pulp: Pour it into ice cube trays and freeze for up to several months. Pop a cube into soup for a bright, herby flavor, or defrost and use the pulp in place of some fresh herbs when making pesto (page 95).

Make prep for this dish easier by dividing it between 2 days. Make the herb oil in advance, and chop the vegetables a day ahead, too. Then on the day of, cook as directed and serve.

If you prefer not to use wine, you may substitute white grape juice or chicken broth.

1. Get Ready

- Fill a large bowl with ice water. Line a fine-mesh strainer with a few layers of cheesecloth and set over a spouted bowl.

2. Prep the Fennel Like a Pro

- Pull all the feathery fronds off the fennel stalks **A**. Set aside 1 cup of the fronds for the herb oil and a few more for serving (if you have a little less than 1 cup that's okay, too). Reserve the fennel bulb for cooking the fish.

3. Blanch the Herbs

- Fill a medium saucepan three quarters full with water and add the salt. Bring it to a boil and add the fennel fronds, basil, and chives. Cook just until the herbs darken and begin to wilt, 15 to 20 seconds **B**. Immediately lift the herbs from the water and transfer to the ice bath **C**. Let stand for a few seconds, until the herbs are cool enough to handle, then drain and squeeze them dry (you want to get rid of as much liquid as possible).

4. Make the Herb Oil (You Can Use This on Lots of Things!)

- Add the blanched herbs to a food processor or high-speed blender and add the oil. Blend on high speed until smooth and bright green, 1 to 2 minutes.
- Put the mixture in the fridge to infuse for 30 minutes or overnight.

these feathery things are fronds →

- Pour the herb oil through the cheesecloth-lined strainer into the spouted bowl or jar **D**. (Resist the urge to squeeze more oil from the cheesecloth—doing so could make it cloudy.) If not using immediately, transfer the oil to an airtight container and refrigerate for up to 1 day.

5. Cut the Fennel

- Using a vegetable peeler, peel off any bruised parts of the outer layer of the bulb **E** (what you are left with after the stalks are cut off). Trim off the root end **F**.
- Cut the bulb in half **G** and, with a sharp knife, remove the core of each half by cutting a "V" shape around it **H**.
- Coarsely chop each half by slicing it and then stacking the slices and chopping. You should get about 2 cups—you can chop up the stalks if you need more. Save the rest of the stalks for the poaching liquid.

6. Sauté the Vegetables

- In a large, straight-sided skillet or Dutch oven over medium heat, add the butter and oil and cook until the butter melts. To the skillet add *half of each* of the fennel, leek, onion, squash, and garlic, plus all of the chile; season with ¾ teaspoon of the salt and the lemon pepper. Cook, stirring occasionally, until soft and tender, 8 to 10 minutes (if the vegetables are developing any color, reduce the heat to medium-low). Scrape the vegetables onto a paper towel–lined plate to drain off excess fat.

7. Make the Poaching Liquid

- Wipe out the pan, then add the remaining chopped fennel (plus any stalks), leek, onion, squash, and garlic, along with the lemon rind, basil sprigs, clam juice, wine, and water; season with 1 teaspoon of salt. Bring the mixture to a boil, then turn down the heat to medium-low until the liquid reaches a simmer. Simmer for 20 minutes to allow the flavors to meld. Drain and discard the vegetables (or use them again to make vegetable broth), then return the liquid to a low simmer over medium-low heat. If it looks like the poaching liquid may not cover your fish, have some hot water ready to add to the pan.

8. Poach the Fish

- Season the fish fillets with the remaining 1½ teaspoons of salt. Gently lower the fish into the barely simmering poaching liquid (if the fish is not completely submerged, add enough hot water to just cover the fillets completely). Cover and gently cook until the fish is translucent and flakes easily, 5 to 7 minutes.
- Lift the fillets from the liquid and transfer to four shallow bowls. Stir the lemon juice into the poaching liquid, then season to taste with salt and/or more lemon juice. Spoon ½ cup poaching liquid into the bowls, then top each with the sautéed vegetables and a generous drizzle of herb oil and a few of the reserved fresh fennel fronds.

SWAP IT

Pretty much any seafood is fair game here. You can sub in firm white fish, like halibut and haddock, but fatty fish like salmon and trout are also delicious. You can even use shellfish like shrimp, clams, mussels, or a combination.

this is called the bulb ↘

A

B

C

Level Up

Fried Cornmeal-Coated Catfish

Serves 4

MARINADE

- 1 cup whole milk
- ¼ to ⅓ cup your favorite hot sauce
- 1 large egg
- Zest and juice of 1 lemon
- 2 tablespoons Dijon mustard
- 1 tablespoon chopped fresh dill
- 1 tablespoon smoked paprika
- 1 tablespoon Old Bay Seasoning
- 2 teaspoons onion powder
- 2 teaspoons garlic powder
- 1 teaspoon kosher salt
- ½ teaspoon freshly ground black pepper
- 2 pounds boneless, skinless catfish fillets

FRYING

- 1½ to 2 quarts neutral oil

CORNMEAL COATING

- 2 cups finely ground cornmeal (see Tini's Tips)
- 1 cup all-purpose flour
- 1 tablespoon chopped fresh dill
- 1 tablespoon smoked paprika
- 1 tablespoon Old Bay Seasoning
- 1 tablespoon kosher salt
- 2 teaspoons onion powder
- 2 teaspoons garlic powder
- 1 teaspoon freshly ground black pepper

FINISHING AND SERVING

- Flaky salt
- Homemade Tartar Sauce (recipe follows) or store-bought
- 4 lemon wedges

This light and crispy fried fish is something Antoine craves on the regular, so I make it often. You can always pan-fry catfish, but deep-frying is no doubt the way to go, especially where I live—some will tell you deep-frying this firm, sweet fish is the *only* way to eat it. Catfish is not always easy to find, though, especially outside the southern United States. You can use this technique of marinating and coating for most types of fish. Tilapia, which is easy to source, works well. It's cheaper, too. Honestly, once you get frying down, you'll be able to fry most anything. I like to serve up these crunchy fillets with some homemade slaw on the side (page 65). Tartar sauce and hot sauce are a must.

TINI'S TIPS

To ensure your coating is crunchy but not gritty, use finely ground cornmeal. If you have a medium- or coarse-grind cornmeal, put it in the blender and run it on high until it is finely ground, like a flour but with a bit more texture than all-purpose wheat flour.

If you are making the homemade tartar sauce, make that before anything else so the flavors can meld while you fry the fish (you can even make it a day or two ahead).

1. Marinate the Fish

- In a large bowl, whisk together the milk, hot sauce, egg, lemon zest and juice, mustard, dill, smoked paprika, Old Bay, onion powder, garlic powder, and the salt and pepper until thoroughly combined.
- Pat the fillets dry with a paper towel. Cut each one down the center lengthwise along the natural seam into 2 fillets.
- Toss the fish in the marinade and, using tongs, move the pieces around until they are completely submerged **A**. Let the fish marinate at room temp while you continue the prep.

2. Heat the Oil

- Pour 1 to 2 quarts of oil in a 6- to 7-quart pot or Dutch oven. You want at least 1½ to 2 inches of oil in the pot. Heat over medium high until the oil reaches 350°F on a candy thermometer.

3. Make the Cornmeal Coating

- In a shallow dish, whisk together the cornmeal, flour, dill, smoked paprika, Old Bay, salt, onion powder, garlic powder, and pepper until thoroughly combined.

4. Dredge and Fry the Fish

- Fit a baking sheet with a wire rack and set aside. Check your oil temp to make sure you're at 350°F; if it's too high or low, adjust the heat as needed.
- Using tongs, remove the fish one piece at a time from the marinade, dredge it in the cornmeal mixture **B**, and then lower it into the hot oil **C**. Add as many pieces as will fit without overcrowding. You want an inch or two between each piece for even cooking.
- Fry the fish until it turns a dark golden brown and an instant-read thermometer reads 145°F. Keep an eye on the oil temp and adjust the heat as needed to maintain 350°F.
- Transfer the fried fish to the wire rack, which will prevent the fish from getting soggy. Sprinkle with flaky salt and repeat with the remaining fish.
- Serve hot with tartar sauce and lemon wedges.

HOMEMADE TARTAR SAUCE

Makes about 1½ cups

- 1 cup mayonnaise
- ½ cup chopped dill pickles
- 2 tablespoons chopped fresh dill
- 2 teaspoons pickle juice
- 2 teaspoons freshly squeezed lemon juice
- 1 teaspoon Dijon mustard
- ¼ teaspoon garlic powder
- Kosher salt and freshly ground black pepper
- 1 tablespoon finely chopped chives (optional)

- In a small bowl, stir together the mayonnaise, pickles, dill, pickle juice, lemon juice, mustard, garlic powder, and salt and pepper to taste. Stir in the chives, if using. Store in an airtight container in the refrigerator for up to 3 days.

Scampi-Style Sautéed Shrimp

Serves 4

MARINADE

2 pounds large peeled and deveined shrimp, tails removed

4 teaspoons Tini's Spice Blend (recipe follows) or store-bought Creole seasoning

1 teaspoon grated lemon zest

¼ teaspoon cayenne pepper

SAUCE

6 tablespoons unsalted butter

Extra-virgin olive oil

10 garlic cloves, finely grated or minced (about ¼ cup)

2 large Fresno chiles, thinly sliced

Kosher salt

1 teaspoon Tini's Spice Blend (recipe follows) or store-bought Creole seasoning

1 cup dry white wine

1 cup low-sodium chicken or vegetable broth

2 lemons, one for 3 tablespoons juice, one for wedges for serving

¼ cup finely chopped parsley

Freshly ground black pepper

SERVING

Cooked linguine or toasted rustic bread

If I'm making shrimp, I'm making it with garlic, and lots of it—scampi-style, but not the authentic way. For my own Tini twist, I add some of my spice blend, but you can also use a pre-mixed Creole seasoning. Because I'm *always* going for big flavor, I add Fresno chiles and lemon zest for a bright kick to the shrimp. Serve this saucy dish over linguine or with bread, because you're going to want something to sop up all the buttery, garlicky deliciousness.

TINI'S TIPS

Shrimp can be purchased peeled and deveined, but if you need to do it yourself, it's simple. Using a paring knife or your fingers, tug at the legs of the shrimp to loosen the shell, then pull it off **A**. Run a paring knife down the back of the shrimp, all the way to the tail, to expose the digestive tract **B**. Sometimes it's already clean, but if you see a dark vein running down the center, go ahead and pull it out **C**.

The amount of salt in Creole seasonings can vary, so I don't give salt amounts in this recipe. Be sure to season to taste.

1. Marinate the Shrimp

- In a medium bowl, toss the shrimp with my spice blend, the lemon zest, and cayenne. Let stand at room temperature for at least 15 minutes, or cover and refrigerate for up to 2 hours.

2. Cook the Shrimp and Vegetables

- In a large skillet over medium-high heat, add 2 tablespoons of the butter and 2 tablespoons olive oil. When the butter is melted, add the shrimp in an even layer, working in batches if necessary. Cook, flipping once, until lightly browned and curled, about 2 minutes per side **D**. Transfer to a plate.
- To the same skillet, add 1 tablespoon butter and 1 tablespoon olive oil. Add the garlic, chiles, and a pinch of salt. Reduce the heat to medium, and cook, stirring occasionally, until softened and browned in places, 6 to 7 minutes. Add the spice blend and cook until fragrant, about 1 minute.

3. Finish the Sauce

- Stir in the wine and broth, then bring to a simmer, scraping up any browned bits from the bottom of the skillet. Cook until reduced by about half, 4 to 5 minutes. Add the lemon juice and the remaining 3 tablespoons butter, and cook just until the butter melts. Taste the sauce and season to taste. Remove the pan from the heat and stir in the cooked shrimp and parsley. Season with a pinch of black pepper and more salt if needed (pop a shrimp in your mouth to test!).
- Serve over plates of linguine or in bowls with warm bread alongside for sopping up the sauce.

SWAP IT

I like to make a creamy version of this dish. Add ¼ cup heavy cream when you add the lemon juice—it will warm up as the butter melts.

TINI'S SPICE BLEND

Use this in place of Creole seasoning.

Makes ⅓ cup

1 tablespoon smoked paprika

1 tablespoon garlic powder

1 tablespoon onion powder

2 teaspoons kosher salt

2 teaspoons dried thyme

1 teaspoon dried oregano

1 teaspoon freshly ground black pepper

½ teaspoon cayenne pepper

- In a small bowl, whisk together the smoked paprika, garlic powder, onion powder, salt, thyme, oregano, pepper, and cayenne. Store in an airtight container for up to 6 months.

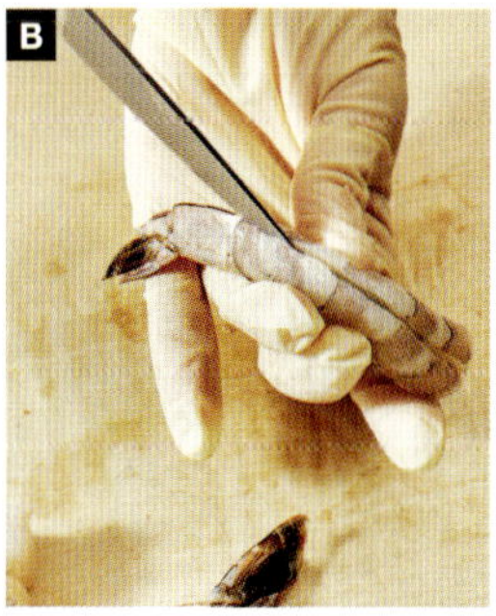

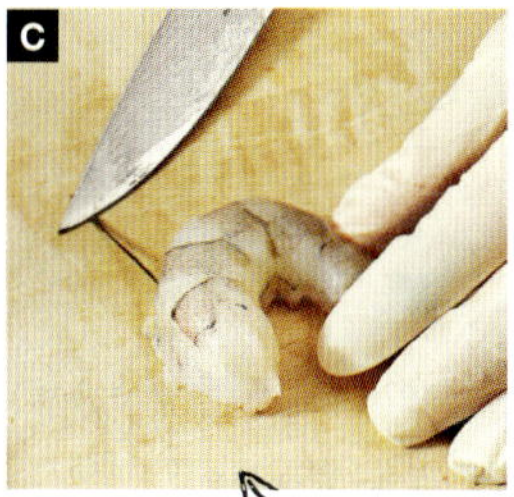

use your knife to get rid of the digestive tract (poop vein)

Bourbon-Maple Bacon-Wrapped Shrimp

Serves 2 as a main / 4 as an appetizer

- 8 slices thin-cut bacon, halved crosswise
- 16 large tail-on shrimp (about ¾ pound), peeled and deveined
- 1¼ teaspoons kosher salt
- ⅔ cup Tini's Homemade Bourbon BBQ Sauce (recipe follows) or your favorite bourbon barbecue sauce
- 1 tablespoon chopped chives, for garnish (optional)
- Lemon wedges, for serving

Bourbon-maple anything is a no-brainer. I brush this winning combo on ham, wings, and especially shrimp. These shrimp are the perfect appetizer at a barbecue. I bet you'll see people poppin' these sweet-spicy-smoky bites into their mouths one after the other. This dish comes together pretty fast, so it's a good one to bring to a cookout, a potluck, or anywhere people want food. I can pretty much promise they'll love you for it.

TINI'S TIPS

If you want a bigger bacon-to-shrimp ratio, you can use medium-size shrimp (instead of large). I do not recommend using extra-large or jumbo shrimp, though, as your ratio will be off. It's better to go smaller if your options are limited.

Salting the shrimp for a few minutes ahead of time helps lock in moisture, which makes them much harder to overcook.

1. Get Ready

- Place a rack in the upper third position of the oven and preheat to 400°F. Line a rimmed baking sheet with foil and an oven-proof wire rack.

2. Cook Up Some Bacon

- Arrange the bacon in an even layer on the wire rack. Bake until the bacon begins to turn golden but is still pliable, about 13 minutes. You want to be able to wrap it around the shrimp, so don't overcook it. It will crisp up some as it cools, so consider this when deciding when to pull it from the oven. (It will cook 5 more minutes with the shrimp as well.) Set the bacon aside until cool enough to handle.

3. Salt the Shrimp

- Meanwhile, in a medium bowl, toss the shrimp with the salt. Let it stand for 15 minutes.

4. Coat the Shrimp

- Add ⅓ cup of the BBQ sauce to the shrimp and toss to coat.

5. Assemble the Shrimp

- Working with one at a time, wrap a piece of bacon around each shrimp, securing the bacon with a toothpick. Return it to the wire rack on the baking sheet.

6. Bake and Glaze the Shrimp

- Bake for 5 minutes, then turn on the broiler to high.
- Brush some of the remaining BBQ sauce mixture over each shrimp. Return the baking sheet to the oven and broil until crisp and golden brown on top, about 1 minute. Flip the shrimp, brush with more sauce, and broil until crisp on the second side, about 1 minute. Keep a close eye on the broiler—they vary widely, so my minute could be different from your minute!
- Sprinkle with chives, if using, and serve immediately with lemon wedges.

TINI'S HOMEMADE BOURBON BBQ SAUCE

Makes a generous ½ cup

- ½ cup Tini's Homemade BBQ Sauce (page 65), or your favorite barbecue sauce
- 4 teaspoons bourbon
- 2 teaspoons pure maple syrup
- 1 teaspoon Worcestershire sauce
- ½ teaspoon grated lemon zest
- 1 teaspoon smoked paprika
- ½ teaspoon freshly ground black pepper
- ¼ teaspoon cayenne pepper

- In a small bowl, whisk together the barbecue sauce, bourbon, maple syrup, Worcestershire sauce, lemon zest, smoked paprika, black pepper, and cayenne.

always serve seafood with lemon, or
some type of citrus, or even citrus zest

Coconut Curry Mussels

Serves 2 as a main / 4 as an appetizer

- 2 pounds mussels
- 2 tablespoons coconut oil or other neutral oil
- 1 large shallot, sliced
- 4 garlic cloves, finely grated
- 1½ teaspoons freshly grated ginger
- 1 to 2 bird's-eye chiles, also called Thai chiles, seeds and membranes removed, minced (see Tini's Tips)
- ¼ cup tomato paste
- 1 to 2 tablespoons curry powder
- 1 teaspoon chili powder
- 1 (13.5-ounce) can full-fat unsweetened coconut milk
- 1 cup seafood stock or clam juice
- 2 teaspoons freshly squeezed lime juice
- Kosher salt and freshly ground black pepper
- Handful of cilantro leaves, for serving
- 1 lime, cut into wedges, for serving
- Focaccia, ciabatta, or baguette, for serving

Coconut curry mussels feel like pure summer to me. They make me think of the beach, sand, and saltwater. I like to plop down a big pan of these mussels in the center of my picnic table for people to dig right into. You can make them as spicy as you want by upping the peppers or curry powder. I always serve curry mussels with lots of focaccia for dipping into the broth. If I didn't, people would be drinking it out of the pan.

TINI'S TIPS

Mussels are alive when you buy them (or at least they should be!). If any are slightly open, lightly pinch them—if they close on their own, you can still use them. If they don't close, toss them, as they are likely dead.

If you notice a clump of dark threads, called the beard, coming from the opening of your mussels, it must be removed (sometimes mussels come de-bearded). You should do this right before cooking, as removing it can kill the mussel **A**.

Chile peppers get their heat from the membranes and seeds, not the flesh. And generally, the smaller the pepper, the hotter it is, like the bird's-eye pepper I call for in this recipe. If you prefer a less fiery dish, seed the peppers before using by cutting them in half lengthwise and cutting the core and seeds out with a spoon.

If you don't have seafood stock or clam juice, go ahead and sub in water—it'll work just fine (although stock and clam juice make it more flavorful).

1. Wash and De-Beard the Mussels

- First, scrub your mussels with a brush under cold, running water to clean the shell, then simply pull the beard out with your fingers or a pair of pliers (see Tini's Tips).

2. Sauté the Aromatics

- To a deep, wide skillet with a lid, add the oil and heat over medium high until it shimmers. Add the shallot, and cook until slightly softened, about 2 minutes. Add the garlic, ginger, and chiles and cook until fragrant, about 1 minute. Stir in the tomato paste, 1 tablespoon of the curry powder, and the chili powder. Cook, stirring constantly, until the mixture darkens and almost caramelizes, about 4 minutes.

3. Steam the Mussels Till They Open Up

- Pour in the coconut milk **B**, seafood stock **C**, and lime juice, and whisk until smooth.
- Bring the liquid to a simmer. Season with salt and pepper, then taste for any needed adjustments. If you'd like more curry powder or salt and/or pepper, add it now.
- Reduce the heat to medium, gently add the mussels, and cover with the lid **D**.
- Steam the mussels, shaking the pan every few minutes, until all or most of the mussels are opened, 5 to 7 minutes, and immediately remove from the heat. The minute they open they are done—you don't want to overcook them. If any of the mussels don't open, discard them **E**.

4. Finish and Serve

- Serve straight from the skillet or transfer the mussels and broth to a serving bowl.
- Top with cilantro leaves and serve with lime wedges and bread on the side for dipping.

← these stringy threads are the beard

B

C

D

E

↑
all your mussels
should be open like this
one on the right—
if they aren't
(like the one on the left),
don't eat them!

Seared Sea Scallops

WITH CORN AND TOMATO

Serves 4

- 3 large ears of fresh corn ($2\frac{1}{2}$ pounds)
- 1 pound fresh sea scallops (16 to 18)
- Kosher salt and freshly ground black pepper
- 1 tablespoon extra-virgin olive oil
- 1 garlic clove, smashed and peeled (see page 23)
- 1 tarragon sprig, plus 1 teaspoon minced leaves
- 3 scallions, thinly sliced, white and green parts separated
- 1 large plum tomato, cored and chopped
- 2 teaspoons freshly squeezed lime juice, plus lime wedges for serving

I have two brothers, Thijs and Tage, who are thirteen months apart. They love my scallops. In fact, they love *all* the seafood I cook. When I was in culinary school, I liked to practice what I learned, so they had lots of chances to eat restaurant-worthy dishes, and plump, pan-seared scallops were one of their favorites. (If you've never cooked scallops, they are probably one of the easiest, if not *the* easiest, seafoods to cook.) The key to creamy, delicate scallops like these is a good sear, which creates a lightly caramelized crust. I sauté corn and tomatoes, too, with some tarragon, which gives just a hint of flavor that goes so well with the scallops. For such a simple meal, it's a really satisfying one, and great to make at the height of summer with farm-fresh produce. I think my brothers know I love them when I make this for them—cooking is how I express my emotions. Seared scallops = love.

TINI'S TIPS

When buying scallops, look for ones that are fresh and NOT stored in a milky liquid. If you see any kind of fluid like this, it usually has a chemical preservative in it.

The fresher your corn, the more likely you are to get some liquid/milk when scraping the cobs.

1. Prep the Corn and Scallops

- Remove the corn husks and silks and cut the kernels from the cobs (see A Tini Tip, page 153); you should have about 3 cups. Transfer the corn kernels to a medium bowl and, holding the corn cobs over the bowl, use the back of a large knife to scrape the cobs to extract as much liquid as you can into the bowl.
- Pat the scallops with paper towels until very dry (this is essential for a good sear). Season the scallops generously on both sides with 2 pinches of salt and a pinch or two of pepper.

Sear the Scallops, look at that sexy crust!

2. Sear the Scallops

- In a large, heavy-bottomed skillet (preferably cast-iron) over high heat, add the olive oil, garlic, and tarragon sprig. Heat until the oil shimmers. Don't be afraid to get the pan really hot. Add the scallops and cook without disturbing (this is really important!), until they are caramelized and dark brown on one side, about 2 minutes. Flip and cook the other side until golden brown, another 1 to 2 more minutes **A**. Transfer the scallops to a plate.

3. Sauté the Vegetables

- Reduce the heat to medium, then add the white parts of the scallions and the corn (including the corn milk) and season generously with salt and pepper. Cook, stirring occasionally to pick up some of the browned bits from the bottom of the pan, until the corn is softened and bright yellow, 4 to 5 minutes. Stir in the tomato and minced tarragon and cook until the tomato just starts to soften and the mixture is fragrant, about 2 minutes. Remove from the heat, discard the garlic clove and tarragon sprig, and stir in the lime juice; season to taste.
- Spoon the vegetables onto plates and top with the scallops. Sprinkle with the scallion greens and serve with lime wedges alongside.

SWAP IT

Spring: Try shallots, sliced asparagus, and fresh shelled peas.

Fall: Swap in red onion, sliced wild mushrooms, and shredded Brussels sprouts.

Winter: Use sweet onion, thinly sliced carrots, and shredded radicchio.

My All-Time Favorite Seafood Boil

Serves 4 to 6

BOIL

- 8 cups water
- 3 (12-ounce) cans of your favorite IPA beer
- Juice of 3 oranges
- Juice of 2 lemons
- ½ cup Old Bay Seasoning, plus more for serving
- ¼ cup Tini's Spice Blend (page 76) or Creole seasoning
- ¼ cup garlic powder
- ¼ cup onion powder
- 2 tablespoons freshly ground black pepper
- 4 large ears of fresh corn, husked and each cut crosswise into thirds
- 1 pound baby red potatoes
- 12 to 16 ounces of andouille sausage, sliced into 1½-inch-long pieces
- 2 to 3 (4- to 6-ounce) lobster tails
- 3 clusters of snow crab legs, defrosted if frozen (see Tini's Tips)
- 1 pound crawfish or unpeeled large shrimp

DIPPING SAUCE

- 2 sticks (16 tablespoons) butter
- 4 garlic cloves, finely grated
- 4 teaspoons of your favorite hot sauce
- Zest and juice of ½ lemon
- Zest of ½ orange
- ½ teaspoon Old Bay Seasoning
- ½ teaspoon smoked paprika

FINISHING AND SERVING

- 2 lemons, cut into wedges
- Handful of chopped parsley leaves

I grew up in Maryland, where steamed crabs are life! We'd dump the cooked crabs out onto a newspaper-covered table and totally get into it, eating the crabs with our hands, dipping the meat in loads of melted butter and Old Bay. It was messy, fun, and delicious. This big pot of seafood is a little different—it's boiled instead of steamed—but equally scrumptious. I like how the corn and potatoes soak up tons of flavor from the cooking liquid, which includes a few beers (I like a citrusy IPA because it goes so well with seafood; Sierra Nevada Hazy Little Thing is my favorite) and a whole bunch of seasonings. The seafood picks up a good bit of flavor, too. The best part is the garlicky butter that gets poured over everything. This boil is a real crowd-pleaser, and it looks so impressive. Be sure to have some wet wipes and lots of napkins nearby—things are about to get messy.

TINI'S TIPS

Timing is everything here. Don't walk away, because a minute or two more of cooking can mean the difference between succulent seafood or disappointingly overcooked crustaceans. Most seafood takes only minutes to cook. I'd worry more about overcooking than undercooking.

Most snow crab legs are sold precooked and frozen, so you are really just reheating them. The seafood will continue to cook after you turn the heat off.

1. Get Ready to Party!

- Decide what tray you are using for serving. You can use a food-safe enamel or metal tray or (my preference) a big disposable aluminum roasting pan/steam tray available from grocery stores. Have a big bowl on hand for shells, and maybe a small bowl or two of water for dipping your fingers into. And definitely lots of napkins (and some trash bags, too . . . you don't want to leave seafood shells and peels in your kitchen garbage can overnight)!

2. Make the Cooking Liquid

- In a very big pot (7 quarts or larger) over high heat, combine the water, beer, orange juice, lemon juice, Old Bay, spice blend, garlic powder, onion powder, and pepper. Bring the liquid to a boil.

3. Boil the Vegetables and Sausage

- Once the water boils, add the corn, potatoes, and sausage and reduce the heat to low so the liquid simmers. Cook until the potatoes are fork-tender, about 20 minutes.

4. Make the Dipping Sauce

- In a medium saucepan over medium heat, melt the butter. Add the garlic and cook until fragrant, about 2 minutes. Add the hot sauce, lemon zest and juice, orange zest, Old Bay, and smoked paprika. Stir until well combined, remove from the heat, and set aside.

5. Cook the Seafood

- Add the lobster tails to the big pot and continue to simmer until they turn bright red, 3 to 4 minutes. Add the snow crabs and crawfish and continue to cook for another 3 minutes. Remove from the heat and allow the seafood to sit for 5 more minutes.

6. Serve

- Using tongs and/or a spider, transfer the cooked seafood and vegetables to the large platter or heatproof tray. For easier eating, you can split the lobster tails in half lengthwise using kitchen shears or a chef's knife. (The meat should be opaque white. If it's at all translucent or jelly-like, throw it back in the pot for a few minutes to cook from the heat of the cooking liquid.)
- Drizzle half of the dipping sauce over the entire tray of food. Garnish with the lemon wedges and parsley and sprinkle with a little more Old Bay if you want. Serve with the remaining dipping sauce and dig in!

Pasta Like a Pro

Tini's Viral Mac and Cheese

Serves 8 to 10

PASTA

- Butter, for greasing the dish
- Kosher salt
- 1 pound dried cavatappi pasta

CHEESE SAUCE

- 16 ounces low-moisture mozzarella cheese, grated (about 4 cups)
- 16 ounces Colby Jack cheese, grated (about 4 cups)
- 8 ounces cheddar cheese, grated (about 2 cups)
- 3 tablespoons unsalted butter
- 1 teaspoon smoked paprika
- ¾ teaspoon kosher salt
- ½ teaspoon garlic powder
- ½ teaspoon freshly ground black pepper
- 3 tablespoons all-purpose flour
- 1 (12-ounce) can evaporated milk
- 2 cups heavy cream
- 1 tablespoon Dijon mustard

GARNISH

- 1 tablespoon chopped chives (optional)

It took me four years to perfect this mac and cheese recipe. Antoine was the judge, and he kept saying my attempts were good but not the best. I tried making it with a roux and without one, used different types of cheeses, even cream cheese (too creamy). I tried swapping out milk for heavy cream, then switched to evaporated milk (the winner) and perfected the seasonings (smoked paprika and Dijon mustard are key). Cavatappi is always the pasta of choice because the sauce gets up into the holes and you get a nice creamy bite every time. I could give you a story behind each ingredient and why, but let's cut to the chase: Trust me and join countless others in making this recipe for the most comforting and satisfying mac and cheese. While most places in this book I'll tell you to be free and get creative—here I say *don't*. If you want Tini's Mac and Cheese, exactly how I make it, follow the directions. Then if you want to do your own thing, I've got you covered (see Swap It, page 91).

*whatever you do, don't f*ck up the roux!*

TINI'S TIPS

Don't use pre-grated cheese—it has anti-clumping preservatives that can prevent it from melting well and will make it grainy. Plus, it's less cost effective.

My mac and cheese actually has French roots—the base of the sauce is a béchamel (page 27), one of the five French mother sauces, which becomes a mornay sauce when I add grated cheese and seasonings.

1. Get Ready

- Preheat the oven to 350°F. Butter a 9 × 13-inch baking dish and set aside.

2. Cook the Pasta

- Fill a large pot three quarters full with water and salt it like the ocean (see page 99). Bring to a boil and cook the cavatappi according to the package directions for al dente (or 1 minute less than the full cooking time); remember, it will keep cooking in the oven so you don't want it too soft! Drain and set aside.

3. Make the Mornay Sauce

- In a large bowl, combine the mozzarella, Colby Jack, and cheddar cheeses.
- BLOOM YOUR SPICES: In a large skillet over medium heat, melt the butter **A** and add the smoked paprika, salt, garlic powder, and pepper. Using a wooden spoon or heatproof spatula, stir and cook until fragrant, about 30 seconds **B**.
- MAKE A ROUX: Add the flour **C** and continue to stir until the mixture becomes a thick paste, 3 to 5 minutes **D**.

recipe continues ››

- Slowly whisk in the evaporated milk, a little at a time, and continue to whisk until the mixture thickens, about 5 minutes **E**. Add the heavy cream and mustard and whisk again until well combined.
- Reduce your heat to low and slowly whisk in 2½ cups of the grated cheese **F**, allowing it to melt before adding another 2½ cups of the cheese (you should have 5 cups of grated cheese left in the bowl). Be patient. If your heat is too high, your sauce will break and curdle, which will make your sauce grainy. Continue to whisk until the sauce is creamy and smooth **G**.
- Stir in the cooked cavatappi and make sure it's completely coated with cheese sauce **H**.

4. Layer and Bake

- To your prepared baking dish, add a layer of cavatappi, then a layer of grated cheese, then repeat with layers of cavatappi and cheese, ending with the cheese on top, until you've used up all the pasta and cheese.
- Bake until the cheese is melted and bubbly, 25 to 30 minutes.

5. Broil

- Remove the baking dish from the oven.
- Move a rack 6 inches from the broiler (or more if needed for your pan to fit) and preheat it to high.
- Return the dish to the oven and broil until golden brown on top, about 2 minutes. Sprinkle with the chives, if using. Leftover mac and cheese may be stored in an airtight container for up to 4 days. To reheat, add a splash of milk to loosen up the pasta, cover with foil, and warm in a preheated 350°F oven until the pasta is warmed through. Top with a sprinkle of grated cheese and broil until the top is golden, another minute or two.

MAKE IT AHEAD

You can easily make mac and cheese a day in advance. Cook the pasta for 1 minute less than the called for cooking time (you want to ensure the cavatappi is al dente).

Do everything, including sprinkling the top with cheese, up until putting the mac and cheese in the oven. Cover tightly with plastic wrap or foil and refrigerate it.

Pull the mac and cheese from the refrigerator 30 minutes before you are ready to cook it (if it's too cold, the cheese might separate and get greasy). Cook as directed in the recipe.

To freeze the mac and cheese, do the same as above, but freeze instead of refrigerate. You can do this up to 3 months in advance. The day before you are going to cook it, move it to the refrigerator to thaw. Then just as above, pull it from the refrigerator 30 minutes before you are ready to cook it.

I always make my mac and cheese a day in advance for the holidays

SWAP IT : MAC AND CHEESE EDITION

Buffalo Chicken Mac and Cheese

- Cut up 1 pound of raw chicken tenders into bite-size pieces and, in a large bowl, toss with 2 teaspoons dried ranch seasoning, 2 teaspoons garlic powder, 1 teaspoon onion powder, 1 teaspoon chili powder, 1 teaspoon smoked paprika, ½ teaspoon cayenne pepper, ½ teaspoon kosher salt, and ½ teaspoon freshly ground black pepper. In a large skillet over medium, heat 2 tablespoons olive oil and sauté the chicken until cooked through, 3 to 5 minutes; set aside.
- Make the roux and stir in the chicken and ½ cup Frank's RedHot sauce into the roux.
- **SWAP OUT THE CHEESES:** 16 ounces Colby Jack cheese, grated; 8 ounces mozzarella cheese, grated; 8 ounces cheddar cheese, grated; and 8 ounces smoked Gouda cheese, grated.
- Serve topped with more Frank's, ranch seasoning, and chopped chives.

Jalapeño Mac and Cheese

- In a sauté pan over medium-high heat, fry 8 slices of bacon until crispy, about 5 minutes per side. Remove the bacon from the pan and, when cool, dice into small pieces. Save the grease in the pan and use it in place of the butter when making the roux.
- **SWAP OUT THE CHEESES:** 16 ounces Colby Jack cheese, grated; 8 ounces mozzarella cheese, grated; 16 ounces pepper Jack cheese, grated.
- Use jalapeño evaporated milk, such as Carnation, instead of plain (if you can't find jalapeño evaporated milk, plain will do just fine).
- Fold the diced bacon and 2 seeded and chopped jalapeños into the sauce.
- Layer and bake as directed. Garnish with slices of jalapeño.

Lobster Mac and Cheese

- When you bloom your spices, include 1 teaspoon Old Bay Seasoning.
- **SWAP OUT THE CHEESES:** 16 ounces mozzarella cheese, grated; 8 ounces Gruyère cheese, grated; 8 ounces fontina cheese, grated; 8 ounces Gouda cheese, grated.
- Substitute whole-grain mustard for the Dijon.
- Fold 1 pound poached lobster, cut into 1-inch pieces, into the sauce.
- Sprinkle a few pinches of Old Bay over the finished dish before baking.
- Bake as directed.

Pesto Rigatoni
with Sun-Dried Tomatoes and Ricotta

Pesto Rigatoni

WITH SUN-DRIED TOMATOES AND RICOTTA

Serves 4

- ½ teaspoon kosher salt, plus more for salting the water
- 16 ounces dried mezzi rigatoni
- 2½ cups fresh spinach or arugula
- 1 (10-ounce) jar oil-packed sun-dried tomatoes, drained and chopped (about 1 cup)
- 1⅓ cups homemade pesto (page 95) or store-bought
- 1 cup Homemade Ricotta (page 97) or store-bought whole milk ricotta
- 1 ounce Parmesan cheese, finely grated (about ½ cup), plus more for serving
- Zest of ½ lemon
- ¼ teaspoon freshly ground black pepper
- Crushed red pepper flakes
- 1 to 2 teaspoons lemon juice, as needed (optional)
- Basil leaves, for garnish (optional)

While I do like to make *everything* from scratch, there are some days I can't, or just don't! You have options here. If you go the store-bought route, buy the best-quality pesto you can afford, and make sure your ricotta is whole milk for the creamiest outcome. I like to use mezzi rigatoni because the ridges on the tubes hold on to the sauce, and they are bite-size, so everything fits nicely onto the fork for a good bite. The savory sun-dried tomatoes add some umami to this simple dish, which gets a nice creaminess from the cheeses. It's perfect for a weeknight dinner and also special enough for guests.

TINI'S TIPS

Mise en place is key here. Have all your ingredients ready to toss with the pasta as soon as it's drained. The heat of the noodles helps wilt the greens and melt the cheeses to create a sauce.

Feel free to sub in your favorite pasta shape—cavatappi or small shells would work well.

1. Cook the Pasta

- Fill a large pot three quarters full with water and salt it like the ocean (see page 99). Bring to a boil and cook the rigatoni according to the package directions. Reserve ½ cup of the pasta cooking water, then drain and set aside.

2. Toss the Pasta

- Return the pasta to the pot and immediately toss in the spinach and sun-dried tomatoes. Using tongs or a spoon, toss the pasta until the spinach is lightly wilted.
- Spoon in the pesto, minus a tablespoon or two, and toss until everything is coated.
- Add ¼ cup of the ricotta, the Parmesan, lemon zest, ½ teaspoon salt, the black pepper, and a generous pinch or two of red pepper flakes. Continue to toss the pasta until the ricotta is smooth and the Parmesan is somewhat melted. You can add a tablespoon of the reserved pasta water, or more, if you want a saucier sauce.

3. Season and Serve

- Taste the pasta and add more seasoning or the reserved pesto as needed. At this point you could add a teaspoon or two of lemon juice if you need some acid.
- Transfer the pasta to individual serving bowls or to a platter and dollop the remaining ¾ cup ricotta evenly over the pasta. Garnish with basil leaves, if using, more Parm, and serve.

Fresh Pesto

Makes about 1 cup

- ⅓ cup pine nuts (about 1½ ounces)
- 4 cups unpacked basil leaves
- 2 garlic cloves, peeled
- 1 ounce Parmesan cheese, finely grated (about ½ cup)
- ½ cup extra-virgin olive oil
- ½ teaspoon grated lemon zest
- 2 to 4 teaspoons freshly squeezed lemon juice
- ¾ teaspoon kosher salt, plus more to taste
- ¼ teaspoon freshly ground black pepper

Made from mostly basil and olive oil, this fragrant sauce is light and fresh and tastes really good. You can put it on chicken or bread or use it for most anything savory. You can make pesto quickly with a food processor, but it is traditionally made using a mortar and pestle. If you do use a pestle, save the olive oil for last, drizzling it in a little at a time and waiting until it's incorporated to continue.

A TINI TIP

Leaving some water clinging to the basil leaves helps mimic the creamier texture you'll get with a mortar-and-pestle-made pesto.

1. Toast the Nuts

- Place the pine nuts in a small, dry skillet over medium-low heat. Toast, shaking the pan occasionally (a good place to practice the well-known chef "pan flip"!), until they are lightly browned and very fragrant, 4 to 5 minutes. Immediately transfer the nuts to a bowl to avoid any carryover cooking. Set aside to cool.

2. Blend the Pesto

- Rinse the basil with cool water, then shake it mostly dry (leave some water clinging to the leaves). Transfer it to a food processor with the garlic, Parmesan, and cooled pine nuts. Pulse until finely minced, 20 to 30 seconds. With the machine running, drizzle in the olive oil and blend until mostly smooth and emulsified. Add the lemon zest, 2 teaspoons of the lemon juice, the salt, and pepper and pulse a few times to combine. Take a taste and add more lemon juice and/or salt as needed. Store in an airtight container in the refrigerator for up to 1 week (drizzle the top with a thin coating of olive oil to help maintain the bright green color for longer).

SWAP IT

Just about any nut or seed can be swapped in for the pine nuts. Walnuts, almonds, cashews, pistachios, sunflower seeds, and pumpkin seeds are great options. Toast them just the same.

Any tender herb will work here, too. Fresh parsley will be just as fresh as basil; a mixture of chives and scallions will give an onion-y kick; and cilantro will give a different vibe, especially when paired with lime instead of lemon.

While Parmesan is classic, feel free to use your favorite aged hard cheeses like Pecorino Romano or Asiago.

A
B
C
D

Homemade Ricotta

Makes 1½ to 1¾ cups

- ½ gallon (8 cups) whole milk, not ultra pasteurized, such as Organic Valley pasteurized
- 1 teaspoon kosher salt
- 3 to 5 tablespoons freshly squeezed lemon juice

SPECIAL EQUIPMENT

Cheesecloth

Fresh homemade ricotta is actually really easy to make, *and* you need only three ingredients. It's one of my favorite things I learned in culinary school. It's kind of like a cool science experiment you can eat—it is simply separated curds and whey. Even though it's not labor intensive, it does take patience. Don't rush heating the milk, because it can easily scorch or bubble over, and that's a nasty mess to clean up. I like to use this smooth, creamy cheese for pesto rigatoni (page 94), and I love tossing it in fresh pasta, too. It's good smeared on a sandwich with some pesto or even with a drizzle of honey for dessert.

TINI'S TIPS

Don't miss this! Look for milk that is processed with HTST pasteurization (high temperature short time) or just "pasteurized" versus ultra-high pasteurization, because the ultra-heating process affects the milk's proteins and prevents them from coagulating. Your ricotta won't work if you use ultra-high pasteurized milk.

Lemons vary in acidity, which is why I give a range for lemon juice. Start on the low end and add more if the ricotta isn't curdling within 15 seconds. If you don't have lemons, you can try subbing in 3 tablespoons of white vinegar.

For seasoned ricotta, stir in a few pinches each of kosher salt and freshly ground black pepper, and a drizzle of olive oil.

1. Heat the Milk

- In a medium saucepan over medium heat, add the milk and salt and bring to a near simmer, which is when small bubbles first start to appear in the milk (about 180°F on an instant-read thermometer) **A**.
- Add 3 tablespoons of the lemon juice and stir for 15 seconds. Curds should begin to form; if not, add more lemon juice, 1 teaspoon at a time, until you see curds **B**. Cover the pot, turn off the heat, and let the milk and juice sit for 20 minutes with the pot still on the burner (stirring occasionally if you have an electric burner) until curds have fully formed **C**.

2. Strain the Curds

- Line a fine-mesh strainer set over a medium bowl with cheesecloth (or paper towels) extending a few inches above the top rim. Using a slotted spoon, transfer the curds from the pot to the sieve **D**. Do not be tempted to pour the liquid into the strainer; a spoon works better to transfer the curds.
- Let the ricotta drain to your desired consistency, 5 to 15 minutes (the longer you drain it, the thicker it'll be).
- When the ricotta is cooled and drained, transfer the cheese to a serving or storage container.

SWAP IT

Play around with different infusions to create different flavors! Add any of the following to the milk when you are warming it and remove when transferring the curds to the sieve:

- 5 large sprigs basil and 2 peeled garlic cloves
- 4 sprigs thyme and the peel of 1 lemon
- 2 sprigs rosemary and the peel of 1 orange
- 2 cinnamon sticks and a pinch of cardamom for a dessert ricotta

Quick Spicy Sausage and Goat Cheese Penne

Serves 4

PASTA

Kosher salt

16 ounces dried penne

SAUCE

2 tablespoons extra-virgin olive oil

1 pound (16 ounces) hot Italian sausage, casings removed (see Tini's Tips)

1 large sweet onion, finely chopped

5 garlic cloves, finely grated

3 tablespoons tomato paste

Kosher salt

1 (28-ounce) can crushed tomatoes

1 sprig basil, plus leaves for serving

½ cup water

1 to 3 teaspoons crushed red pepper flakes, plus more for serving (optional)

1 (10.5-ounce) log goat cheese

I think of this as my everything-must-go sauce—when I have odds and ends in the fridge about to expire, I just throw them in a pan with a can of crushed tomatoes and serve it over pasta. I use hot Italian sausage here, but you could use whatever protein you have: chicken sausage, ground pork, even tofu. Goat cheese adds the perfect amount of creaminess to this spicy sauce, but if you've got cream or cream cheese or anything creamy that you've got to use up, toss that in instead. I am the biggest fan of fresh pasta (page 103), but sometimes I just don't feel like making it. When it comes to dried pasta, I'm not picky. I just buy whatever is on the store shelf. As with most of my recipes, try my way first, then start making your own substitutions. Think of dried pasta as your blank canvas.

TINI'S TIPS

Whenever cooking pasta, always reserve a cup of the salty, starchy water *before* draining it. Even a few tablespoons can nicely thicken a sauce and help it bind better to the noodles.

To remove sausage from its casing, cut a thin, shallow slit lengthwise in the sausage. The casing (skin) should pop apart. Then, using your fingers, peel it away, releasing the meat from the casing. Dispose of the casing.

SALT YOUR PASTA WATER! A LOT!

If you watch my videos, you've heard me say "Salt your water like the ocean." Seasoning food is important on every level, from the inside out and as you go. Salting pasta water can make a big difference in the taste of your final dish. You may need a lot more than you think. You should use 1 to 2 tablespoons of kosher salt per gallon of water. So, while it may not be quite the same salinity of the ocean, you get the idea. Add the salt just as the water comes to a boil, so it dissolves, *then* add your pasta.

1. Cook the Pasta

- Fill a large pot three quarters full with water and salt it like the ocean (see below). Bring to a boil and cook the penne according to the package directions for al dente. Reserve 1 cup of the pasta cooking water, then drain and set aside.

2. Make the Sauce

- In a large, deep-sided skillet over medium-high heat, add the olive oil. Add the sausage and cook, breaking up the meat into small pieces with a wooden spoon, until golden brown but not quite cooked through, 5 to 7 minutes. Using a slotted spoon, transfer the sausage to a bowl and leave the rendered fat in the pan.
- Add the onion to the skillet and reduce the heat to medium. Sauté, stirring occasionally, until softened and beginning to brown, 4 to 5 minutes. Stir in the garlic, tomato paste, and a pinch of salt, and cook until fragrant, 1 to 2 minutes.
- Add the crushed tomatoes, basil sprig, water, and another pinch of salt. Return the sausage to the skillet and bring the mixture to a boil. Taste the sauce and add red pepper flakes to your desired spice level. Reduce the heat to medium-low and simmer, partially covered, until thickened slightly, 15 to 20 minutes.

3. Finish and Serve

- Discard the basil sprig from the sauce, reduce the heat to low, and then crumble in half of the goat cheese. Stir until smooth and melted. Stir in the cooked pasta and ¼ cup of the reserved pasta water, stirring until the sauce coats the pasta, about 1 minute (add more pasta water a splash at a time, as needed). Season with more salt to taste.
- To serve, crumble the remaining goat cheese over the pasta and top with a few fresh basil leaves and another pinch of pepper flakes, if desired.

Mushroom Alfredo Sauce

WITH HOMEMADE FETTUCCINE

Serves 4 to 6

Kosher salt

1 stick (8 tablespoons) unsalted butter

2 tablespoons extra-virgin olive oil

16 ounces baby bella mushrooms, sliced (about 5 generous cups)

Freshly ground black pepper

2 cups packed baby leaf spinach (about 3 ounces)

4 garlic cloves, finely grated

1¼ cups heavy cream

1 tablespoon chopped basil, plus a few leaves for garnish

1 tablespoon chopped parsley, plus a few leaves for garnish

3 ounces Parmesan cheese, finely grated (about 1½ cups)

1 recipe Homemade Pasta Dough (page 103), cut into fettuccine, or 1 pound store-bought fresh fettuccine

I really love a creamy, very cheesy Alfredo sauce—especially with fettuccine noodles because they are wide and the sauce adheres so well. Fettuccine Alfredo was actually the first thing I made for Antoine, before we were boyfriend and girlfriend. It was also the first time I'd ever made the dish, and it was the most memorable meal (I suppose Antoine had something to do with it, but I swear, this combo is the best). I made it again when we were engaged, then again when we were married (and lots more times in between). I hope you like this comfort food meal as much as we do.

1. Get Ready

- Fill a large pot three quarters full with water and salt it like the ocean (see page 99). Bring the water to a boil while you make the sauce and it'll be ready to go.

2. Make the Sauce

- In a large, straight-sided skillet over medium heat, add 3 tablespoons of the butter and the olive oil. Once the butter is melted, add the mushrooms and sprinkle with 2 pinches each of salt and pepper. Sauté until just softened, 3 to 4 minutes. Next, add the spinach and stir until wilted, about 1 minute. Toss in the garlic and stir until it becomes fragrant, about 1 minute.
- Add the remaining 5 tablespoons butter and stir until it's melted, then slowly whisk in the heavy cream. Stir in ¾ teaspoon salt and ¼ teaspoon pepper.
- Simmer the heavy cream until slightly thickened, 5 to 7 minutes. Stir in the basil, parsley, and 1 cup of the Parmesan until smooth. Turn off the heat and let the sauce sit while you cook the pasta.

3. Cook the Pasta

- Using tongs, transfer the fresh noodles to the boiling water, stirring them slightly to loosen any that are stuck together. Cook until al dente, 2 to 3 minutes.
- Using tongs, transfer the cooked noodles to the skillet with the sauce (don't discard the water), tossing to combine, and adding a few splashes of the reserved pasta water as needed to create a sauce that coats the noodles. Season with salt and pepper to taste.

4. Garnish and Serve

- Transfer the pasta to a serving platter (or serve it straight from the skillet). Sprinkle with the remaining ½ cup Parmesan and garnish with the basil and parsley leaves. Serve immediately.

if you're feeling fancy, grate some truffle on top, or if you're not a mushroom person, leave them out for a basic creamy Alfredo sauce

Homemade Pasta Dough

Serves 3 to 4, depending on your recipe (Makes almost 1 pound)

- 2 cups / 260g 00 flour, plus more for rolling
- 3 large eggs, at room temperature
- 1 tablespoon extra-virgin olive oil
- ½ teaspoon kosher salt

I like making pasta from scratch. I think it tastes ten times better than dried pasta. I really like the texture homemade dough gives pasta; there's a good chewiness to the noodles. I think of it like making fresh bread—it just tastes fresher. Many years ago, the first time I made pasta, I didn't understand how thinly I should roll out the dough, and my noodles were not good. Really try to get the dough as thin as you can. You can do it by hand with a rolling pin, but a machine does make it much easier.

TINI'S TIPS

You can also make the pasta dough in a food processor. Simply dump all the ingredients in and pulse until a dough ball forms, 5 to 6 pulses. Wrap and rest as directed.

00 flour has a finer texture than all-purpose flour, so it's ideal for making fresh pasta because it makes a tender dough that is easy to roll yet not so tender that it tears. You can use all-purpose flour; the noodles just won't be as tender.

you know your pasta dough is done when you slightly press it and the dent bounces back

1. Make the Dough

- Mound the flour onto a clean work surface (or in a large bowl) and use your hands to form a well in the center. Add the eggs, olive oil, and salt to the well. Using a fork, beat the eggs to break up the yolks. Gradually begin to incorporate the flour until the dough turns into a shaggy mixture.

2. Knead It

- Once the dough becomes too tough for the fork, use your hands to bring it together into a ball **A**. Knead the dough by pushing the dough ball forward with the heel of your hand **B**, then turning it a quarter turn and repeating until it's soft, supple, and smooth, about 5 minutes—dust the surface lightly with more flour as needed to keep the dough from sticking, but don't add so much that the dough becomes dry and hard to knead. You'll end up with a smooth ball **C**. When it's ready, the dough should spring back when gently pressed with your fingertip.

3. Wrap and Rest

- Divide the dough in half and shape each half into a flat square. Wrap each in plastic wrap and let stand at room temperature for at least 30 minutes and up to 2 hours **D**. Pasta dough can be wrapped tightly and refrigerated for up to 1 day. Bring it to room temperature before rolling.

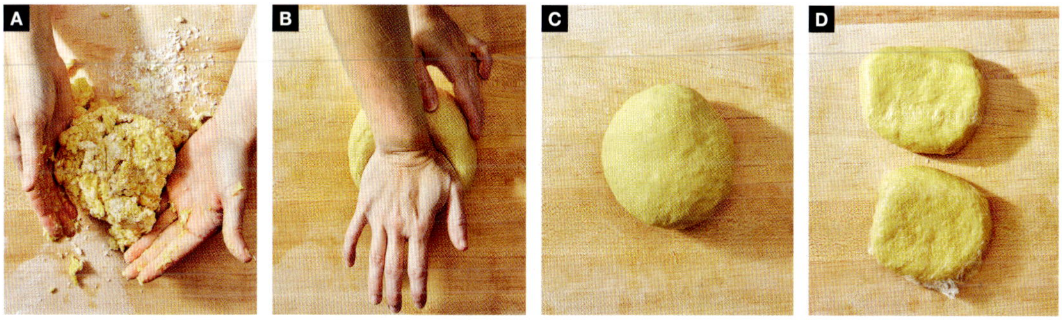

recipe continues ▸▸

4. Roll the Dough

- Lightly dust your work surface with flour and, using a rolling pin, roll out one dough half (keep the other piece of dough covered with plastic wrap so it doesn't dry out) to a large rectangle, about 20 × 12 inches **E**—it should be thin enough that you can see the outline of the palm of your hand through it **F**. If you have a pasta maker or pasta roller attachment for your stand mixer, you can use that, passing the dough through each number twice up to 7 (if using a machine, you'll need to cut the dough halves into quarters).

5. Cut the Dough

- **FOR FETTUCCINE:** Arrange the rectangle of rolled dough on your work surface and dust lightly with more flour if it's at all tacky (cut it into more manageable pieces if needed). Using a sharp knife or pizza cutter, slice the dough into long ¼-inch-thick strands **G** or, if your pasta maker has a fettuccine-cutting attachment, you can use that. Transfer the noodles to a baking sheet and gently toss with a bit more flour to keep the strands from sticking to one another as you gently let them fall into a small nest. Repeat the rolling and cutting process with the second piece of dough.

6. Storing Fresh Pasta

- Homemade fresh pasta noodles can be made up to 1 day ahead, although they are best cooked within a few hours (store-bought fresh pasta has a longer shelf life than homemade). Sprinkle the baking sheet with extra flour (you can use a little semolina, too), cover with plastic wrap, and refrigerate.
- For longer storage, you can freeze cut noodles. It works really well. You can dust them with flour and twirl them into little nests. Let the nests dry on the counter for about an hour, then transfer them to an airtight container (in a single layer), cover, and freeze.

7. Cooking Fresh Pasta That's Been Frozen

- You can cook frozen pasta directly from the freezer. Just add to boiling water and cook as you would fresh pasta. Do not defrost frozen pasta before cooking, because it can affect the texture; the noodles will likely get sticky and clump together.

Potato Gnocchi

WITH BROWN BUTTER AND FRIED SAGE

Serves 4 to 6

GNOCCHI

2 pounds Yukon Gold potatoes

1 teaspoon kosher salt, plus more for salting the water

2 cups / 260g 00 flour or all-purpose flour, plus more for the work surface

2 large egg yolks

BROWN BUTTER SAGE SAUCE

6 tablespoons unsalted butter

Freshly ground black pepper

8 large sage leaves

Kosher salt

SERVING

1 ounce Parmesan cheese, finely grated (½ cup)

To prepare myself for competing on *Next Level Chef,* I watched the entire first season. The contestants were all making gnocchi, so for a week, I made it till I nailed it. I worked really hard to perfect it—I will toot my horn on this one. The cloud-like pillows of potato are soft, light, and tender and are my kind of comfort food. I make different types of sauces depending on the season: pumpkin or squash in fall, lemon and herb in spring, and pesto or a creamy Alfredo year-round. I like my gnocchi a little crunchy, so after boiling them, I fry them up in the brown butter, then sprinkle them with the crispy sage leaves.

TINI'S TIPS

If you're a beginner cook, don't be tempted to boil your potatoes for this recipe. Boiling them introduces moisture that will change the amount of flour needed. You may cook them in the microwave, though: Using a fork, prick the potatoes several times and cook on high until they are fork-tender, 7 to 10 minutes, flipping halfway through the cooking time.

It's VERY important to break up your potatoes by using a potato ricer, grating them, or pushing them through a fine-mesh strainer. Do not just mash them.

1. Bake and Peel the Potatoes

- Preheat the oven to 400°F. Prick the potatoes all over with a fork and place them on a foil-lined baking sheet. Bake until they are fork-tender, 45 to 50 minutes. Let the potatoes cool to the touch, then peel them using a paring knife or peeler.

2. Boil Some Water

- Fill a large pot three quarters full with water and salt it like the ocean (see page 99). Bring the water to a boil while you make the dough.

3. Make the Dough

- Into a large bowl, press the baked potatoes through a potato ricer **A**. If you don't have one, grate the potatoes using the large holes of a box grater or press them through a fine-mesh strainer.
- Add the flour, egg yolks, and the 1 teaspoon salt. Using a rubber spatula, stir until the mixture becomes stiff and you can't stir it anymore **B**.
- Using your hands, bring the dough together and transfer it to a floured surface. Knead the dough, pushing the dough ball forward with the heel of your hand, then turning it a quarter turn, and pushing again, repeating until it's soft, supple, and smooth, about 10 minutes—dust the surface lightly with more flour as needed to keep the dough from sticking **C**. When it's ready, the dough should spring back when gently pressed with your fingertip.

recipe continues ▸▸

4. Shape and Cut the Dough

- Cut the springy dough ball into 4 equal pieces **D**. Using your hands, on a lightly floured surface, roll one of the dough pieces into an 18-inch-long rope **E**. Using a bench scraper, cut the rope into ½-inch-thick pieces that resemble little pillows **F** and put them on a floured baking sheet. Repeat the process with the remaining 3 pieces of dough.
- THIS IS OPTIONAL: If you'd like to add the grooved texture you see on traditional gnocchi, dip a fork in flour, and hold the fork upright at a slight angle with the tines pressing into the counter and the backside facing up. Place a piece of gnocchi at the top of the backside of the fork, press down slightly with your thumb, and slowly slide the dough down your fork, letting it roll right off to create a lined texture **G**. (These ridges help the sauce stick to the pasta.) Repeat this with all the pieces of gnocchi.

5. Brown the Butter, Fry the Leaves

- Place the butter in a large stainless or light-colored skillet over medium heat (you want to be able to see the butter as it changes color, see page 244). Once it's melted, add a few big pinches of pepper and cook, swirling the pan occasionally, until the butter is golden and beginning to smell nutty, 3 to 4 minutes. You should see milk solids starting to turn dark on the bottom of the pan. Add the sage leaves and cook until crisp and fragrant, 15 to 30 seconds, using tongs to turn them. Remove the sage leaves from the butter and reserve them as a garnish. Turn the heat off under the skillet.

6. Cook the Gnocchi and Plate

- Using a spider or slotted spoon, lower the gnocchi into the boiling water and cook at a simmer. When the gnocchi floats, simmer until the pasta is cooked through, another 2 to 3 minutes.
- Again, using a spider or slotted spoon, transfer the cooked gnocchi to the brown butter sauce **H** (be careful, it may spatter), tossing to combine and adding a few splashes of pasta water as needed to create a sauce that coats the pillows. Season to taste with salt and pepper. Transfer the pasta to a serving platter, garnish with the fried sage leaves, and sprinkle with the cheese. Serve immediately.

SWAP IT

Almost any type of starchy vegetable will work to make gnocchi. Switch out the potatoes for the same amount of butternut squash, sweet potatoes, pumpkin, or beets.

Sunday Red Sauce

WITH MINI MEATBALLS

Serves 6 to 8
(Makes 2 quarts of sauce and 38 mini meatballs)

SAUCE

- ½ stick (4 tablespoons) unsalted butter
- 1 tablespoon extra-virgin olive oil
- 2 shallots, minced
- 7 to 9 garlic cloves, finely grated or minced
- 2 tablespoons chopped basil, plus more for serving
- 2 teaspoons chopped thyme
- 1 tablespoon balsamic vinegar
- 2 (28-ounce) cans whole peeled tomatoes in their juice
- 1 (28-ounce) can fire-roasted crushed tomatoes
- 1 sweet onion, quartered **A**
- 2 teaspoons kosher salt
- ½ teaspoon freshly ground black pepper

MEATBALLS

- ⅓ cup whole milk
- ¾ cup Italian bread crumbs
- 1 pound ground beef
- 1 pound ground pork
- 3 large eggs
- 1 ounce Parmesan cheese, finely grated (about ½ cup), plus more for serving
- ¼ cup minced sweet onion
- 2 tablespoons chopped basil, plus whole leaves for garnish
- 3 to 4 garlic cloves, finely grated
- 2 teaspoons kosher salt
- 1 teaspoon chopped thyme
- ¾ teaspoon freshly ground black pepper
- ½ teaspoon garlic powder
- ½ teaspoon onion powder

I like a one-bite meatball. If you have a small mouth, it might be two bites, but in any case I firmly believe you shouldn't have to cut a meatball with a knife and fork. You definitely need only a fork for these babies, because they are perfectly tender but not so soft that they fall apart. I cut down on cooking time by browning the meatballs under the broiler, which is more efficient (and less messy!) than cooking on the stovetop. Where I don't cut time, though, is with my thick, rich sauce. The key is slow cooking (perfect for a Sunday!), which allows the flavors to develop. The garlic and onion mellow and become sweet along with the tomatoes. These meatballs can hold their own without pasta, but a little spaghetti never hurt no one.

TINI'S TIPS

For tender meatballs, be gentle—do not overmix or press hard!

To freeze meatballs, place them in a single layer on a parchment-lined baking sheet in the freezer, then when solid, transfer to resealable bags and keep for up to 3 months.

During the summer, I use fresh tomatoes. I roast them (see page 145) to deepen their flavor, then peel and deseed them. In the winter, or when I have less time, I use canned.

1. Make the Sauce

- In a large Dutch oven or pot over medium heat, add the butter and oil and cook until the butter melts. Add the shallots and garlic, and cook until the shallots are translucent, about 3 minutes. Stir in the basil and thyme and cook for 1 minute. Add the vinegar and bring it to a boil. Add all the tomatoes, the quartered onion, salt, and pepper **B**.
- Bring the sauce to a boil. Reduce the heat to low and simmer, partially covered, stirring occasionally to avoid sticking, for 2 hours **C**. Remove the pot from the heat and using a potato masher, break up the tomatoes and onion, mashing until you get a chunky sauce. You may remove any large onion pieces that don't break down (or leave them—they are nice and sweet!).

2. Make the Meatballs

- In a small bowl, combine the milk and the bread crumbs and stir until all the bread crumbs are moistened.
- In a large bowl, combine the beef, pork, eggs, Parmesan, onion, basil, garlic, salt, thyme, pepper, garlic powder, and onion powder. Add the moistened bread crumbs.
- With your hands, gently squeeze the mixture to combine (you might want to wear gloves!), rubbing any clumps of bread crumbs between your thumb and forefinger to evenly disperse them. Get all in there to make sure everything is evenly mixed, but once it is, stop to avoid overmixing.
- Using your hands, make golf-ball-size meatballs (a heaping tablespoon or just over 1 ounce each). You should get 36 to 38 meatballs. Line them up on a rimmed baking sheet, or two if you need, with just less than an inch between each one **D**.

3. Brown the Meatballs

- Move a rack about 6 inches from the broiler and preheat to high. Broil the meatballs until browned, about 6 minutes. Then, using a spatula, gently turn them over and brown the other side, about another 6 minutes.

4. Add the Meatballs to the Sauce

- Using a spatula, tilt the pan and slide the browned meatballs into the sauce, scraping in any juices or browned bits that have accumulated. You may also add a tablespoon or two of water to thin the sauce if necessary. Bring the sauce to a simmer over medium-low and cook until the meatballs are cooked through (when an instant-read thermometer is inserted into the center of a meatball, it will read 145°F), 5 to 10 minutes.

5. Garnish and Serve

- Transfer spoonfuls of the meatballs with sauce to shallow bowls and top with lots of Parmesan and a few basil leaves.
- Leftover sauce can be refrigerated for up to 3 days or frozen for up to 3 months.

SWAP IT

To make spaghetti and meatballs, reserve two cups of sauce without meatballs. Cook 1 pound of spaghetti and transfer it back to the pot after draining, add the reserved 2 cups of sauce, and, using tongs, toss to combine. Serve the pasta in bowls, with cooked meatballs and more sauce on top.

A

B

C

D

No-Fail Bacon Carbonara

Serves 4

Kosher salt

1 large egg plus 3 large egg yolks, at room temperature

1½ ounces Pecorino Romano cheese, finely grated (about ¾ cup), plus more for serving

½ ounce Parmesan cheese, finely grated (about ¼ cup)

Freshly ground black pepper

4 slices thick-cut bacon, cut into ½-inch pieces

12 ounces dried spaghetti

After you nail my creamy Alfredo (page 100), I encourage you to move on to this carbonara, another classic pasta sauce, but made with only bacon, eggs, and Parmesan and pecorino cheeses. The sauce is so rich and silky—it is downright indulgent. It does take some skill to make something so good with so few ingredients, though. If you move too fast, or cook the eggs over high heat, you'll scramble them, and your sauce will go from smooth to curdled. The secret to no-fail carbonara is timing and room-temp eggs.

TINI'S TIPS

Traditional carbonara is made with guanciale, a cured meat made from pork jowl. Bacon has a similar rich, smoky flavor and is easier to come by, so I mostly use that, but if you happen to see guanciale in your grocery store, you can use the same amount for a more authentic carbonara.

If you want to cook a full pound of pasta (this recipe calls for ¾ pound), set aside a quarter of cooked pasta for later. To prevent the noodles from sticking together, toss with olive oil before putting them in a storage container. Then you've got a base for a quick lunch or single-serve meal.

1. Get Ready

- Fill a large pot three quarters full with water and season with salt (use about half of what you normally would when cooking pasta, as the cheese and bacon add a lot of the saltiness for this dish, so go easy—more like brackish water than the ocean). Bring the water to a boil.
- Fill a large bowl with very hot water. Set aside.
- In a small bowl, using a fork, whisk together the egg, egg yolks, pecorino, Parmesan, and a small pinch of salt and pepper until well combined **A**. Set aside. (We are doing this now to ensure everything is room temp!)

2. Cook the Bacon

- In a large skillet over medium heat, add the bacon and cook, using tongs to stir occasionally, until crisp and the fat has rendered, 8 to 10 minutes **B**. Move the bacon to one side of the skillet and, with a pair of tongs, grip some paper towels and blot out some of the excess grease from the skillet, leaving no more than 1 tablespoon behind. Turn off the heat and leave the skillet on the burner until you are ready for the pasta.

3. Cook the Pasta

- While the bacon cooks, add the pasta to the boiling water and cook according to the package directions for al dente.
- Turn the heat under the skillet with the cooked bacon back to low. Using tongs, lift the cooked pasta from the water and transfer it to the skillet, tossing it over low heat for 1 minute (it's okay if some water is still clinging to the noodles) **C**.
- Add 2 tablespoons of the pasta cooking water to the bowl with the egg and cheeses and whisk until smooth. Reserve 1 cup more of the pasta water.

4. Emulsify the Sauce and Serve

- Dump the now-warm water out of the large bowl from earlier, thoroughly wipe it dry, then add the pasta and bacon.
- Drizzle the egg mixture over the pasta **D**, vigorously tossing with tongs until the sauce coats every strand of spaghetti. If needed, add another splash of the reserved pasta water to loosen.
- Season to taste with salt, then serve immediately, topped with another generous pinch of pepper and more pecorino.

The Best Beans and Grains

How to Cook Beans
(PLUS A VINAIGRETTE!)

Makes 5 to 6 cups of beans and about ⅔ cup vinaigrette

BEANS

- 1 pound dried beans, such as pinto, kidney, black, navy, or black-eyed peas (about 2 cups)
- 2 tablespoons kosher salt
- 1 teaspoon extra-virgin olive oil
- 1 yellow onion, halved
- 1 head of garlic, halved crosswise
- 1 small Fresno chile, halved and seeded (optional)
- 8 sprigs parsley, plus 2 tablespoons finely chopped leaves
- 2 dried bay leaves
- 1½ teaspoons whole black peppercorns
- 2 celery stalks, cut into 3-inch pieces
- 12 cups water

VINAIGRETTE

- ¼ cup freshly squeezed lemon juice
- 1 tablespoon Dijon mustard
- 1 teaspoon whole-grain mustard
- ⅓ cup extra-virgin olive oil
- Kosher salt and freshly ground black pepper

SPECIAL EQUIPMENT

Cheesecloth

TBH, I rarely cook beans from scratch because it feels like a pain to me. Everything about it takes a while—the soaking, the cooking. My go-to is always beans from a can. I do know, though, that good home-cooked beans are *really good.* When you simmer dried beans with aromatics, it infuses them with flavor that you won't get from canned beans, plus you can control the texture. Beans also freeze well, so you can cook up a big batch at once. And dried beans are more economical than their canned counterparts. If you've never cooked dried beans, I say go for it. Make a batch and decide for yourself if it's worth it. To make these beans extra flavorful, I toss them in a vinaigrette when they are warm.

TINI'S TIPS

Forgot to soak your beans? Save time by pouring boiling water over the dried beans and letting them sit for 2 hours before draining and proceeding with the recipe.

If you don't have cheesecloth for the herb sachet, throw the whole herbs in the pot and replace the peppercorns with ½ teaspoon ground black pepper.

Leaving the skins on the onion and garlic adds flavor.

1. Sort, Rinse, and Soak the Beans

- Place the beans in a colander and pick through and discard any stones or dried out and shriveled beans that you see **A**. Rinse well under cool water, then transfer to a large bowl and stir in 1 tablespoon of the salt.
- Add enough water so that the beans are covered by 3 inches **B**, then seal the bowl with plastic wrap. Move the beans to the refrigerator and let them soak overnight **C**. Drain and rinse again **D**.

2. Char the Aromatics

- In a large stockpot over medium-high heat, add the olive oil and heat until it shimmers. Add the onion and garlic, cut-sides down, and the chile (if using). Cook until well charred (there will be visible black spots), about 5 minutes.

3. Cook the Beans

- Meanwhile, place the parsley sprigs, bay leaves, and peppercorns in a small piece of cheesecloth and tie into a bundle, securing with a piece of twine. Add the herb bundle, celery, the remaining 1 tablespoon salt, and the water to the pot, then stir in the drained beans.
- Bring the mixture to a boil, skimming off any foam that rises to the surface. Reduce the heat to low, cover, and simmer until the beans are tender and creamy, 1½ to 2 hours. Drain the beans and discard the onion, garlic, chili, celery, and herb sachet (or whole herbs if not using a sachet).

4. Make the Vinaigrette

- In a large bowl, whisk together the lemon juice and both mustards. While whisking, gradually drizzle in the olive oil until thick and emulsified. Season to taste with salt and pepper.
- Gently stir in the beans while they're warm, tossing to coat in the vinaigrette. Season again with salt and pepper to taste (don't be shy!). Serve warm or at room temperature.

SWAP IT

For an added burst of smoky flavor, add a 1-pound smoked ham hock to the pot when you add the water—since the ham hock is very salty, reduce the salt in this step to 1½ teaspoons (and omit the salt when soaking). To the vinaigrette, if using, replace the lemon juice with cider vinegar and add ½ teaspoon sweet paprika before tossing with the beans. Serve big bowls with a poached or fried egg, the ham hock (shredded, if desired), and a generous drizzle of hot sauce, and you've got yourself a satisfying meal perfect for brunch, lunch, or dinner.

A

B

C

D

Marinated Three-Bean Salad

WITH HEARTS OF PALM

Serves 6

VINAIGRETTE

- ¼ cup red wine vinegar, plus more to taste
- ½ red onion, thinly sliced
- 2 to 3 garlic cloves, finely grated
- 2 teaspoons sugar
- 1½ teaspoons chopped fresh oregano or ½ teaspoon dried oregano
- 1 teaspoon fresh thyme leaves
- ¼ teaspoon crushed red pepper flakes
- ½ cup extra-virgin olive oil
- 2 teaspoons kosher salt, plus more for salting the water
- ½ teaspoon freshly ground black pepper

SALAD

- Kosher salt
- 10 ounces green beans, trimmed
- 1 (15.5-ounce) can kidney beans, drained and rinsed
- 1 (15.5-ounce) can chickpeas, drained and rinsed
- 1 (14-ounce) can hearts of palm, drained and cut into 1-inch pieces
- Freshly ground black pepper

SERVING

- ½ cup packed basil leaves, torn

Using a couple of techniques like marinating and blanching can turn a simple salad into something special. Leaving the beans and vegetables in the fridge overnight gives them time to soak up the dressing and for the flavors to meld (you can also shorten the marinating time by leaving them out at room temp). Hearts of palm, which kind of look like white asparagus, are pretty mild and really take on the marinade's flavors. They are usually sold in cans or glass jars and are a great pantry staple. They add an interesting crispy yet tender texture when added to pastas and salads.

A TINI TIP

Shocking vegetables in an ice-water bath stops the cooking and prevents them from becoming overcooked and mushy.

1. Make the Vinaigrette

- In a large bowl, stir together the vinegar, onion, and garlic. Let stand for 10 minutes. Add the sugar, oregano, thyme, and red pepper flakes. Whisk in the olive oil. Season with the salt and black pepper. Taste the dressing—it should be tangy and a bit sweet. If it's not, add more vinegar and/or sugar to taste.

2. Blanch and Shock the Fresh Beans

- Fill a large bowl with ice and water.
- Bring a medium pot of salted water to just a boil.
- Add the green beans to the boiling water and cook until bright green and just tender, about 1 minute after the water comes back to a boil.
- Using a slotted spoon or spider, immediately transfer the beans to the bowl of ice water. Swish them around until they are cool and use a spider or slotted spoon to remove them from the water. Pat them dry and cut into 1-inch pieces.

3. Assemble the Salad

- Add the green beans to the bowl with the dressing. Add the kidney beans, chickpeas, and hearts of palm. Season with salt and pepper.

4. Marinate

- Let the salad marinate at room temperature for up to 1 hour or in the refrigerator overnight. Taste for seasonings after marinating, and sprinkle with the basil leaves just before serving.

SWAP IT

Make it any bean—replace the chickpeas or kidney beans with your favorites. Black-eyed peas are great, as are white beans and even edamame! If you can find wax or Romano beans, use them in place of or in addition to the green beans.

Creamy Grits

WITH SAUTÉED MUSHROOMS AND BUTTERNUT SQUASH

Serves 4

GRITS

- 2 cups water
- 2 cups whole milk
- 2 tablespoons unsalted butter
- ½ teaspoon kosher salt
- ¼ teaspoon freshly ground black pepper
- 1 cup stone-ground white corn grits
- 6 ounces mild cheddar cheese, coarsely grated (1½ cups)
- 2 ounces Parmesan cheese, finely grated (1 cup)

VEGETABLES

- ¼ cup extra-virgin olive oil
- 1 pound butternut squash, peeled, seeded, and diced
- 1¼ teaspoons kosher salt
- 12 ounces cremini mushrooms, stems trimmed and quartered
- 1 medium red onion, chopped
- 1 large garlic clove, smashed and peeled (see page 23)
- 2 teaspoons minced thyme leaves
- 2 teaspoons Tini's Spice Blend (page 76) or Creole seasoning
- ¼ teaspoon crushed red pepper flakes

SAUCE

- 1 cup vegetable broth
- ¼ cup cider vinegar
- ½ stick (4 tablespoons) cold unsalted butter, cut into small pieces
- 1 teaspoon cornstarch
- Fresh parsley leaves, for garnish (optional)

When I was little, I didn't like oatmeal and I hated grits. It was a texture thing. Then in culinary school I was introduced to cheesy grits. Now I like grits a lot. They are comforting, and I eat them any time of day—breakfast, lunch, or dinner. I always make them savory, though. No sweet grits for me. I like to top grits with andouille sausage, an egg, even just hot sauce. Here I make them rich and hearty with squash and mushrooms and a buttery cider sauce that soaks into the grits. I don't think anyone will miss the meat.

TINI'S TIPS

The easiest way to break down a butternut squash: First, remove the top and bottom with a large knife so that the squash can stand up flat. Then run a Y-shaped vegetable peeler down the sides of the squash to remove the skin **A**. Slice the squash in half vertically **B**, then use a spoon to scoop out the seeds **C**.

The squash can be chopped **D** and refrigerated in an airtight container, covered with a damp paper towel, for up to 2 days.

Drizzle hot sauce on this dish for an extra kick.

1. Make the Grits

- In a medium saucepan over medium-high heat, combine the water, milk, butter, salt, and pepper and bring to a boil, then reduce the heat to low and, using a whisk, stir in the grits. Cover the pan and let the grits simmer, stirring occasionally, adding more water if the grits become too stiff or dry, until they are creamy and soft, 15 to 20 minutes.
- After the grits have softened, stir in the cheddar and Parmesan until melted, and set aside with the lid on the pan to keep them warm.

2. Sauté the Vegetables

- In a large skillet over medium-high heat, add 2 tablespoons of the olive oil and heat until it shimmers. Add the butternut squash and ½ teaspoon of the salt and cook, stirring occasionally, until golden and tender, 10 to 13 minutes. Transfer to a plate and set aside.
- Add the remaining 2 tablespoons olive oil, then add the mushrooms, onion, garlic, and ½ teaspoon salt to the skillet. Cook, stirring occasionally, until golden and tender, 6 to 8 minutes. Stir in the thyme, spice blend, and red pepper flakes and cook until fragrant and toasted, about 1 minute.

3. Make the Sauce and Serve

- Stir in the broth and vinegar and bring to a vigorous simmer. Add the butter, a few small pieces at a time, stirring until fully melted and smooth.
- **MAKE A SLURRY:** Transfer 1 tablespoon of the broth mixture to a small bowl and whisk in the cornstarch (it's important to dissolve the cornstarch with the broth first; if you add it directly to the sauce it can form lumps). Add the slurry to the skillet and stir for a few seconds, just until beginning to thicken.
- Return the squash to the skillet, then remove from the heat and season with the remaining ¼ teaspoon salt.
- Divide the grits among four shallow bowls, tapping the bottoms with the palm of your hand to even them out, then top with the sautéed vegetables and their sauce. Garnish with parsley, if using, and serve.

A

B

How to Cook the Perfect Rice

Makes about 3 cups

- 1 cup long-grain rice, such as basmati or jasmine
- ½ teaspoon kosher salt
- 1¾ cups water
- 1 tablespoon unsalted butter (optional)

If you think it's weird that I have a recipe for white rice in this book, let me tell you why I do—because this is a learning book. I want to teach you from the basics up. Making properly cooked white rice is not as easy as it seems. It's a building block for many recipes, including some in this book.

Here's how I do it:

I don't really measure things if I don't have to, even rice. I like to use the fingertip method when cooking rice. First, I add rice to the pot, put in my index or middle finger to touch the top of the rice **A**, then add water up to the first knuckle on my finger **B**. This recipe uses a ratio of slightly less liquid than 2:1, which keeps the grains of rice really light and fluffy. Rinsing the rice until the water runs clear also washes away extra starch, which can make rice mushy. Sometimes I make Antoine cook the rice because he always makes it perfectly!

TINI'S TIPS

For extra flavor, swap the water for a flavorful chicken or vegetable stock, or throw in one or two bouillon cubes when adding the water.

This recipe can also easily be doubled—just use a medium saucepan instead!

1. Rinse the Rice

- Place the rice in a medium bowl and cover completely with cool water. Swish the rice and water around with your fingers, then drain through a fine-mesh strainer. Continue rinsing and draining a few more times, until the water runs clear. Drain again.

2. Cook the Rice

- In a small saucepan, combine the rinsed rice, salt, and water. Bring to a boil over medium-high heat, then reduce the heat to low and cover. Simmer, undisturbed, until the liquid is completely absorbed and the rice is fluffy and tender, 15 to 18 minutes.
- Add the butter, if using, then cover again and remove from the heat. Let the rice stand for 10 minutes, then fluff with a fork and serve. Leftover rice can be cooled completely, then stored in airtight containers in the refrigerator for up to 3 days or in the freezer for up to 3 months. If freezing, thaw in the refrigerator overnight before using.

Easy Rice Pilaf

Serves 4
(Makes a generous 3 cups)

- 1 cup long-grain rice, such as basmati or jasmine
- 3 tablespoons unsalted butter
- 1 small yellow onion, finely chopped
- 2 scallions, thinly sliced, white and green parts separated
- 3 garlic cloves, finely grated
- ¾ teaspoon kosher salt
- ½ teaspoon freshly ground black pepper
- ¼ teaspoon smoked paprika
- ¼ teaspoon chili powder
- 1¾ cups low-sodium chicken broth or water
- ½ teaspoon grated lemon zest

Pilaf is a great side to chicken (page 43) or fish (page 70), or even beans. Plus, it's really pretty easy. There are many kinds of pilaf in this world—it's a very global dish in which rice or a type of grain is sautéed in a fat like butter or oil, then cooked with stock, and usually meat or vegetables are added. The technique makes the grains very fluffy, and flavorful, too. It's definitely worth the little bit of added effort to make rice go from boring to not. And if you are a rice lover, you might just love it all on its own.

1. Rinse the Rice

- Place the rice in a medium bowl and cover completely with cool water. Swish the rice and water around with your fingers, then rinse through a fine-mesh strainer. Continue rinsing and draining a few more times, until the water runs clear (washing the grains removes extra starch, which results in fluffier rice). Drain again, then set aside.

2. Sauté the Aromatics

- In a medium skillet over medium heat, melt the butter. Add the onion, white parts of the scallions, and garlic and season with ½ teaspoon of the salt. Cook, stirring occasionally, until softened and beginning to brown in places, 8 to 10 minutes.

3. Bloom the Spices

- Add the pepper, smoked paprika, and chili powder and cook until very fragrant, about 2 minutes.
- Add the drained rice, stirring to coat in the butter and spices. Cook for 1 minute.

4. Simmer the Pilaf and Serve

- Stir in the chicken broth and the remaining ¼ teaspoon salt and bring to a boil. Reduce the heat to low and cover. Simmer, undisturbed, until the liquid is completely absorbed and the rice is fluffy and tender, 18 to 20 minutes.
- Remove from the heat and let the rice stand, covered, for 10 minutes, then fluff with a fork, stir in the scallion greens and lemon zest, and serve.

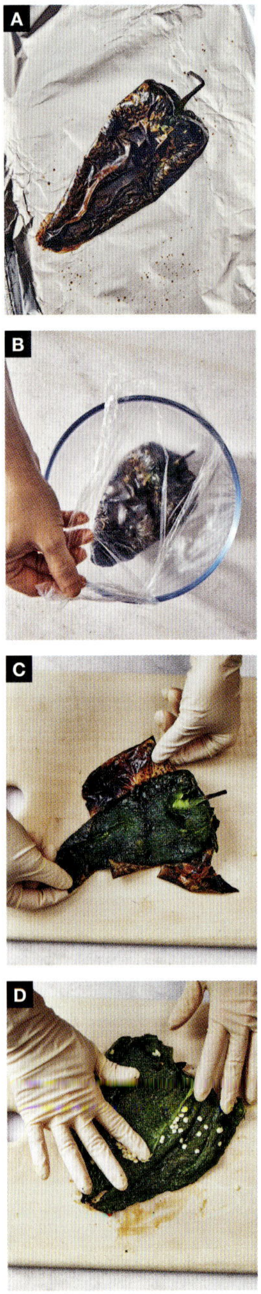
A
B
C
D

Baked Rice

WITH BROCCOLI AND ROASTED POBLANO CREAM SAUCE

Serves 4 to 6

- 1 large poblano pepper
- 2 tablespoons unsalted butter
- 1 medium yellow onion, chopped
- 3 garlic cloves, chopped
- 2 teaspoons smoked paprika
- 2 teaspoons kosher salt
- ½ teaspoon freshly ground black pepper
- ¼ teaspoon freshly grated nutmeg
- 1 cup heavy cream
- 1 tablespoon Dijon mustard
- 1 cup medium-grain white rice, rinsed
- 3 cups low-sodium chicken broth, plus more as needed
- 1 large broccoli crown (about ¾ pound), roughly chopped
- 8 ounces sharp cheddar cheese, grated (about 2 cups)
- 8 ounces Monterey Jack cheese, grated (about 2 cups)

I think cheese and broccoli go well together—it's a classic combination, kind of like bacon and eggs. Who's going to question it? Make me a cheese and broccoli casserole and I would be thrilled. This is a take on that hot dish idea. The broccoli and rice cook together with a comforting poblano cream until they are tender, and then you stir in the cheese and it melts all in, making it cheesy and satisfying, and something I want to eat more of. It's kind of like a mac and cheese made with rice and broccoli. It's exactly the kind of comfort food I like.

A TINI TIP

For a pretty presentation, leave about a third of the broccoli in medium-size florets—you can arrange those toward the top of the dish before broiling.

1. Roast the Pepper

- Move a rack about 6 inches from the broiler and preheat it to high. Place the poblano on an aluminum-foil-lined baking sheet. Broil, flipping the pepper occasionally with tongs, until well charred all over, 10 to 12 minutes **A**. Transfer to a small bowl, cover with a plate or plastic wrap, and let stand for 15 minutes **B**. Once cool enough to handle, peel away the skin **C** and remove the stem, ribs, and seeds **D**. Set aside.

2. Sauté the Aromatics

- In a 12-inch ovenproof skillet with a lid, melt the butter over medium heat. Add the onion and garlic and cook, stirring occasionally, until softened and browned in places, 6 to 8 minutes.

3. Bloom the Spices

- Add the smoked paprika, ¾ teaspoon of the salt, the pepper, and nutmeg and cook, stirring to coat the onion and garlic with the spices, until fragrant, about 1 minute. Remove from the heat and let cool slightly.

4. Blend the Cream Sauce

- In a high-speed blender, combine the charred poblano, sautéed onion mixture, heavy cream, and mustard. Blend on high until smooth and creamy, about 1 minute.

5. Cook the Rice

- To the same skillet in which you cooked the aromatics, add the poblano cream, rice, chicken broth, broccoli, and the remaining 1¼ teaspoons salt, stirring to combine and scraping the bottom of the pan to release any cooked spices. Bring the mixture to a boil, then reduce the heat to low, cover, and simmer until the rice and broccoli are tender. This can vary widely depending on your heat source. Start checking for doneness after 18 minutes, then continue checking every few minutes until the rice is cooked (it shouldn't be sticky or mushy). If the mixture seems dry, you can add a splash of broth or water.
- Set aside ½ cup of each cheese, then uncover the skillet and stir in the remaining cheese until melted. Sprinkle the reserved cheese evenly over the top.

6. Broil the Cheese

- Move a rack about 8 inches from the broiler and preheat it to high.
- Place the skillet under the heat and broil until the cheese is melted and browned in spots, 5 to 8 minutes (keep a close eye on this). Let cool for at least 15 minutes before serving.

SWAP IT

Use your own unique mix of cheeses—cheddar is a good one to keep, since it melts well, but the Monterey Jack can be swapped with Gruyère, Parmesan, Manchego, fontina, and more.

Want to spice things up? Swap the smoky poblano pepper for 2 large finely minced jalapeños and throw them in to cook when you sauté the aromatics.

Cajun-Inspired Andouille and Rice

Serves 4

- 1 tablespoon vegetable oil
- 14 ounces andouille pork sausage, cut on the diagonal into ¾-inch slices
- 1 green bell pepper, diced
- 1 yellow onion, diced
- 3 ribs of celery, diced
- 3 garlic cloves, finely grated
- 1 to 2 tablespoons Tini's Spice Blend (page 76) or store-bought Creole seasoning, plus more to taste
- 2 teaspoons smoked paprika
- 1 (14.5-ounce) can fire-roasted diced tomatoes
- 1½ cups chicken broth
- 1 cup long grain rice, rinsed and drained
- 2 bay leaves
- ½ teaspoon kosher salt, plus more to taste
- ¼ teaspoon freshly ground black pepper, plus more to taste
- 2 scallions, for garnish

I love New Orleans. It's one of my top three favorite cities I've been to—everyone was nice, even a little mysterious. There was a real vampire-type vibe. I especially love their flavor-packed Cajun-style cuisine. I can still remember walking down Bourbon Street and taking in all the restaurants' inviting aromas. This dish is my ode to that city. Andouille is smoky and spicy and has its roots in Cajun cooking. (If you can't find it, you can sub in kielbasa.) Combine it with the holy trinity of Cajun or Creole food (equal parts green pepper, onion, and celery), add some rice and seasonings, and you've got yourself a (big) easy meal.

1. Brown the Sausage

- In a large, straight-sided skillet or pot over medium heat, add the oil and heat until it shimmers. Add the sausage and cook until browned on both sides, about 3 minutes per side.

2. Sauté the Aromatics

- To the skillet, add the pepper, onion, and celery and cook, stirring occasionally, until the onion is softened and translucent, 5 to 7 minutes.

3. Bloom the Spices

- Add the garlic, 1 tablespoon of the spice blend, and the smoked paprika and stir until the spices and garlic are fragrant, about 1 minute. Depending on the spiciness of your sausage and your personal heat preference, add more spice blend as desired.

4. Cook the Rice

- Add the tomatoes, chicken broth, rice, bay leaves, salt, and pepper and stir until combined. Bring the liquid to a boil, then reduce the heat to low, cover, and simmer until the rice is tender. This can vary widely depending on your heat source. Start checking for doneness after 15 minutes, then continue checking every few minutes until the rice is cooked (it shouldn't be sticky or mushy). If the mixture seems dry, you can add a splash of broth or water.

5. Garnish and Serve

- When the rice is done cooking, remove the skillet from the heat and let it sit, covered, for about 5 minutes. While the rice rests, thinly slice the scallions on the bias, which means to cut them diagonally, or at a 45-degree angle. (It makes them look pretty and professional!). Uncover, remove the bay leaves, and fluff the rice with a fork. Taste for seasonings and add salt, pepper, and more spice blend as needed. Garnish with the scallions and serve.

SWAP IT

Add cooked shrimp, chicken, tofu, or other proteins in addition to, or in place of, the sausage.

look how cool
it is when they
curl

Shrimp Fried Rice

Serves 4 to 6

MARINADE

1 pound raw large tail-on shrimp, peeled and deveined

1 tablespoon soy sauce

1 tablespoon oyster sauce

½ teaspoon toasted sesame oil

2 teaspoons rice vinegar

Kosher salt

STIR-FRY

5 tablespoons neutral oil, such as canola or vegetable

3 large eggs, lightly whisked

Kosher salt and freshly ground black pepper

1 large white onion, diced

2 scallions, white parts chopped and the greens reserved for garnish (to curl, see Tini's Tips)

1 large red bell pepper, chopped

3 garlic cloves, finely grated

4 cups cooked white rice, preferably a day old

FINISHING AND SERVING

3 tablespoons soy sauce

1 tablespoon oyster sauce

½ teaspoon toasted sesame oil

2 tablespoons unsalted butter, softened

Chili crisp (optional)

This one-pan dish is a brilliant way to use up leftovers, especially if you have a container of rice from takeout somewhere in your fridge. You want day-old rice, because the grains are drier and don't clump together when cooked. Sometimes I add so many things other than rice, you wouldn't even know it's a rice dish. Follow my proportions, though, and you'll get a balanced dish. And I'm just saying: Mise en place is your best friend here. Get everything chopped, cut, and prepped, and then it takes only minutes for the dish to come together. If you don't, you may end up thinking, "I should've listened to Tini."

TINI'S TIPS

If you want to make the rice the same day, you can spread out just-cooked rice on a baking sheet to allow the moisture to evaporate, then cool it in the fridge.

To get curly scallion greens like you'd see at a fancy restaurant, take your scallion greens (after you've used the whites in the recipe) and cut them in half crosswise to get roughly 2-inch pieces **A**. With the tip of your knife, cut those pieces lengthwise into thin strips **B**, the thinner they are, the curlier they'll get **C**. Submerge the strips in a small bowl of ice water for a minute or two and watch them curl **D**!

1. Marinate the Shrimp

- In a medium bowl, combine the shrimp with the soy sauce, oyster sauce, sesame oil, vinegar, and a pinch of salt. Toss gently and let sit at room temperature for 10 minutes.

2. Cook the Shrimp

- In a wok or large nonstick skillet over high heat, add 2 tablespoons of the neutral oil, then the shrimp and their liquid. Cook, turning halfway through the cooking time, until pink but not fully cooked through, about 1 minute per side. Transfer to a plate using a slotted spoon.

3. Scramble the Eggs

- Add 1 tablespoon neutral oil to the same pan and heat until it shimmers. Pour in the eggs, sprinkle with a pinch of salt and pepper and, using a rubber spatula, stir and scramble the eggs until just set, 1 to 2 minutes. Transfer to a small bowl.

4. Stir-Fry the Vegetables and Rice

- In the same pan, add 1 tablespoon of neutral oil and heat until it shimmers. Add the onion and scallion whites. Cook over medium-high heat until softened and translucent, about 3 minutes.
- Add the bell pepper and garlic and cook until slightly softened and fragrant, 2 minutes more.
- Using your spoon or spatula, push the vegetables to one side and add the remaining 1 tablespoon neutral oil to the clear spot in the pan; heat until it shimmers. Add the rice, breaking up any clumps with your spoon. Stir to coat in the oil and then stir in the vegetables and eggs. Cook undisturbed for 2 to 3 minutes to allow the rice to crisp slightly.

5. Finish and Serve

- Add the soy sauce, oyster sauce, and sesame oil to the pan with the rice. Return the shrimp to the pan and stir in the butter.
- Stir continuously for 2 to 3 minutes, until everything is well combined and the shrimp are cooked through.
- Spoon into bowls and serve immediately. Sprinkle with scallion greens and a drizzle of chili crisp, if using.

SWAP IT

Instead of shrimp, feel free to swap in one pound of any lean, quick-cooking protein, as long as it's cut into roughly 1-inch cubes. Try it with sirloin steak, chicken breasts, extra-firm tofu, pork tenderloin, or even bacon!

Asparagus Lemon Risotto

WITH CRISPY CAPERS

Serves 2 to 3 as a main / 4 as a side dish

Neutral oil, such as canola or vegetable, for frying

1 pound asparagus, ends trimmed and cut into 1-inch pieces and tips separated from the stalks

3 tablespoons capers, drained and rinsed

4 cups low-sodium chicken broth

1 cup water

3 tablespoons unsalted butter

2 tablespoons extra-virgin olive oil

Kosher salt and freshly ground black pepper, to taste

2 large shallots, finely chopped

3 garlic cloves, finely grated

1 cup Arborio rice

½ cup dry white wine

3 ounces Parmesan cheese, finely grated (about 1½ cups), plus more for serving

1 tablespoon freshly squeezed lemon juice

Basil leaves, for serving

Lemon wedges, for serving (optional)

Risotto, which I see on menus at fancy restaurants, is almost the opposite of rice pilaf (page 122), in which separated grains are key. You *want* the short-grain Arborio rice to get creamy and silky (but not mushy). Even though I think of this as a total comfort food, it still feels light and fresh to me. I get a little cheffy here and separately fry up the asparagus tips and capers for a crispy, briny topping that complements the brightness of the lemon and the nuttiness of the Parmesan. Risotto is very adaptable. It's kind of like pasta: You can switch out or add most any vegetable or protein.

A TINI TIP

The ends of asparagus tend to be woody and fibrous (not pleasant to eat). Each spear has a natural point that separates those woody ends from the rest. Hold an asparagus spear in both hands and simply snap it. You can then use that asparagus as a guide to know where to cut the rest.

1. Shallow-Fry the Topping

- In a medium, heavy-bottomed skillet over medium-high heat, pour in about ½ inch of neutral oil and heat until it sizzles when you dip in a chopstick or the end of a wooden spoon.
- Pat the asparagus tips and capers dry with paper towels. Add the asparagus tips to the hot oil and cook until crisp and golden, 3 to 5 minutes. Using a slotted spoon, transfer the asparagus to a paper towel–lined plate. Fry and drain the capers the same way–they should take 1 to 2 minutes to cook. Set aside.

2. Heat the Liquid

- In a medium saucepan over medium-high heat, combine the chicken broth and water. Bring it to a simmer, then reduce the heat to low and cover to keep warm.

3. Sauté the Asparagus

- In a large, straight-sided skillet over medium heat, melt 1 tablespoon of the butter. Cook until the butter begins to brown slightly and smell nutty, 1 to 2 minutes. Stir in 1 tablespoon of the olive oil. Add the remaining asparagus to the skillet and season with a pinch or two each of salt and pepper. Cook, stirring occasionally, until bright green and tender, 4 to 5 minutes. Transfer to a plate and set aside.

4. Cook the Risotto

- Add 1 tablespoon butter and the remaining 1 tablespoon olive oil to the same large skillet (still over medium heat), then add the shallots and cook, stirring occasionally, until softened, 3 to 4 minutes. Add the garlic and cook until fragrant, about 1 minute.
- **TOAST THE RICE:** Add the rice and cook, stirring frequently, until the grains are lightly toasted and some begin to pop in the pan, 2 minutes. Add the wine and cook until mostly evaporated, about 1 minute **A**.
- **STIR CONTINUOUSLY:** Stir in 2 cups of the warm broth and a pinch of salt **B**. Gently simmer, stirring continuously, until the liquid is almost completely absorbed, 6 to 8 minutes. If the risotto is bubbling too vigorously at any point, reduce the heat to medium-low. Continue adding more stock, ½ cup at a time **C**, and stirring until the rice is cooked but still slightly al dente, all of the liquid has been used, and the risotto is very smooth and creamy, about 25 minutes.

5. Finish the Risotto

- When the risotto is nice and creamy **D**, remove it from the heat and stir in the asparagus pieces (not tips), Parmesan, lemon juice, and the remaining 1 tablespoon butter. Take a taste and season with salt and pepper as needed.
- To serve, divide the risotto among shallow bowls and top with more cheese, the fried asparagus tips and capers, and a few fresh basil leaves. Serve with lemon wedges on the side, if using. To reheat, transfer to a small saucepan with enough broth or water to loosen. Cook over medium-low heat until warmed through, about 5 minutes.

SWAP IT

Spring: Swap in English peas and leafy greens like spinach.

Summer: Try sweet corn, zucchini, and tomatoes.

Fall: Swap the water for 1 cup canned pumpkin puree, and fry sage leaves for a garnish (see page 105).

Winter: Add some roasted winter squash and cooked crumbled sausage.

you can use whatever veg you have to top risotto

Soup School

How to Make Chicken Stock

Makes 2½ to 3 quarts

- 1 roast chicken carcass, skin and meat removed
- 2 celery stalks, cut into thirds
- 1 large unpeeled yellow onion, quartered
- 1 large carrot, halved and split lengthwise
- 1 unpeeled head of garlic, halved crosswise
- ½ bunch of parsley
- ½ bunch of thyme
- 3 small sprigs of rosemary
- 4 quarts water

Homemade chicken stock is liquid gold: You can use it for much more than soups, like making sauces richer or rice more flavorful (page 125). When making stock, you can add all kinds of things to enhance the flavor. I like to use whatever is in my fridge—it may be leeks or lemons or shallots. Herbs can also be switched out; you could even try cilantro for a more Southwestern-style stock. I like to freeze quarts of it so I always have stock on hand for homemade soup. The flavor is more complex than store-bought and adds depth to whatever I'm making.

TINI'S TIPS

The longer you cook the stock, the richer and more flavorful it will become.

Leaving the skin on the onion when cooking the stock adds to its rich golden color.

Freezing the stock in a zip-top bag makes for easier storage and faster defrosting.

When using fresh parsley, freeze leftover stems and use them for making stock. Parsley stems are loaded with flavor.

1. Cook the Stock Until It's Golden

- To a large stockpot or pasta pot over high heat, add the chicken carcass, celery, onion, carrot, garlic, parsley, thyme, rosemary, and water **A**. Bring to a boil, then reduce the heat to medium-low to gently simmer. Partially cover and cook until the stock is reduced by about 25 percent of its volume and is a dark golden color, about 1 hour and 30 minutes **B**. Remove from the heat and let the stock cool slightly.

2. Strain the Stock

- Strain the stock through a fine-mesh strainer into a medium pot and discard the vegetables (or eat them if you want a mushy veggie snack!). Allow the stock to fully cool before transferring to storage containers.

3. Store the Stock

- The stock may be stored in an airtight container in the refrigerator for up to 4 days, or in the freezer for a few months. For easy freezer storage, transfer the stock to zip-top plastic bags. After sealing the bags, lay them flat on a half baking sheet so they freeze flat.

if you want to add more collagen and gelatin to your broth, add chicken feet when cooking

A

B

← most store-bought broths are light like this

↙ you can make homemade stock dark, rich, and more flavorful

Chicken Soup
WITH HOMEMADE NOODLES

Serves 6 to 8 (Makes 3½ quarts)

CHICKEN

- 2 bone-in, skin-on split chicken breasts, about 1½ pounds (see Tini's Tips)
- 2 tablespoons extra-virgin olive oil
- 1 teaspoon kosher salt
- 1 teaspoon garlic powder
- 1 teaspoon onion powder
- ¼ teaspoon freshly ground black pepper

SOUP

- 3 tablespoons unsalted butter
- 2 tablespoons extra-virgin olive oil
- 3 carrots, diced
- 1 large yellow onion, diced
- 2 celery stalks, diced
- 2½ teaspoons kosher salt, plus more to taste
- 1 teaspoon freshly ground black pepper, plus more to taste
- 5 garlic cloves, minced
- ½ teaspoon dried thyme
- Pinch of dried oregano
- 3 quarts homemade chicken stock (page 134) or store-bought
- 2 tablespoons chopped fresh dill

NOODLES

- 2 cups / 280 grams all-purpose flour
- 1 teaspoon / 3 grams kosher salt, plus more for the pasta water
- 1 large egg plus 1 large egg yolk
- ⅓ cup water

I really like chicken noodle soup. It's comforting and homey, and makes me feel good when I eat it. The balance of flavors makes it so nothing is all up in your face; the ingredients go well together—the tender carrots and celery are mellow; the dill and thyme add a bright layer of flavor; the shredded chicken just tastes good, especially because it's roasted first (SO much better than cooking it in the soup, or eating those weird meat cubes in canned soup). The homemade noodles, well, they might surprise you because they are chewy yet soft and are really satisfying. I think of this as an all-year-round soup, not just one to serve in winter. I make it on repeat, and I hope you do, too.

TINI'S TIPS

If you don't feel like making noodles yourself, skip that step and buy store-bought egg noodles. Still cook them separately, though. Cooking noodles in the soup, whether store-bought or homemade, makes the stock too starchy. If you *are* making homemade noodles and don't have a rolling pin, a wine bottle works great for rolling out the dough.

If you can't find bone-in chicken breasts, boneless work—you may just need to reduce the cooking time. You can even use 3 cups leftover cooked chicken.

1. Get Ready

- Preheat the oven to 375°F. Line a baking sheet with parchment paper.

2. Roast the Chicken

- Put the chicken breasts on the baking sheet and drizzle with the olive oil. Sprinkle the salt, garlic powder, onion powder, and pepper evenly over the chicken.
- Roast until the chicken reaches 165°F on an instant-read thermometer, or the juices run clear when a knife is inserted into the center of the breast, 30 to 35 minutes.
- Let the chicken rest at room temp so the juices reabsorb into the meat, about 10 minutes. Using two forks, remove the skin and discard (or eat!), and shred the chicken meat on the baking sheet. Set aside.

3. Make the Soup

- To a large soup pot or Dutch oven over medium heat, add the butter and olive oil. When the butter is melted, add the carrots, onion, and celery, 2 teaspoons of the salt, and the pepper. Cook, stirring frequently, until the carrots and celery are slightly softened, 8 to 10 minutes. Add the garlic, thyme, and oregano and cook until fragrant, about 1 minute.
- Slowly add the chicken stock, stirring to scrape up any browned bits from the bottom of the pot. Add the dill and bring the soup to a boil. Reduce the heat to medium-low and partially cover. Gently simmer until the vegetables are soft and the soup is slightly reduced, about 30 minutes.

4. Make the Noodles (You Won't Regret It!)

- In a large bowl, whisk together flour and salt with a fork. Make a small well in the center of the flour mixture and add the egg, egg yolk, and the water. Using a fork, whisk together until a shaggy dough forms **A**.
- Once the dough has just come together, transfer it to a floured surface and knead **B** until it forms a smooth ball **C**, about 3 minutes. Cover the dough with plastic wrap and let it rest at room temperature for at least 15 minutes.
- Cut the dough in half, then with a floured rolling pin, roll each piece into an 8 × 12-inch rectangle, about ¼ inch thick **D**. With a pizza cutter or sharp knife, slice the rectangle lengthwise into three even panels **E**. Then, working one panel at a time, cut crosswise into slender ribbons, each about 3 inches long and ½ inch wide, to form rustic, hand-cut noodles **F**.

5. Cook the Noodles

- Fill a large pot three quarters full with water and salt it like the ocean (see page 99). Bring the water to a boil. Cook the noodles until just tender and floating to the top, about 3 minutes. With a slotted spoon or spider, transfer the noodles directly to the large pot of soup.

SERVING

- 1 to 2 tablespoons freshly squeezed lemon juice (optional)
- Pinch or two of cayenne pepper (optional)
- 2 tablespoons chopped parsley

6. Finish and Serve

- Add the shredded meat and any accumulated juices to the pot. Add the remaining ½ teaspoon salt and more seasoning to taste. Stir in the lemon juice and/or cayenne, if using, and top with parsley right before serving.

SWAP IT

For creamy chicken soup, add ¼ cup all-purpose flour to the pot when you add the garlic in step 3. Cook it for an extra minute or two, then proceed with the recipe as written. At the very end of the recipe, right after you've removed the pot from the heat, add 1 cup of heavy cream.

For some greens, in the last 2 minutes of cooking, add 10 ounces baby spinach and stir until wilted.

you can't go wrong with homemade chicken noodle soup because it just makes the soul feel warm

Chicken and Chive Dumplings Soup

Serves 6
(Makes about 3 quarts)

CHICKEN

- 2 bone-in, skin-on split chicken breasts, about 1½ pounds (if you have leftover chicken, you can skip this step and use 3 cups shredded chicken)
- 1 tablespoon extra-virgin olive oil
- ½ teaspoon kosher salt
- ½ teaspoon garlic powder
- Freshly ground black pepper

DUMPLINGS

- 1¼ cups / 175g all-purpose flour
- 1 teaspoon baking powder
- 1 teaspoon garlic powder
- ¼ teaspoon kosher salt
- 2 tablespoons unsalted butter, cut into small cubes
- ½ cup plus 1 tablespoon whole milk
- ¼ cup sour cream
- 2 tablespoons chopped fresh chives

SOUP

- 1 to 2 tablespoons extra-virgin olive oil
- 3 celery stalks, chopped
- 1 medium yellow onion, diced
- 2 medium carrots, peeled and chopped
- 1 medium shallot, diced
- 1½ teaspoons kosher salt, or more to taste
- ¼ teaspoon freshly ground black pepper
- 3 garlic cloves, finely grated

It normally doesn't snow in south Georgia, but one day it did, and I really wanted chicken and dumplings soup. It's even cozier and heartier than my chicken noodle soup. To me, this all-American creamy comfort food seems kind of old-fashioned—in a good way. This recipe *does* take hours to make if you include cooking the homemade stock (page 134), but feel free to use store-bought. And the same goes for the chicken: Use up leftovers or even buy a rotisserie chicken. For those of you new to Southern-style dumplings, they are like a fluffy boiled drop biscuit. I add chives, inspired by the flavor of sour cream and onion potato chips. What could inspire your own twist on these dumplings?

TINI'S TIPS

If you don't have sour cream for the dumplings, you can use whole milk Greek yogurt.

For the soup, you may sub in whole milk for the evaporated milk.

1. Roast the Chicken

- Preheat the oven to 375°F. Line a baking sheet with parchment paper.
- Put the chicken breasts on the baking sheet and drizzle with the olive oil. Sprinkle the salt, garlic powder, and a few pinches of pepper evenly over the chicken.
- Cook until the chicken reaches 165°F on an instant-read thermometer, or the juices run clear when a knife is inserted into the center of the breast, 30 to 35 minutes.
- Let the chicken rest at room temp so the juices reabsorb into the meat, about 10 minutes. Using two forks, remove the skin and discard (or eat!), and shred the chicken meat on the baking sheet. Set aside.

2. Make the Dumpling Dough

- In a medium bowl, combine the flour, baking powder, garlic powder, and salt.
- Toss in the butter and, using your hands or a pastry cutter or two knives, cut it in (see page 186) by pressing the pieces of butter into smaller pieces until it has a coarse texture, about the size of peas.
- Gently stir in the milk, sour cream, and chives until combined. Cover and set aside.

3. Make the Soup

- **SAUTÉ THE VEGETABLES:** In a Dutch oven or soup pot over medium heat, add the olive oil and heat until it starts to shimmer. Add the celery, onion, carrots, shallot, salt, and pepper. Cook until the onion is softened and translucent, 5 to 7 minutes.
- Add the garlic and cook, stirring, until it becomes fragrant, about 1 minute.

recipe and ingredients continue ▸▸

3 tablespoons unsalted butter

3 tablespoons all-purpose flour

1 (12-ounce) can evaporated milk

4 cups homemade chicken stock (page 134) or store-bought, plus more as needed

1 teaspoon chicken bouillon powder

1 tablespoon chopped rosemary or 1 teaspoon dried rosemary

1 teaspoon thyme leaves or ½ teaspoon dried thyme

1 teaspoon smoked paprika

SERVING

Handful of parsley leaves and/or 2 tablespoons chopped chives

- MAKE A ROUX: Add the butter and stir until it melts **A**. Sprinkle in the flour **B**, and keep stirring until a thick paste forms, about 2 minutes **C**.
- Slowly whisk in the evaporated milk **D**, a little at a time. Continue to whisk until it is all incorporated, then add the chicken stock **E** and the bouillon powder, rosemary, thyme, and smoked paprika.
- Stir in the shredded chicken.
- Cover the pot and continue to cook on medium heat to allow the flavors to develop, about 10 minutes.

4. Cook the Dumplings and Serve

- After the soup has cooked, using two dinner spoons, drop large spoonfuls of the dumpling dough (about the equivalent of two heaping tablespoons) into the soup **F** until all the dough is used **G**. Cover the pot again and simmer over medium heat until the dumplings are cooked through, 15 to 20 minutes **H**.
- If needed, add more stock, ¼ cup at a time, to thin out the soup. Taste and season as needed.
- Ladle the soup into individual serving bowls and garnish with a few sprinkles of parsley and/or chives.

BUILDING FLAVORS = A DELICIOUS BITE

I want every bite of a dish to be loaded with flavor. When we're cooking, there are many ways to make this happen, and layering flavors and textures is one of them. Herbs and aromatics are always a good place to start as they enhance other ingredients. Toasting foods like nuts and seeds adds depth of flavor to a dish. Using wine or broth to deglaze the fond from a pan (see page 28) adds complexity to a dish, and a drizzle of olive oil or other fat can enhance the mouthfeel. Pickled foods like onions or jalapeños can add some good acid notes, and balsamic may introduce a hint of sweet along with acid. Mustard is often used for its subtle tang, and of course salt—never underestimate the power of salt. With just a few pinches, it can intensify the flavor of a dish beyond belief. Thinking about textures is important, too, especially when it comes to soup. Sometimes a creamy puree needs a little crunch for interest. For me, croutons (page 145) almost always do the job.

Loaded Baked Potato Broccoli Soup

Serves 8
(Makes about 3 quarts)

SOUP

- 8 bacon slices, cut into ½-inch pieces
- 5 tablespoons unsalted butter
- 1 yellow onion, chopped
- 4 garlic cloves, finely grated
- Kosher salt and freshly ground black pepper
- 1 tablespoon garlic powder
- 1 tablespoon onion powder
- 2 teaspoons smoked paprika
- ¼ cup all-purpose flour
- 4 cups chicken stock, plus more as needed
- 1½ cups whole milk
- 1 cup heavy cream
- 2½ pounds Yukon Gold potatoes (6 to 8 medium), cut into 2-inch pieces
- 1 broccoli crown, cut into small florets (3 cups)
- 8 ounces mild cheddar, grated (about 2 cups)
- 8 ounces smoked Gouda, grated (about 2 cups)

SERVING

- 8 ounces (1 cup) sour cream
- ¼ cup minced chives
- Braided pretzel twists

This hearty soup has the feel-good flavors of a loaded baked potato (and some may say their childhood): sour cream, cheddar cheese, bacon, and chives. I add broccoli because it adds to the nostalgic flavors (think broccoli cheddar soup). There's something about this soup that makes you want to dip into it with more than a spoon, so I always serve it with a loaf of crusty bread, or even some store-bought pretzels will do the job.

1. Cook the Bacon

- Put the bacon in a large pot and turn the heat to medium-high (starting in a cold pan helps the fat render more slowly, so the meat doesn't burn before the fat is rendered off). Cook, stirring occasionally, until the fat is rendered and the bacon is crisp, about 12 minutes. Using a slotted spoon, transfer the bacon to paper towels to drain.

2. Sauté the aromatics

- In the pot with the bacon fat, melt 2 tablespoons of the butter. Reduce the heat to medium and add the onion and garlic. Season with a few pinches each of salt and pepper. Cook, stirring occasionally, until softened and beginning to brown, 5 to 7 minutes.

3. Bloom the Spices

- Add the garlic powder, onion powder, and smoked paprika and cook, stirring, until fragrant, 1 to 2 minutes.

4. Make the Roux

- Add the remaining 3 tablespoons butter and stir until it melts. Sprinkle in the flour and stir until a thick paste forms, about 2 minutes. Slowly drizzle in the chicken stock, whisking constantly. Stir in the milk, heavy cream, potatoes, and broccoli and season again with another pinch or two of salt and pepper **A**. Bring the mixture to a boil, then reduce the heat to medium-low. Cover and simmer until the potatoes and broccoli are fork-tender and the soup is thickened slightly, about 20 minutes **B**.
- Remove from the heat and, using a potato masher, mash up about one third of the potatoes to thicken the soup further. Add the cheeses and stir until melted, then stir in half of the bacon. If needed, add more stock, ¼ cup at a time, to thin out the soup (you may need to heat up the soup for a few). Season to taste with salt and pepper.

5. Garnish and Serve

- Divide the soup among bowls and top with the sour cream, chives, and the remaining bacon. Serve with pretzel sticks for dipping.

SWAP IT

For more of a German beer cheese vibe, add up to 8 ounces of a light-bodied ale or pilsner after you stir in the cheeses.

potatoes are a natural thickener

A

B

Roasted Tomato and Basil Soup

Serves 4
(Makes 1½ to 2 quarts)

- 2 heads of garlic
- 4 pounds plum, vine-ripened, beefsteak or other tomatoes, halved or quartered if large
- 1 large yellow onion, cut into eighths
- ¼ cup extra-virgin olive oil
- 2 tablespoons balsamic vinegar
- 1 tablespoon kosher salt, plus more to taste
- 1 teaspoon smoked paprika
- 1 teaspoon freshly ground black pepper, plus more to taste
- ¼ cup packed fresh basil leaves, plus more for serving
- Pinch of dried oregano
- 2 pinches of fresh thyme leaves
- 1 to 2 pinches of crushed red pepper flakes, or more as desired
- ½ cup heavy cream, plus more for serving
- ½ ounce Parmesan cheese, finely grated (about ¼ cup), plus more for serving
- ¼ to 1 cup vegetable broth, if needed
- Homemade Croutons (recipe follows) or store-bought croutons, for serving (optional)

I was a guest at a chef's table when I was served the best smoky tomato soup. The chef told me she roasted the vegetables to get the deep flavor I tasted. I find most chefs, if they have time, will talk about the history of their dishes. Sitting at a chef's table, although usually somewhat pricey, can be very inspiring. The personal interaction can be a kind of training in itself. You can always send a compliment to a chef on a slow night, and who knows where it may lead—the back of the kitchen? (Did you watch *The Bear*?) My experience with a generous chef led to the inspiration for this fresh and still satisfying soup.

TINI'S TIPS

Straining the soup in a fine-mesh strainer after you puree it in Step 3 gives you a really silky texture, but feel free to skip straining to keep it a little rustic.

You can leave this recipe open to using nearly any kind of tomato—I have used all sorts of combinations including plum, vine-ripe, and campari tomatoes. Just make sure they are cut the same size, and if you use cherry tomatoes, leave them whole!

1. Get Ready

- Preheat the oven to 425°F.
- Cut the garlic heads in half crosswise, through the entire head. No need to peel or separate the cloves.

2. Roast the Tomatoes

- On a baking sheet, combine the tomatoes, onion, and halved garlic heads. Drizzle with the olive oil and vinegar, then sprinkle with the salt, smoked paprika, and black pepper and toss to coat. Place the garlic heads cut-side down, and roast until the tomatoes are completely tender and charred in spots, about 45 minutes.

3. Puree

- Remove the roasted garlic heads and set aside to cool slightly. Carefully transfer the remaining contents of the baking sheet to a blender, plus any juice that has accumulated. Working in batches if necessary, blend on medium speed until smooth, about 2 minutes.
- Squeeze the soft roasted garlic cloves out of their peels into the blender. Add the basil, oregano, thyme, and red pepper flakes. Blend the soup again until smooth, about 1 minute.

4. Finish and Serve

- Transfer the soup to a medium pot over medium heat, and stir in the heavy cream and Parmesan. Taste for seasonings and add salt and pepper as needed. If the soup seems too thick, add a little vegetable broth to slightly thin.
- Heat the soup until it is warmed through, about 5 minutes. Serve in bowls, top with a drizzle of cream, more Parmesan, basil, and garlic croutons (if using).

HOMEMADE CROUTONS

My favorite crispy topping for any soup!

Makes 3 cups

- 1 medium loaf sourdough or crusty bread, cut into 1-inch cubes (about 3 cups)
- 2 to 3 tablespoons extra-virgin olive oil, plus more as needed
- Kosher salt and freshly ground black pepper

- Preheat the oven to 450°F.
- Spread the bread cubes on a rimmed baking sheet and drizzle with the olive oil. Sprinkle with a generous pinch of salt and pepper and toss to coat. If you need more olive oil to coat, add another drizzle.
- Bake, tossing halfway through, until well toasted and golden brown,10 to 12 minutes. Let the croutons cool before using.

SWAP IT

To make garlic croutons, add 2 grated garlic cloves (or ¾ teaspoon garlic powder) to the oil before drizzling. Bake as directed.

To make herb croutons, add a teaspoon or two of chopped fresh herbs, such as rosemary or thyme, or a combo.

Curried Pumpkin Soup

Serves 4 to 6
(Makes to 2 to 2½ quarts)

1 (3-pound) sugar pumpkin (see Tini's Tips)

SPICE MIX

1 tablespoon curry powder

2 teaspoons garlic powder

1½ teaspoons ground cumin

1½ teaspoons ground cinnamon

¼ teaspoon smoked paprika

¼ teaspoon dried sage

¼ teaspoon ground allspice

¼ teaspoon freshly ground black pepper

PUMPKIN SEEDS

1 teaspoon pure maple syrup or packed light brown sugar

½ teaspoon extra-virgin olive oil

Kosher salt

SOUP

3 tablespoons extra-virgin olive oil

3 medium shallots, chopped

Kosher salt and freshly ground black pepper

4 garlic cloves, finely grated

1 (2-inch) piece fresh ginger, peeled and grated (1 heaping tablespoon)

4 teaspoons red curry paste, plus more as desired

½ teaspoon smoked paprika

4 cups vegetable stock or chicken stock, plus more as needed

This soup has real fall vibes. Not just because it's pumpkin (or any winter squash—you can swap the pumpkin for butternut, acorn, or kabocha) but because it's loaded with warming spices and curry paste. And we're not letting the seeds go to waste. Roasting them with the spice mix makes a flavorful topping. To garnish like I would in a professional kitchen, I put some extra coconut milk in a squeeze bottle. Then I can make decorative circles and dots with the milk before serving. I top it off with a little pile of greens, like cilantro. If you can get your hands on them, microgreens look pretty fab, too. A teeny bit of smoked paprika finishes off the look like a real pro.

TINI'S TIPS

You can sub in 2¼ pounds (8 cups) cubed winter squash or pumpkin for the whole sugar pumpkin.

When peeling something with a very tough skin, like pumpkin, place the segments flat on the cutting board so that you have a flat surface to work with. If the pumpkin is rolling around on your cutting board, you'll be more likely to cut yourself.

If your pumpkin or squash doesn't have many seeds, feel free to use store-bought pepitas instead of or in addition to.

1. Break Down the Pumpkin

- Remove the stem. Cut the pumpkin in half through the stem end **A**, then scoop out the seeds **B**, pulling them away from the slimy membranes (it's okay if some of the membrane remains attached, you should have about ½ cup of seeds) **C**; set aside.
- Divide the pumpkin into more manageable pieces **D**, then use a sharp knife or vegetable peeler to slice off the tough outer skin **E**. Cut the pumpkin into 1-inch cubes (you should have about 8 cups) **F**. Set aside.

2. Make the Spice Mix

- In a small bowl, combine the curry powder, garlic powder, cumin, cinnamon, smoked paprika, sage, allspice, and pepper.

3. Roast the Pumpkin Seeds

- Preheat the oven to 375°F. On a parchment-lined rimmed baking sheet, toss the pumpkin seeds with the maple syrup, olive oil, 1½ teaspoons of the spice mix, and a pinch of salt. Spread into an even layer.
- Roast, stirring occasionally, until crisp and golden brown, 10 to 12 minutes. Remove from the oven and let cool completely.

4. Make the Soup

- **SAUTÉ THE AROMATICS:** In a large saucepan or Dutch oven over medium-high heat, add the olive oil and heat until it shimmers. Add the shallots and season with salt and pepper. Cook, stirring occasionally, until softened and browned in places, 3 to 5 minutes.
- **BLOOM THE SPICES:** Add the garlic, ginger, curry paste (add up to 2 teaspoons more if you like it spicy), smoked paprika, and the remaining spice mix. Cook until very fragrant, 1 to 2 minutes. Add the cubed pumpkin and stir to coat in the spices.
- **SIMMER THE SOUP:** Stir in the vegetable stock. Reserve 2 to 3 tablespoons of the coconut milk and stir the rest of it in, along with the bay leaves, water, and a big pinch of salt. Bring the mixture to a boil, then reduce the heat to medium-low, partially cover, and simmer until the pumpkin is fork-tender, almost falling apart, about 20 minutes. Remove from the heat, discard the bay leaves, and let cool for 5 minutes.

5. Puree and Serve

- Working in batches, transfer the soup to a high-speed blender and run on high until smooth and creamy (alternatively, blend the soup in the pot using an immersion blender), about 2 minutes. Return the blended soup to the pot and stir in the lime juice; season to taste with salt and pepper. (If you prefer a thinner soup, stir in hot water or more stock, ½ cup at a time, until it reaches your desired consistency.)
- Ladle the soup into bowls and serve with a light drizzle of the reserved coconut milk, a sprinkle of roasted pumpkin seeds and cilantro, a pinch or two of smoked paprika (if using), and lime wedges alongside.

1 (13.5-ounce) can full-fat unsweetened coconut milk

2 dried bay leaves

2 cups water

3 tablespoons freshly squeezed lime juice

SERVING

Handful of cilantro leaves or microgreens

A few pinches of smoked paprika, for garnish (optional)

Lime wedges

SWAP IT

Sub the pumpkin with regular old sweet potatoes for an even sweeter alternative.

If you love coconut, lean into that flavor by swapping the pumpkin seeds with ½ cup coconut flakes (try toasting them, too).

if you have the time and patience, take the green seeds, called pepitas, out of the crunchy white shells before roasting by crushing them lightly with a rolling pin and boiling them for 5 minutes, the pepita should easily separate from the hull

Curried Pumpkin Soup

French Onion Soup

WITH HOMEMADE CROUTONS

Serves 4
(Makes about 2 quarts)

- 6 tablespoons unsalted butter
- 4 large yellow onions (about 3 pounds), thinly sliced (about 12 cups)
- 4 large garlic cloves, thinly sliced
- 4 teaspoons kosher salt
- 2 teaspoons sugar
- ¼ cup all-purpose flour
- 3 tablespoons brandy or sherry
- ½ cup dry white wine, such as sauvignon blanc
- 6 cups beef broth
- 1 teaspoon freshly ground black pepper
- 5 sprigs thyme
- 2 sprigs rosemary
- 2 dried bay leaves
- 1 cup Homemade Croutons (page 145) (see Tini's Tips)
- 4 ounces Swiss cheese, grated (about 1 cup)
- 4 ounces smoked Gouda, grated (about 1 cup)

If you want the best method for not crying while cutting onions, simply close your eyes. Just kidding. I don't have a best practice for you. I wish I did. There are lots of theories. Wear goggles, put a piece of bread in your mouth, use a sharp knife. I say, sometimes you just gotta cry. You won't be crying once you try this soup, though. There are plenty of sweet caramelized onions in the rich, beefy broth so you get a nice big spoonful of them every time. And while most French onion soups don't call for garlic, I can't make a soup without it, so there's that, too. Plus, the combo of Swiss and Gouda makes for one magnificent cheese pull.

TINI'S TIPS

If you don't have small ovenproof bowls, you can pour the finished soup into one large oven-safe dish to broil the cheese and croutons, *then* ladle it into smaller serving bowls.

If you don't want to make croutons, you can sub them out with 4 slices of toasted French baguette.

1. Slowly Cook the Onions

- In a large pot or Dutch oven over medium heat, melt the butter. Reduce the heat to medium-low, then add the onions, garlic, 2 teaspoons of the salt, and the sugar **A**. Cook until the onions start to soften **B**, then stir every 10 minutes or so, until they are a deep golden brown **C**. This could take up to an hour or even longer (see **D** for color), and it's worth every minute. If the onions seem like they may burn, add a splash of water.

2. Thicken the Soup

- Add the flour to the onions and stir to incorporate. Cook until the flour is fully hydrated (meaning you don't see any more white), about 1 minute. Add the brandy and cook until the liquid is almost entirely evaporated, about 30 seconds. Add the wine and again let it cook until almost entirely evaporated, another 30 seconds or so.
- Slowly add the beef broth, whisking constantly. Add the remaining 2 teaspoons salt and the pepper, thyme, rosemary, and bay leaves. Bring the soup to a boil over medium high, then reduce the heat to medium. Partially cover and simmer, whisking occasionally, until the broth is thickened and slightly darkened, about 30 minutes.

3. Broil the Cheese and Serve

- Move a rack about 6 inches from the broiler (or more if needed for your bowls to fit) and preheat it to high.
- Remove the bay leaves and the thyme and rosemary stems from the soup.
- Ladle the soup into 4 ovenproof bowls, top with a handful of croutons, and layer equal amounts of the cheeses to cover the surface. Broil the soup until the cheese is melted and bubbling, about 2 minutes. Serve hot.

these are onions at 10, 20, and 35 to 40 minutes, or more because stoves vary, timing may too!

Creamy Corn and Jalapeño Chowder

Serves 4 to 6
(Makes about 2½ quarts)

- 3 ears of fresh corn or 3 cups frozen
- 3 Yukon Gold potatoes (about ¾ pound)
- 8 bacon slices, cut into 1-inch pieces
- 1 tablespoon smoked paprika, plus more for garnish (optional)
- 2 teaspoons chipotle chili powder
- 2 tablespoons all-purpose flour
- 1 yellow onion, diced
- 2 jalapeños, seeded and diced
- 1½ teaspoons kosher salt, plus more to taste
- ¾ teaspoon freshly ground black pepper, plus more to taste
- 6 garlic cloves, chopped
- 4 cups vegetable or chicken stock
- 1 (12-ounce can) evaporated milk
- 1½ cups heavy cream
- 4 ounces sharp cheddar cheese, grated (about 1 cup)
- 2 scallions, white and green parts, thinly sliced, for serving

While I like to make this soup during the height of the summer when corn is at its sweetest, there's no reason you can't make it with frozen corn any time of year. When I *do* have cobs, though, I throw them in the pot to simmer out some extra flavor, although one thing this soup doesn't lack is flavor! There's some nice spice from the jalapeño, and the chipotle chili powder, which also gives it some smokiness, along with the paprika. And bacon: The salty, fatty addition is *always* a plus. The potatoes thicken the broth up some, as does the cheese and cream. After the flavors have cooked and developed, I sometimes like to blend this soup super smooth—some might even call it velvety.

A TINI TIP

If you want to use an immersion blender instead of a blender, strain the blended soup through a fine-mesh strainer to eliminate the fibrous skins of the corn kernels and get an extra-smooth finish.

1. Prep the Corn and Potatoes

- Remove the corn husks and silks. Hold the corn vertically in a wide, shallow bowl and, using a sharp knife, cut downward, stripping the kernels off the cobs (you should have about 3 cups) **A**. Save the cobs for cooking.
- Cut the potatoes into large chunks (about 2-inch pieces) and put them into a bowl of water to prevent them from browning.

2. Cook the Bacon

- Put the bacon in a large pot and turn the heat to medium high. Cook, stirring occasionally, until the fat is rendered and the bacon is crisp, 15 to 18 minutes. Using a slotted spoon, transfer the bacon to paper towels to drain.

3. Bloom the Spices

- Reduce the heat to medium and add the smoked paprika and chipotle powder, and cook, stirring, until fragrant, 1 to 2 minutes.

4. Make the Roux

- Sprinkle the flour into the pot and cook, stirring until a thick paste forms, about 2 minutes.

5. Sauté the Aromatics

- Stir in the onion, jalapeños, and corn, then sprinkle with 1 teaspoon of the salt and the black pepper. Cook until just softened, about 5 minutes. Add the garlic and cook until fragrant, about 1 minute.

6. Add the Liquids, Potatoes, and Cobs and Simmer

- Slowly pour in the vegetable stock, 1 cup at a time, stirring constantly. Stir in the evaporated milk and heavy cream. Drain the potatoes and add, along with the reserved corn cobs and bring the mixture to a boil.
- Reduce the heat to medium-low. Cover and simmer until the potatoes are fork-tender and the soup is thickened slightly, about 30 minutes. Season with the remaining ½ teaspoon salt and more black pepper (and salt) to taste. Remove the corn cobs from the soup.

7. Mash or Puree, Your Choice! And Serve

- Here you can either (1) use a potato masher to mash up the soup some or (2) puree all the soup in a high-speed blender until it's very smooth. (If using an immersion blender, see A Tini Tip.)
- To serve, ladle the soup into bowls and top evenly with the cheese, scallions, and the reserved bacon. If you want, sprinkle with the tiniest bit of smoked paprika for color.

SEASONING
For Seafood, Poultry, Salads, Meats
Same great taste
since 1939

Lessons in Vegetables

Roasted Maple-Dijon Vegetables

Serves 4

VEGETABLES

12 ounces new baby potatoes, halved

12 ounces carrots (2 to 3 medium large), cut into 1½-inch chunks (if very thick, cut lengthwise first)

3 tablespoons extra-virgin olive oil

1 teaspoon kosher salt

12 ounces Brussels sprouts, trimmed and halved

1 medium sweet onion, quartered and separated

3 to 4 garlic cloves, finely grated (about 1 tablespoon)

SAUCE

2 tablespoons Dijon mustard

2 tablespoons pure maple syrup

1 tablespoon extra-virgin olive oil

1½ teaspoons fresh thyme leaves or ½ teaspoon dried thyme

1 teaspoon kosher salt

¾ teaspoon smoked paprika

½ teaspoon freshly ground black pepper

½ teaspoon garlic powder

½ teaspoon onion powder

Everyone seems to love a sheet pan dinner, especially people who don't cook for a living, because it's easy and usually pretty quick and healthy(ish). I do get a little extra with this roast, though, and add the vegetables to the pan in stages, because timing is everything here. Carrots and potatoes go first because they need more time, followed by Brussels sprouts, onions, and the chopped garlic. It's especially important to keep an eye out for the alliums (onions and garlic): They can get bitter when overcooked, so always add them a bit later. During fall, I like to use maple syrup in everything, so I add it to the sweet-savory-salty sauce, which is tossed with the browned, crispy veggies after roasting. It makes all the flavors shine a bit more. This roast makes a great holiday side dish, too!

TINI'S TIPS

Cut your vegetables with at least one flat side (halve Brussels sprouts and baby potatoes, cut large carrots in chunks) so a flat surface touches the hot pan to brown and get crispy!

Cut your vegetables the same size to ensure they cook evenly.

1. Toss and Roast the Root Vegetables

- Preheat the oven to 425°F.
- In a medium bowl, combine the potatoes, carrots, and 2 tablespoons of the olive oil and season with ½ teaspoon of the salt. Spread the vegetables out on a baking sheet so a flat side of each piece is facing down. Roast for 15 minutes.

2. Toss and Roast the Softer Vegetables

- In the same medium bowl, combine the Brussels sprouts, onion, and garlic with the remaining 1 tablespoon olive oil and the remaining ½ teaspoon salt. Remove the baking sheet from the oven and add the Brussels sprouts mixture. Roast all the vegetables for another 15 minutes.

3. Make the Maple-Dijon Sauce

- In a small bowl, whisk together the mustard, maple syrup, olive oil, thyme, salt, smoked paprika, pepper, garlic powder, and onion powder.

4. Add the Sauce and Finish Roasting

- Take the pan out of the oven and pour the maple mixture over the vegetables and toss well. Spread the vegetables evenly out on the pan, and roast until the carrots, potatoes, and sprouts are fork-tender and the onion quarters are slightly charred on the ends, about 10 more minutes. Serve hot.

SWAP IT

Replace the Brussels sprouts and potatoes with equal amounts of parsnips and butternut squash.

you can throw everything on the pan, then in the oven, and call it a day!

A

B

C

D

Lemon-Parmesan Broccoli

WITH GARLIC CHIPS

Serves 4

GARLIC CHIPS

8 garlic cloves, thinly sliced

½ cup extra-virgin olive oil

BROCCOLI

1 large head of broccoli (about 1¼ pounds)

Kosher salt and freshly ground black pepper

DRESSING

1 large egg yolk

½ teaspoon Dijon mustard

½ teaspoon grated lemon zest

2 tablespoons freshly squeezed lemon juice

¼ teaspoon smoked paprika

⅛ teaspoon cayenne pepper

1 ounce Parmesan cheese, finely grated (about ½ cup)

1 tablespoon minced chives

Kosher salt and freshly ground black pepper

When I was younger, if we didn't want to eat something, my mom would let us put chocolate sauce on it, hoping we would then try it. I don't think I ever had to put chocolate sauce on broccoli, though. As far back as I can remember, I always liked it. I usually pair it with cheese, because it's a classic combo, but this feels a little more like broccoli for adults. Here we're going to elevate simple steamed broccoli—which I know can seem bland—with golden-fried garlic chips and a creamy, zesty dressing to a place you won't believe. And why steam as opposed to roast or fry? For variety, not to mention that the super simple stovetop technique helps preserve vegetables' nutrients. The lemony-garlicky dressing is made by emulsifying an egg yolk with oil as in a traditional Caesar. I then sprinkle it all with Parmesan (I couldn't totally let go of the idea of cheese). One bite and I hope you get it about how good broccoli is—and don't need any chocolate sauce.

TINI'S TIPS

Don't throw away the broccoli stems! When peeled and thinly sliced, they can cook right alongside the florets and steam in the same amount of time.

If you don't have a steamer basket, you can make one by placing a colander in a pot with a lid (make sure the colander sits in the pot, not partway out). Note that steaming may take longer this way if your setup isn't "sealed" and steam escapes while cooking.

1. Fry the Garlic

- In a small skillet over medium heat, combine the garlic and olive oil **A**. Once the garlic begins to sizzle around the edges, continue cooking, stirring frequently, until the garlic is crisp and golden brown, about 4 minutes **B**. Using a slotted spoon, lift the garlic from the oil and transfer to it paper towels to drain. Set the oil aside to cool completely.

2. Prep the Broccoli

- Using a sharp knife, separate the broccoli crowns from the stems. Cut the crowns into florets. Peel the stems **C** and thinly slice **D**.

3. Steam the Broccoli

- Add about 1 inch of water to a large, deep pot and place a steamer basket on top. Bring to a simmer over medium heat, then add a few pinches of salt. Put the broccoli in the steamer basket. Tightly cover the pot and cook until the broccoli is bright green and tender, 8 to 10 minutes.

4. Whip Up the Garlicky Dressing and Serve

- Meanwhile, in a medium bowl, whisk together the egg yolk, mustard, lemon zest, lemon juice, smoked paprika, and cayenne until smooth. Gradually drizzle in ⅓ cup of the cooled garlic-infused oil, whisking constantly, until smooth and thickened slightly. Stir in 2 tablespoons of the Parmesan and the chives, then season to taste with salt and black pepper.
- Arrange the steamed broccoli on a platter and sprinkle with the remaining Parmesan, allowing it to melt. Drizzle with half of the dressing and sprinkle with about ½ the garlic chips (reserve the rest in an airtight container in the fridge to sprinkle over vegetables or pastas or, if you like things really garlicky, use them all on the broccoli!). Serve with the remaining dressing and/or garlic oil on the side.

SWAP IT

Steaming works for just about any vegetable you like, including cauliflower, carrots, asparagus, sugar snap peas, green beans, beets, white potatoes, and sweet potatoes.

Fresh lime juice or mild vinegars like apple cider or white wine vinegar can be swapped for the lemon juice.

Sautéed Southern Succotash

Serves 4
(Makes about 3 cups)

- 2 tablespoons unsalted butter
- 1 small yellow onion, diced
- 2 garlic cloves, finely grated
- 1 teaspoon kosher salt, plus more to taste
- ½ teaspoon freshly ground black pepper, plus more to taste
- ½ (10-ounce) package frozen baby lima beans, partially defrosted
- 1 (10-ounce) container multicolor cherry tomatoes, halved
- 1 medium zucchini or yellow squash, diced
- 2 ears of fresh corn, kernels removed (see Tini's Tips)
- ¼ cup basil leaves, sliced chiffonade-style (see page 25)

My second-to-last round as a contestant on *Next Level Chef*, I made succotash with fried pork tenderloin. Although succotash may not have the best memories for me (it was too close to my elimination round), I think there's something especially beautiful about it, and not in a way you might think. It's about the history. This side dish, made up of a combination of corn, beans, and squash, comes from Native American traditions of planting certain crops—these they called "the three sisters"—together for the health and benefit of each other. Today, this combination is still going strong, especially in the South. I've added tomatoes to the traditional combination for a nice burst of freshness. There's true beauty in the simplicity of this dish.

TINI'S TIPS

To remove the kernels from the ears of corn, place the tip of the ear in the center of a shallow bowl and use your knife to shave them off the cobs (see page 153).

If you can't find lima beans, frozen edamame (shelled) makes a great substitute!

1. Sauté the Aromatics

- In a large skillet over medium-high heat, melt the butter. Add the onion, garlic, salt, and pepper and cook, stirring, until softened and translucent, about 3 minutes.

2. Add the Vegetables

- Add the lima beans and cook for 2 minutes. Stir in the tomatoes and cook until slightly softened, about 2 minutes. Stir in the zucchini and corn, and cook until brightly colored and tender and the lima beans are cooked through, 5 to 8 minutes.

3. Finish with Herbs

- Stir in the basil and season with more salt and pepper if needed.

SWAP IT

For a smoky twist, add 4 strips of thick-cut bacon cut into ½-inch pieces. In the large skillet over medium heat, cook the bacon, stirring occasionally, until crisp and the fat is rendered, about 8 minutes. Transfer the bacon to paper towels to drain. Pour off all but 1 tablespoon of fat. Proceed with the recipe using 1 tablespoon butter instead of 2 tablespoons. Sprinkle the bacon on top of the succotash at the end.

Sautéed Green Beans

WITH WHIPPED GOAT CHEESE AND POMEGRANATE

Serves 4

1 medium shallot, thinly sliced into rings

3 tablespoons freshly squeezed lemon juice

Kosher salt

Pinch of sugar

8 ounces goat cheese, softened

¼ cup extra-virgin olive oil, plus more as needed

1½ teaspoons grated lemon zest

3 tablespoons unsalted butter

¼ teaspoon freshly ground black pepper

1 pound green beans, stem ends trimmed

1 small garlic clove, finely grated

⅓ cup fresh pomegranate seeds

If you want to make your family something that feels fancy (and is *really* good), make this dish. I love how the bright green beans, sautéed in a peppery butter sauce, sit on the swirled lemony goat cheese with pops of red pomegranate seeds and pickled shallot. You see, my family is *not* fancy. They're just happy when I make them delicious food: They don't care if it's plated, or garnished, or pretty. But I like to make things pretty, and this dish automatically elevates any spread. Plus, it tastes fresh, light, and just how my family, fancy or not, likes it—delicious.

A TINI TIP

To break down a fresh pomegranate, slice off about ½ inch from the top, then use a paring knife to score 5 or 6 lines down the sides of the fruit **A**, spacing them evenly. Don't cut all the way through to the seeds, but cut deeply enough to split the skin. From there, pull the pomegranate into sections **B** and plunge them into cold water **C**, shaking gently to agitate and release the seeds (which are actually called arils if you want to get technical) **D**. Peel off any membranes still attached, drain, and enjoy!

1. Quick Pickle the Shallot

- Place the shallot in a small bowl with 2 tablespoons of the lemon juice, a pinch of salt, and the sugar. If the liquid doesn't cover the shallot, add a tablespoon of water (or more if needed). Set aside.

2. Whip the Goat Cheese

- In a food processor, combine the goat cheese, 3 tablespoons of the olive oil, and ½ teaspoon of the lemon zest. Blend until fluffy and smooth, adding more oil as needed to bring it together. Season to taste with salt.
- Spread the whipped goat cheese onto a serving platter. Set aside.

3. Sauté and Serve

- In a large skillet over medium-high heat, combine the remaining 1 tablespoon olive oil and 1 tablespoon of the butter. Once the butter melts, add the pepper and cook, stirring, until very fragrant, 1 to 2 minutes. Add the green beans and ½ teaspoon salt and cook, stirring occasionally, until crisp-tender and beginning to brown in places, 4 to 5 minutes. Add the remaining 2 tablespoons butter, the remaining 1 tablespoon lemon juice, the remaining 1 teaspoon lemon zest, and the garlic, stirring until the butter is melted and coats the beans.
- Pile the beans on top of the whipped goat cheese. Lift the shallot slices from the pickling liquid and scatter them and the pomegranate seeds over the top. Serve.

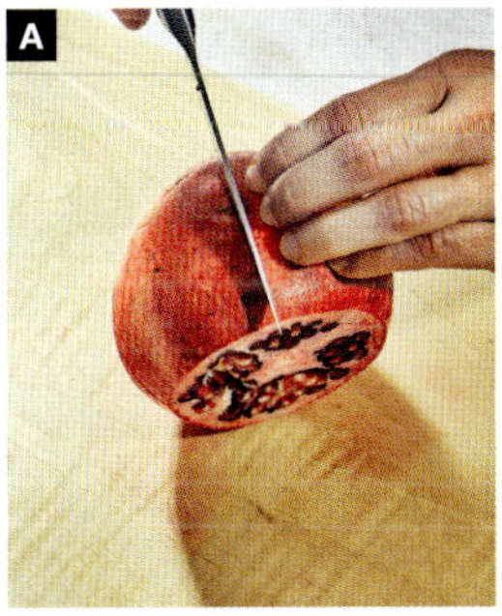

Quick Pickles

Makes 1 quart

- 4 to 5 Kirby cucumbers (about 1 pound)
- 1½ cups distilled white vinegar
- ¾ cup water
- ¼ cup sugar
- 1 tablespoon kosher salt
- 4 to 5 sprigs dill
- 3 garlic cloves, smashed and peeled (see page 23)
- 2 teaspoons whole black peppercorns

SPECIAL EQUIPMENT

32-ounce heatproof jar

I like pickles so much I eat them straight from the jar. To me, a pickle is so much more than a brined cucumber. Here I encourage you to get really creative. Switch up the seasonings, the fruit or vegetable, or whatever you might try to pickle. You can make them much more interesting than what you usually find on the supermarket shelf, plus they are way fresher and crispier, and they just taste brighter. I especially like pickling sweet things—peaches are a favorite. Butternut squash makes a stellar pickle too (see Swap It). Do keep in mind these are "quick pickles" as opposed to fermented pickles, which are lacto-fermented and take days, if not weeks, to make.

A TINI TIP

While pickles are traditionally made with Kirby cucumbers, anything from hothouse (English) to mini Persian cucumbers will work. Kirby and long English cucumbers do best in rounds or half-moons, while Persian cucumbers can either be sliced into rounds or quartered lengthwise to create spears.

1. Prep the Cucumbers

- Using a sharp knife or a mandolin slicer, cut the cucumbers into rounds, slightly thicker than ⅛ inch.

2. Pickle the Cucumbers

- **MAKE THE PICKLING LIQUID:** In a small saucepan over medium-high heat, combine the vinegar, water, sugar, and salt. Bring the liquid to a boil, stirring until the sugar and salt are dissolved. Remove from the heat and add the cucumbers. Let stand for 15 minutes.
- To a 32-ounce heatproof jar, add the dill, garlic, and peppercorns. Ladle, spoon, or pour the cucumbers and pickling liquid into the jar. (If you don't have enough liquid to cover the cucumbers completely, add a combination of more vinegar and water and give it a little stir.)
- Let the liquid cool completely, then seal the jar and refrigerate for at least 4 hours (preferably overnight) before enjoying. Keep the pickles sealed in the refrigerator for up to 1 month.

SWAP IT

To make pickled radishes, swap the cucumber with radishes; cut them into quarters. Plunge the radishes into boiling water and cook for 1 minute, then drain and add to the pickling liquid. Swap the peppercorns with 1½ teaspoons brown mustard seeds and 1 teaspoon coriander seeds. Use the pickled radishes for dipping into creamy dips and as an addition to cheese boards, or slice them thin and add to sandwiches.

To make pickled butternut squash, peel 1 pound of butternut squash, then scoop out the seeds. Cut into ½-inch cubes and use in place of the cucumbers. Plunge the squash into boiling water and cook for 1 minute, then drain and add to the pickling liquid. Swap the white vinegar for champagne vinegar, the garlic for 1 small thinly sliced shallot, and the dill for thyme sprigs; increase the sugar to ⅓ cup and add 1 whole cinnamon stick, 2 whole star anise, 6 whole cloves, and 2 cracked cardamom pods to the jar. Add the pickled squash to autumnal grain bowls and hearty salads with leafy greens like kale or spinach.

To make pickled banana peppers, slice 1 pound of fresh banana peppers (sometimes called yellow wax peppers) into ⅛-inch-thick rings. Swap the white vinegar for rice vinegar, omit the dill, and add 1 teaspoon each of celery seeds and coriander seeds to the jar. Use them to add a punch to Greek salads, or use some of the pickling liquid in place of vinegar for your next homemade salad dressing.

My Favorite Dressings and Vinaigrettes

I used to toss salads for eight hours a day. At that restaurant job, I learned to toss salads with my hands (I used gloves, of course!). It helps make sure every piece of whatever you are tossing is coated. I like to use sunflower seed oil for my vinaigrettes because it's light and neutral and doesn't weigh down delicate greens. I usually use a simple spring mix. I also highly recommend seasoning a salad like you would any other vegetable or meat: After you toss your salad with dressing, sprinkle the leaves with salt and pepper and give them another toss—it makes all the difference. When I use a thicker dressing like ranch (my all-time favorite dipping sauce, too!), I opt for a sturdier lettuce, like romaine, because the leaves don't wilt under the weight of the dressing. If serving salads to guests, wait until everyone is ready to eat, and toss it then. All the vinaigrettes and the dressing can be stored in an airtight container in the refrigerator for up to 3 days.

TINI'S TIPS

Sub the sunflower oil with another neutral oil, like avocado or safflower; extra-virgin olive oil will work as well, although it will change the flavor.

If you don't have a high-speed blender, you can whisk together any of these dressings that call for one. Finely mince the herbs, and finely chop the fruits, then set aside. Combine the shallot and vinegar (or lime juice) and let stand for 15 minutes. Whisk the mustard into the vinegar (or honey into the lime juice), then slowly drizzle in the oil and whisk until fully combined. Stir in the herbs and fruits, then season to taste with salt and pepper.

PEACH-ROSEMARY VINAIGRETTE

Makes about 2 cups

- 1 (6-ounce) ripe peach, peeled, pitted, and chopped
- 1 small shallot, chopped
- 2 teaspoons minced rosemary
- ⅓ cup champagne vinegar or white wine vinegar
- 2 teaspoons whole-grain mustard
- 1 cup sunflower seed oil
- Kosher salt and freshly ground black pepper

▸ In a high-speed blender, combine the peach, shallot, rosemary, vinegar, and mustard and blend until very smooth. With the machine running, slowly drizzle in the sunflower seed oil and blend until fully combined. Season to taste with salt and pepper.

HERBY MANGO VINAIGRETTE

Makes about 1½ cups

- 1 small ripe mango (6 ounces), peeled, pitted, and chopped
- 1 small shallot, chopped
- ⅓ cup fresh lime juice
- 1 cup packed tender herbs, such as basil, cilantro, mint, and parsley
- 2 teaspoons honey
- ¼ teaspoon crushed red pepper flakes
- 1 cup sunflower seed oil
- Kosher salt and freshly ground black pepper

▸ In a high-speed blender, combine the mango, shallot, lime juice, herbs, honey, and red pepper flakes and blend until very smooth. With the machine running, slowly drizzle in the sunflower seed oil and blend until fully combined. Season to taste with salt and black pepper.

LEMONY GARLIC VINAIGRETTE

Makes about 1⅓ cups

- 1 teaspoon lemon zest
- ⅓ cup freshly squeezed lemon juice (about 1½ lemons)
- ½ garlic clove, finely grated
- 1½ teaspoons Dijon mustard
- 1 cup sunflower seed oil
- 1 tablespoon minced basil
- 1 tablespoon minced chives
- Kosher salt and freshly ground black pepper

▸ In a medium bowl, whisk together the lemon zest, lemon juice, garlic, and mustard until smooth. Slowly drizzle in the sunflower seed oil and whisk until fully combined. Stir in the basil and chives, then season to taste with salt and pepper.

use vinaigrettes and lighter dressings to toss delicate greens

get all in there with your hands to toss

every leaf should be lightly coated with dressing

never hesitate to season a salad

ITALIAN VINAIGRETTE

Makes about 1⅓ cups

- ⅓ cup red wine vinegar
- 1½ teaspoons whole-grain mustard
- ½ teaspoon dried oregano
- ½ teaspoon dried parsley
- ¼ teaspoon dried thyme
- 1 small garlic clove, finely grated
- ¼ teaspoon crushed red pepper flakes
- 1 cup extra-virgin olive oil
- Kosher salt and freshly ground black pepper

‣ In a medium bowl, whisk together the vinegar, mustard, oregano, parsley, thyme, garlic, and red pepper flakes until smooth. Slowly drizzle in the olive oil and whisk until fully combined. Season to taste with salt and black pepper.

BALSAMIC VINAIGRETTE

Makes about 1⅓ cups

- ⅓ cup balsamic vinegar
- 1 tablespoon Dijon mustard
- ¼ teaspoon garlic powder
- ¼ teaspoon sugar
- 1 cup extra-virgin olive oil
- Kosher salt and freshly ground black pepper

‣ In a medium bowl, whisk together the vinegar, mustard, garlic powder, and sugar until smooth. Slowly drizzle in the olive oil and whisk until fully combined. Season to taste with salt and pepper (be generous with the pepper in this one).

RANCH DRESSING

Makes about 1½ cups

- ½ cup buttermilk
- ½ cup mayonnaise
- ¼ cup sour cream
- 2 tablespoons pickle juice
- 2 tablespoons freshly squeezed lemon juice
- 2 tablespoons chopped dill
- 2 tablespoons chopped chives
- 2 tablespoons minced parsley
- 1 teaspoon garlic powder
- 1 teaspoon onion powder
- 1 teaspoon kosher salt
- ½ teaspoon freshly ground black pepper

‣ In a medium bowl, whisk together the buttermilk, mayonnaise, sour cream, pickle juice, lemon juice, dill, chives, parsley, garlic powder, onion powder, salt, and pepper until smooth.

‣ Transfer to a lidded jar. Let the flavors meld for at least 20 minutes, or refrigerate overnight, before serving.

balsamic
ranch
lemony garlic

peach-rosemary
Italian
herby mango

Maryland-Style Potato Salad

Serves 4

- 1 pound red potatoes (about 3 medium)
- 1 pound Yukon Gold potatoes (about 3 medium)
- ½ cup plus 1 tablespoon distilled white vinegar
- Kosher salt
- ⅔ cup mayonnaise
- 2 tablespoons pickle juice
- 4 teaspoons Dijon mustard
- 1 tablespoon Old Bay Seasoning
- 2 teaspoons Tini's Homemade Hot Sauce (page 38) or store-bought
- 1 teaspoon smoked paprika
- ¾ teaspoon garlic powder
- ¼ teaspoon celery seeds
- 2 celery stalks, finely chopped
- 1 small red onion, finely chopped
- ⅓ cup finely chopped dill
- ¼ cup finely chopped dill pickles (my Quick Pickles, page 164, work great here!)
- 2 tablespoons minced chives
- Freshly ground black pepper to taste

I'm from Maryland, and we put Old Bay on almost everything, including potato salad. Some people think the savory spice mix is just for seafood, but I find that the blend of eighteen spices, including paprika and celery salt, complements vegetables, chicken, eggs, and, like I said, most things. Old Bay even did a collab with an ice cream company! The seasoning, along with hot sauce, gives this salad a little kick. I also use a mix of red and gold potatoes because it looks pretty. I don't reserve this classic for summer cookouts—I serve it for game day, holidays, basically any day.

A TINI TIP

Seasoning starts with the water you use to boil, just like with pasta. The most important addition is salt—and plenty of it—but I also add vinegar to the cooking water to help the potatoes absorb a nice hit of acid well before they're tossed with the dressing.

1. Boil the Potatoes

- Cut the potatoes into 1-inch pieces and put them in a medium saucepan. Cover with about 2 quarts water, then stir in the ½ cup vinegar and 3 tablespoons salt. Bring the liquid to a boil, then reduce the heat to a simmer, stirring occasionally, until the potatoes are fork-tender, 12 to 14 minutes.
- Drain the potatoes, then transfer to a medium bowl. Season with ½ teaspoon salt and the remaining 1 tablespoon vinegar, tossing gently to coat. Let cool to room temperature, 30 to 40 minutes.

2. Make the Dressing and Serve

- In a large bowl, whisk together the mayonnaise, pickle juice, mustard, Old Bay, hot sauce, smoked paprika, garlic powder, celery seeds, and ½ teaspoon salt until smooth and well combined. Add the cooled potatoes, celery, onion, dill, and pickles and stir gently until everything is evenly coated in the dressing. Taste and season with more salt, if needed, then cover and refrigerate for 1 hour minimum to allow the flavors to meld (it's even better the next day!).
- Before serving, sprinkle the chives over the top and a few grinds of pepper.

SWAP IT

Take a cue from German potato salad and turn this into a mayo-free dish. Cook 4 slices diced bacon in a medium skillet over medium heat, stirring occasionally, until crisp and golden, 8 to 10 minutes. Drain on paper towels. Sauté 1 chopped yellow onion in the bacon grease until softened, about 5 minutes. Toss the onion, bacon, and any remaining bacon fat with the potatoes and the remaining ingredients in the recipe minus the mayonnaise, onion, and dill.

I'll sprinkle Old Bay on most anything, including my potato salad

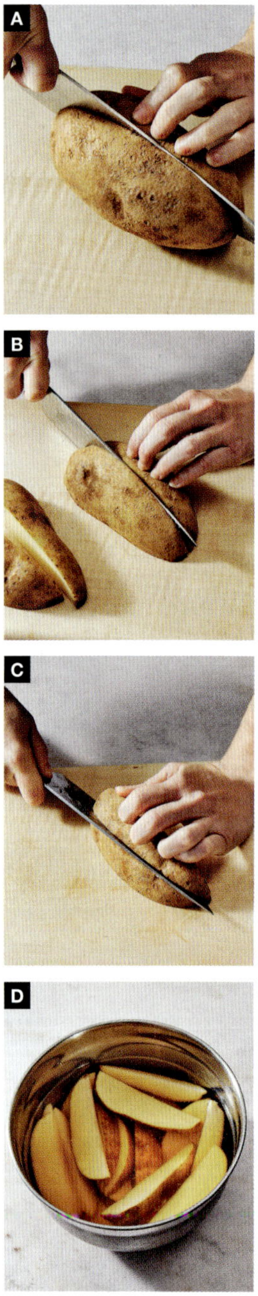
A
B
C
D

Oven-Baked Boardwalk Fries

Serves 4

FRIES

- 3 large russet potatoes (about 1½ pounds)
- 1½ cups distilled white vinegar
- ½ cup malt vinegar
- 3½ teaspoons kosher salt
- ¼ cup extra-virgin olive oil
- 1 tablespoon Old Bay Seasoning
- 2 teaspoons garlic powder
- ½ teaspoon freshly ground black pepper
- Ketchup, for serving (optional)

MALT VINEGAR MAYO

- ⅔ cup mayonnaise
- 4 teaspoons malt vinegar
- 1 tablespoon roasted garlic (page 23)
- ½ teaspoon Dijon mustard
- Kosher salt and freshly ground black pepper

Malt vinegar is the hero of this recipe. It's a classic in Ocean City, Maryland, where you'll find boardwalk fries everywhere. In fact, you'll find malt and vinegar fries with Old Bay in most any tavern in Maryland. My oven-baked version is a great recipe for someone who loves fries but doesn't want to deal with hot oil (just yet! I encourage you to try my Belgian fries when you are ready, page 174). I cut the potatoes into wedges so there's lots of golden surface area for the Old Bay and garlic powder (always a must!). Soaking the potatoes in a salty, acidic brine helps break down starches that could otherwise make the fries mushy, but instead results in a nice crispy wedge. The vinegar and salt also make these fries tasty from the inside out. You could serve these alongside so many things: pulled pork sandwiches (page 63), or even a charred strip steak (page 50). And if you're tempted to skip the malt vinegar mayo, trust me, don't.

TINI'S TIPS

This isn't the place for overly strong vinegars like balsamic, sherry, or red wine, so stick to more basic (and affordable) vinegars like distilled white and malt when soaking the potatoes.

For the mayo, if you don't have time to roast garlic, you can always sub in fresh and it will be punchier.

1. Cut the Potatoes into Wedges

- Cut the potatoes in half lengthwise **A**, then lay both pieces flat-side down and cut them in half again lengthwise **B**. Turn over the potato quarters and cut each quarter in half again lengthwise, right down the center, so you get ¾-inch wedges **C**.

2. Soak the Potatoes

- In a large bowl, cover the potatoes with both vinegars, 2 teaspoons of the salt, and enough room temperature water to cover completely **D**. Let stand at room temperature for 1 hour, then drain. Transfer to paper towels and thoroughly pat dry.

3. Roast the Potatoes

- Preheat the oven to 425°F. Place a rimmed baking sheet on the lower third rack; let it heat for 15 minutes.
- In a large bowl, toss the dried potatoes with the olive oil, Old Bay, garlic powder, pepper, and the remaining 1½ teaspoons salt. Carefully remove the baking sheet from the oven and add the potatoes in an even layer. Roast for 20 minutes, then flip the potatoes and continue roasting until golden brown on both sides and tender on the inside, 15 to 20 more minutes.

4. Make the Mayo and Serve

- In a small bowl, whisk together the mayonnaise, malt vinegar, garlic, and mustard. Season to taste with salt and pepper.
- Serve the potatoes hot with the malt vinegar mayo and ketchup, if desired.

SWAP IT

Oven-Baked Parmesan Fries with Herby Garlic Butter

When soaking the potatoes, replace the malt vinegar with more distilled white vinegar. Omit the Old Bay and garlic powder from the potatoes and toss with ½ cup finely grated Parmesan cheese instead. Roast as directed; the cheese should melt and crisp up to a golden brown around the edges of the potatoes. While the potatoes cook, melt 4 tablespoons unsalted butter in a small saucepan over medium heat. Once melted, add 1 tablespoon minced garlic (from 2 large cloves) and cook until fragrant, about 1 minute. Let cool slightly, then stir in 2 tablespoons each finely chopped parsley and minced chives. Once the potatoes come out of the oven, drizzle the garlic-herb butter over the top and toss gently to coat.

↑

these are killer

Level Up

Belgian-Style Fries

Serves 6

- 3 to 4 cups ice, for chilling the water
- 7 russet potatoes (about 3 pounds)
- 2 to 3 quarts neutral oil, such as vegetable or peanut (duck fat works great, too!)
- Flaky salt or Old Bay Seasoning, for serving

I'm not going to lie—making these fries is a process. I learned to make them in culinary school, and will never, ever make them any other way (and my mom wouldn't eat them any other way either—she *loves* them!). Every step is well worth the result: a crispy yet tender fry that is fluffy and soft inside, with a great potato flavor, all of which Belgian-style fries are known for. Putting peeled potatoes in water prevents them from oxidizing and turning brown; soaking the potatoes draws out the starch; chilling the fries helps dry them out; and double-frying (a Belgian-style must!) is no joke: It makes them perfectly golden. Do it and you'll thank me. If you can get your hands on some duck fat, fry your fries in that. You'll double thank me!

> **A TINI TIP**
> Serve these fries with a selection of dipping sauces; try my homemade aioli (page 54) and curry mayo (page 40).

1. Cut the Potatoes and Submerge in Ice Water

- Fill a large bowl halfway with water and add the ice.
- Peel the potatoes and put the whole potatoes in the water.
- Cut one of the potatoes in half lengthwise **A**. Turn one of the halves flat-side down (this makes cutting easier) and slice the potato half into ¼-inch slices **B**. Stack two or three of the slices and slice them again into ¼-inch sticks/fries **C**.
- Immediately put the cut fries in the ice water and repeat until each potato is sliced and back in the water. I usually let my cut fries sit in water for 1 hour before rinsing—this removes excess starch **D**. After you rinse your fries, return them to the bowl and fill it with cool tap water again (or as many times as needed) until the water remains clear and is not clouded by the starch.

whatever you do, don't skip the blanching step!

2. Chill the Fries

- Line a large baking sheet with paper towels and transfer the fries to the tray. Pat them dry with more paper towels **E**. Switch out the bottom paper towel for a dry one if needed. Chill the fries in the fridge for 30 to 60 minutes.

3. Blanch the Fries

- Line a baking sheet with fresh paper towels and set aside.
- In a large 6- or 7-quart pot or Dutch oven, pour in the oil (you should have at least 1½ to 2 inches of oil) and heat to 300°F on a candy thermometer **F**. Divide the fries into two or three batches and using a spider, lower the fries into the oil. Cook until the potatoes are softened but without any change in color, about 5 minutes; the fries will be limp **G**. Transfer immediately to the paper towel–lined baking sheet and allow the fries to cool for 30 minutes.

4. Fry the Fries Again and Serve

- Once the fries have cooled, heat the oil to 375°F. Working again in batches, fry them, moving them around with a wire-mesh spider, until golden brown, 5 to 7 minutes **H**. (See page 39 for deep-frying tips on monitoring temperature and more.)
- Transfer the cooked fries to a paper-towel-lined sheet tray and season immediately with flaky salt (or Old Bay!). Serve hot.

E

F

G

H

The Breakfast Course

Bananas Foster French Toast

Serves 4
(Makes 8 slices)

FRENCH TOAST

- 2 large eggs
- ⅔ cup whole milk
- ½ teaspoon pure vanilla extract or vanilla bean paste
- ½ teaspoon ground cinnamon (optional)
- 2 tablespoons unsalted butter, plus more as needed
- 8 slices Banana Bread, ½ inch thick (page 238)

BANANAS FOSTER

- 6 tablespoons unsalted butter
- ½ cup packed light brown sugar
- ½ teaspoon ground cinnamon
- ¼ teaspoon kosher salt
- 2 medium ripe but still firm bananas, cut into ¼-inch slices
- ¼ cup of your favorite white (or aged) rum (I often use Captain Morgan's Spiced Rum because my mom likes it!), plus more as needed
- 1 teaspoon pure vanilla extract

SERVING

- 1 cup prepared Vanilla Whipped Cream (page 222)
- 1 to 2 tablespoons powdered sugar
- 1 cup strawberries, sliced or whole (optional)

At culinary school, the first thing I flambéed was bananas Foster, a dessert that came out of New Orleans in the 1950s, and I liked it a lot. We had the warm, buttery bananas on top of homemade honey ice cream—and the honey was fresh from our garden program. I admit, I love to flambé, which is basically pouring alcohol on something and lighting it on fire. I like making fire in a fun way—it impresses people! At restaurants, it's often done tableside. If you do it this way at home, make sure the area is clear; otherwise it's probably best done on the stovetop, and only if you have a ventilation hood. Kitchen safety is no joke—commercial kitchen or not, you should always have a fire extinguisher and fire blanket nearby.

TINI'S TIPS

You can easily sub 1-inch-thick brioche bread for the banana bread. However, you'll need to submerge it a little longer, so you may have enough soaking liquid for only 6 pieces of bread.

If it's your first time flambéing, have someone ready with a match or lighter to ignite the rum right after you add it to the pan. It can be hard to move that quickly when you are just learning.

if you have a gas burner, instead of using a lighter, gently tilt your pan to catch the flame

1. Make the Egg Mixture

- Preheat the oven to 200°F.
- In a medium, shallow bowl, whisk together the eggs, milk, vanilla, and cinnamon.

2. Dip and Cook

- In a large skillet over medium heat, melt 1 tablespoon of the butter.
- Dip each side of the bread into the egg mixture. Do not fully submerge the slice. Place as many pieces of the dipped bread into the pan that will fit. Cook until golden on both sides, 3 to 4 minutes per side.
- Transfer to a baking sheet and keep warm in the oven. Repeat with the remaining bread and 1 tablespoon butter, adding more butter to the pan as needed.

4. Flambé

- In the same skillet over medium heat, melt the butter. Add the brown sugar and wait for it to melt **A**. Do not stir. Once the brown sugar is melted, stir in the cinnamon and salt.
- Add the bananas and cook until the bananas are heated through, stirring occasionally, and the sauce is smooth and caramelly (as opposed to a grainy consistency) **B**.
- Add the rum **C**, reduce the heat to low, and, using a lighter, carefully ignite the sauce in the pan. If you need a splash more rum to get it lit, go for it! Shake the pan and continue to cook until the alcohol has cooked off and the flame dies, 1 to 2 minutes. Be careful!
- Remove from the heat and stir in the vanilla

5. Plate and Serve

- Cut the warm French toast into triangles and line 4 pieces up in a (mostly) standing row on each plate.
- Spoon the cooked bananas over the French toast **D** and top each with a generous spoonful of whipped cream. Using a small sieve, sprinkle sifted powdered sugar over the top and garnish with the strawberries (if using). Serve immediately.

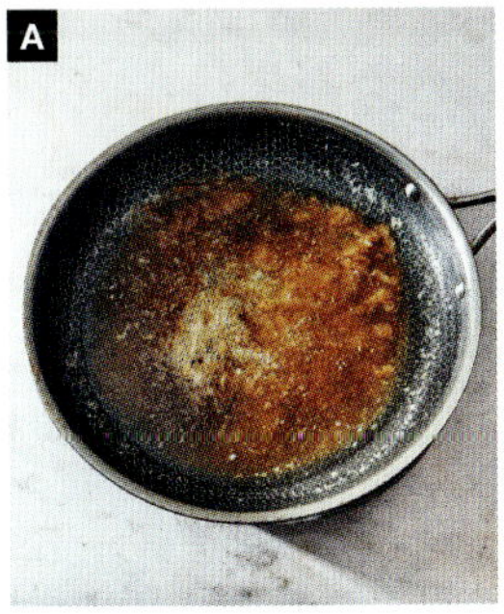
A

B

C

D

Cinnamon Waffles
WITH CARAMELIZED APPLES

Makes 8 (3½ × 4-inch) Belgian waffles

CARAMELIZED APPLES

- 1 stick (8 tablespoons) unsalted butter
- 1 cup packed light brown sugar
- 4 teaspoons freshly squeezed lemon juice
- 1 teaspoon kosher salt
- 4 of your favorite variety crisp apples, peeled and cut into ½-inch wedges
- ¼ cup heavy cream

WAFFLES

- 2¼ cups / 315g all-purpose flour
- 2 tablespoons / 25g granulated sugar
- 2¾ teaspoons/ 11g baking powder
- 1½ teaspoons / 6g kosher salt
- ¾ teaspoon ground cinnamon, plus more for garnish
- 2 large eggs
- 1½ cups / 360g milk
- ½ stick (4 tablespoons) / 56g unsalted butter, melted and cooled
- 4 tablespoons / 60g neutral oil, such as vegetable or sunflower
- 2 teaspoons / 10g pure vanilla extract
- Vegetable oil cooking spray, for the waffle iron

SERVING

- 4 to 8 scoops No-Churn Vanilla Ice Cream (page 257) or store-bought vanilla ice cream (optional)

SPECIAL EQUIPMENT

Waffle iron

In Maryland, where I grew up, there are four distinct seasons, and in fall, apple picking was a thing. I'll never forget my fifth-grade field trip picking apples to make apple pancakes. Plucking them straight from the tree was the best. In Georgia, where I live now, there's no colorful apple/pumpkin-picking fall for me. I miss picking apples, but I still eat plenty of them. I'm a Honeycrisp and Granny Smith girl. And with apples, I love cinnamon. Lots of cinnamon. (You may notice I add cinnamon to most things I bake.) Here I add it to crisp yet tender waffles topped with softened apples that have been cooked in a gooey, sweet caramel-butter sauce. Now these will make any place feel like fall!

TINI'S TIPS

Make a double batch of the waffles and freeze the leftovers; they reheat great in a toaster or air fryer.

Adding cream to the caramel stops the cooking and keeps it liquid-y—otherwise, it would harden at room temperature.

1. Make the Caramelized Apples

- In a large skillet over medium heat, melt the butter. Add the brown sugar, lemon juice, and salt.
- Cook, constantly stirring, until the sugar dissolves, then bring the mixture to a boil and cook for 1 minute.
- Add the apples and cook, stirring occasionally, until they begin to soften and brown a bit and the liquid thickens, 6 to 8 minutes. Slowly pour in the heavy cream (it will bubble up, so be careful!) and cook until the sauce slightly thickens, about 2 minutes. Remove from the heat, cover, and set aside.

2. Make the Waffle Batter

- Preheat the oven to 250°F. Line a rimmed baking sheet with a cooling rack.
- In a large bowl, whisk together the flour, granulated sugar, baking powder, salt, and cinnamon. Make a well in the center and add the eggs, whisk a bit, then add the milk, butter, oil, and vanilla and whisk until just combined (there will be some lumps).

3. Make the Waffles

- Heat your waffle iron and make the waffles according to the manufacturer's instructions. (If you have no instructions, coat the iron with baking spray. Ladle the batter onto the iron. Close the iron and cook until the waffles are golden brown and crisp, 3 to 5 minutes.)
- Transfer the waffles to the rack on the baking sheet and keep warm in the oven. Repeat with remaining batter.

4. Serve

- Serve warm waffles with caramelized apples and a scoop of ice cream (if using), dusted with cinnamon.

A Folded Omelet

WITH GOAT CHEESE AND HERBS

Serves 4
(Makes 2 omelets)

HERBED GOAT CHEESE

- 4 ounces goat cheese, softened
- 1/3 cup loosely packed mixed tender herbs, such as chives, dill, and parsley, finely chopped, plus more for serving
- 1 scallion, white and green parts, coarsely chopped
- 1 teaspoon freshly squeezed lemon juice
- 1/8 teaspoon freshly ground black pepper

OMELETS

- 6 large eggs
- 1/2 teaspoon kosher salt
- 1 tablespoon water
- 4 teaspoons clarified butter (see Tini's Tips)

I've made plenty of omelets, and that's the secret to a great omelet—practice. It takes time to learn the visual clues for cooking a proper omelet, like if the eggs are whisked enough, or if they are ready to be folded. Here we're going to use clarified butter, which is butter that the milk solids have been removed from, because it keeps the eggs from browning or sticking to the pan. I like stuffing my omelets with lots of different things, from bacon and cheddar to mushrooms and chives (I've eaten even *more* omelets than I've made!). And this one is a fluffy American-style omelet, which is folded, and easier for beginners (unlike French omelets, which are rolled, and tend to have less filling, if any). I use herbed goat cheese, which may resemble Boursin to those who know that creamy cheese spread with the green logo (growing up, I always thought it was butter).

TINI'S TIPS

If you can't find clarified butter at the supermarket, you can easily make it at home (and it keeps in the refrigerator for months!). In a small saucepan, melt 1 stick of unsalted butter over medium heat. Let the butter bubble. After a few minutes, the milk solids will rise to the surface, leaving the clarified butter on the bottom of the pan. Use a spoon to scoop the solids off the top, then cool the butter and store refrigerated in an airtight container for up to 3 months.

The homemade herbed goat cheese takes a simple omelet up a notch. If you don't have a food processor or blender, you can finely chop up the herbs and scallions and fold them into the cheese by hand. And feel free to substitute with store-bought herbed goat cheese or Boursin.

1. Make the Herbed Goat Cheese

- To a food processor or blender, add the goat cheese, herbs, scallion, lemon juice, and pepper and pulse until fully combined and smooth.

2. Whisk the Eggs

- In a medium bowl or large, spouted measuring cup, use a fork to whisk together the eggs, salt, pepper, and the water just until no large streaks of egg whites remain.

3. Cook the Omelet

- In an 8-inch nonstick skillet over medium-high heat, melt 2 teaspoons of the clarified butter, swirling the pan to coat the surface. Give the eggs another quick whisk and pour half of them into the pan (the measuring cup is helpful here so your omelets turn out evenly). Let stand until the edges *just* start to set, about 1 minute **A**. Start scraping around the sides of the skillet with a rubber spatula and tipping the skillet to allow the runny eggs to flood into those empty spaces, until no longer runny but still slightly wet, about 2 minutes.
- **FOLD THE OMELET:** Crumble half of the herbed goat cheese over the top of the eggs **B**. Use the spatula to fold one side of the omelet over the filling to create a half-moon shape **C**.

4. Finish and Serve

- Slide the omelet onto a warm plate and tent with aluminum foil to keep warm while you cook the second omelet using the remaining eggs and 2 teaspoons clarified butter.
- Cut each omelet in half and serve immediately, sprinkled with more herbs.

SWAP IT

Fill the omelet with leftover roasted vegetables, cooked crumbled sausage, bacon, or sautéed mushrooms.

Substitute the herbed goat cheese for any good melting cheese, like mozzarella, pepper Jack, or cheddar.

A
B
C

make sure you see these little bubbles before flipping!

Fluffy Chocolate Chip Pancakes

WITH SPICY OVEN-BAKED BACON

Serves 4
(Makes 12 pancakes)

PANCAKES

- 2⅔ cups / 372g all-purpose flour
- 4 teaspoons granulated sugar
- 4 teaspoons baking powder
- 1 teaspoon baking soda
- ¾ teaspoon kosher salt
- 2⅔ cups / 604g buttermilk, at room temperature
- 3 large eggs, at room temperature
- ½ stick (4 tablespoons / 56g) unsalted butter, melted, plus more softened for serving
- 1 teaspoon / 5g pure vanilla extract
- 1 cup / 240g semisweet chocolate chips, plus more for topping (optional)
- Neutral oil or nonstick pan spray
- Pure maple syrup, for serving

BACON

- 12 bacon slices
- 2 tablespoons pure maple syrup
- 2 tablespoons packed light brown sugar
- 1 teaspoon smoked paprika
- ¾ teaspoon freshly ground black pepper

I'm not going to argue with anyone who says pancakes from a mix are easy to make. They are, I get it. I use a boxed mix sometimes. But I *will* argue if they say homemade pancakes are *hard* to make. You simply combine a few dry ingredients and stir them into the wet. And you control the quality of the ingredients! This recipe makes a great classic pancake. There isn't a lot of mess from the bacon because you bake it, *and* it makes the house smell so good (and that's your cue for when bacon is about to be done: when it really starts waking up everyone still in bed). My nose is my timer. Learning to time by smell comes with experience. Both the bacon and pancakes will smell toasty when they are done. If you pay attention to the smells as well as visual cues when food is cooking, it'll help you depend less on timers and more on your intuition.

TINI'S TIPS

No buttermilk? No problem. As long as you have milk, you can make your own. For this recipe, combine 2½ cups milk with 2 tablespoons of fresh lemon juice or cider vinegar. Let it stand at room temperature for about 5 minutes, until it thickens slightly.

Letting the batter rest before cooking allows for it to fully hydrate (and it should take care of any dry lumps, since you never want to overmix pancake batter, which can make your pancakes tough). It also gives the leaveners time to activate for fluffier pancakes.

Make your own pancake mix by combining the dry ingredients and storing them in a jar or airtight container. Then add the wet ingredients when you are ready to cook.

1. Make the Pancake Batter

- In a large bowl, whisk together the flour, granulated sugar, baking powder, baking soda, and salt. In medium bowl, whisk together the buttermilk, eggs, butter, and vanilla until smooth. Add the dry ingredients to the wet and stir with a rubber spatula until halfway combined. Add the chocolate chips and continue stirring just until no large dry spots remain (lumps are encouraged; see Tini's Tips). Let the batter rest at room temperature for 15 minutes.

2. Cook the Bacon

- While the batter rests, move a rack to the upper third of the oven. Preheat the oven to 400°F.
- Set a wire rack inside of a foil-lined rimmed baking sheet. Arrange the bacon in an even layer on the rack. Bake for 10 minutes.
- In a small bowl, whisk together the maple syrup, brown sugar, smoked paprika, and pepper. Brush half of this mixture over the top of the bacon, then return to the oven and bake until the strips start to curl, 5 to 8 minutes. Flip the bacon and brush the other side with the remaining maple glaze. Bake until cooked through and caramelized in places, 5 to 8 minutes. Remove from the oven. Reduce the oven temp to 300°F, leaving it on in case you need to warm up the bacon after cooking the pancakes.

3. Cook the Pancakes

- Heat a large nonstick griddle or skillet over medium-low heat. Brush the surface very lightly with oil (or spray with nonstick pan spray).
- Working in batches, add ⅓-cup mounds of batter to the griddle, using the back of a small spoon to spread into approximate 5-inch circles. Sprinkle a few more chocolate chips over the top, if desired. Cook until the bottoms are golden brown, the tops are puffed, and the edges are bubbly, about 3 minutes **A**. Flip the pancakes and cook until golden on the second side, about 2 minutes **B**.
- Stack the pancakes on plates and top with pats of butter, more chocolate chips, and a drizzle of maple syrup. If the bacon has gotten cold, pop it back in the oven for about 2 minutes, then serve with the pancakes.

SWAP IT

Try pairing the chocolate chips with other flavors that go well with them—substitute half of the chips for chopped fresh banana, peanut butter chips, or chopped pitted fresh cherries.

Or swap the chocolate chips for something else entirely, like fresh or frozen blueberries, raspberries, bananas, or tropical fruits.

Buttery Biscuits

WITH STRAWBERRY COMPOTE

Makes 8 biscuits
2 cups compote

COMPOTE

1 pound fresh strawberries, trimmed and quartered

⅔ cup granulated sugar

1 tablespoon freshly squeezed lemon juice

Kosher salt

BISCUITS

3 cups / 420g all-purpose flour, plus more for rolling

2 tablespoons / 16g cornstarch

2 tablespoons / 25g granulated sugar

1 tablespoon / 11g baking powder

1 teaspoon / 3g baking soda

1½ teaspoons / 6g kosher salt

1 stick (8 tablespoons / 113 g) cold unsalted butter, cut into ½-inch pieces, plus 4 tablespoons melted, for brushing, and 2 tablespoons softened, for serving (they're called buttery for a reason!)

1¼ cups / 300g cold buttermilk, well shaken

Coarse sanding sugar, for topping

When I'm looking for morning comfort food, nothing compares to a homemade buttery biscuit—unlike the ones my dad makes from a box, which are as hard as a rock! Folding and stacking the dough creates layers that let you easily pull these biscuits apart (do it when they're warm and the layers will be steaming!). I brush my biscuits with an extra coating of butter when they come out of the oven for an even richer flavor. I like to spoon on a sweet homemade compote, usually made of strawberries, but you can sub in any seasonal fruit.

A TINI TIP

Compote should be a little looser than jam or preserves. If you prefer a thicker spread, use ¾ cup of sugar per pound of strawberries and cook the mixture for an extra minute or two.

1. Make the Strawberry Compote

- In a medium saucepan, stir together the strawberries, granulated sugar, lemon juice, and salt. Using a potato masher or fork, mash the berries just until some are broken down slightly and begin releasing their juices.
- **SIMMER THE COMPOTE:** Bring the mixture to a boil over medium-high heat, then reduce the heat to medium and simmer, stirring frequently, until syrupy, 4 to 5 minutes (the liquid should drip off the spoon slowly, but not be jam-like just yet).
- Transfer to a medium heatproof bowl and let cool completely. Use immediately or store in an airtight container in the refrigerator for up to 1 week.

2. Make the Biscuit Dough

- Preheat the oven to 425°F and line a baking sheet with parchment paper.
- In a large bowl, whisk together the flour, cornstarch, granulated sugar, baking powder, baking soda, and salt.
- **CUT IN THE BUTTER:** Add the butter pieces and using a pastry cutter, cut the butter into small pieces about the size of peas **A**. Use your hands to toss the butter with the flour to coat, pressing pieces of butter into the dough until it has a coarse texture **B**.
- Drizzle the buttermilk over the mixture **C** and stir with the fork until a shaggy dough forms.
- Dump the dough out onto a lightly floured work surface and knead gently a few times to bring it together **D**. Working quickly, pat the dough into an 8 × 10-inch rectangle **E**. Using a bench scraper, fold one short side of the dough in half to meet the other edge. **F**
- Repeat the patting and folding process two more times **G**, dusting lightly with more flour as needed, then pat the dough out to a ¾-inch thickness.
- Using a 3-inch round biscuit cutter, cut out circles of dough **H** and transfer them to the prepared baking sheet an inch apart. Press the scraps together, re-roll, and cut out more biscuits. Brush the tops with ½ the melted butter and sprinkle lightly with sanding sugar.

3. Bake the Biscuits

- Bake on the center rack until puffed and golden brown, 14 to 16 minutes. Remove from the oven and brush with the remaining melted butter.
- Let the biscuits cool slightly, then serve warm, with more butter on the side, and the strawberry compote.

A
B
C
D
E
F
G
H

Level Up

Poached Eggs

WITH HOMEMADE ENGLISH MUFFINS AND OLD BAY HOLLANDAISE

Makes 8 muffin halves with eggs

HOLLANDAISE

- 4 large egg yolks, at room temperature
- 1 tablespoon freshly squeezed lemon juice, plus more to taste, at room temperature
- 2 sticks (16 tablespoons) unsalted butter
- 1 teaspoon Old Bay Seasoning, plus more for garnish (optional)
- Kosher salt and freshly ground black pepper

SERVING

- 4 Homemade English Muffins (page 191) or store-bought
- ½ stick (4 tablespoons) unsalted butter, softened
- 2 tablespoons chopped fresh chives

POACHED EGGS

- 2 tablespoons white vinegar or white wine vinegar
- 8 large eggs

I can't tell you how many people tell me poached eggs are intimidating to make. But I promise, just like with making omelets, it's all about practice. Once you get the hang of it, and a feel for how quickly and easily the eggs cook, you'll be ready to plate a brunch-worthy spread complete with a beautiful golden-yellow hollandaise. The classic French "mother" sauce, made from egg yolks, butter, and lemon juice, is probably the trickiest part of this recipe. It definitely takes practice to create an emulsion (check out the Tini's Tips for how to save a broken sauce). I'm not going to lie: It may take you a few times to get it right, but once you do, you're golden!

TINI'S TIPS

If you've never poached eggs, before cooking them for someone else, maybe invest in a dozen eggs and practice gently sliding them into the swirling vortex.

To create a stable emulsion **A** (incorporating two unlike liquids), add the butter very, very slowly at first. The general rule is that you can't add more fat to the egg yolk than the volume that already exists, so start with the tiniest of drips, gradually adding more as a creamy sauce forms.

If you add the butter too quickly and the mixture breaks **B**, or if the mixture doesn't thicken, pour it out of the blender into a measuring cup, rinse the blender with very hot water, add 1 new egg yolk and 1 teaspoon of hot water and run the blender until the yolk and water are warmed. Slowly, drop by drop, add the broken or thinned mixture back into the blender and the mixture should thicken up. Go slowly!

If you don't have a blender, you can make the hollandaise with an immersion blender in a takeout quart container, or you can whisk it by hand as well.

1. Make the Hollandaise

- In a large saucepan over high heat, bring 3 quarts water to a boil for poaching the eggs.
- While waiting for the water to boil, combine the egg yolks and lemon juice in a high-speed blender (if you have different sizes of blender jars, the smaller the better). Run on high speed until combined and the mixture is slightly warm (the blender causes friction that gives off some heat), about 1 minute.
- **MELT THE BUTTER:** In a microwave-safe container, add the butter and microwave on high until melted, about 45 seconds (or melt the butter on the stovetop).
- **EMULSIFY THE BUTTER:** Immediately, with the blender running on low, through the top of the blender lid, add the hot butter, drop by drop. Take this slowly. You are emulsifying the butter so it will combine smoothly with the egg yolks and thicken. The goal is a creamy consistency, a little thinner than mayonnaise.
- Keep adding the butter until it's all incorporated. Transfer the thickened sauce to a bowl and stir in the Old Bay. Taste, and add more lemon juice, salt, pepper, and/or Old Bay as needed. See Tini's Tips if your sauce did not thicken or it "broke." If it's *too* thick, add a teaspoon or two of warm water and stir to thin.

this is a curdled, broken sauce; see Tini's Tips for how to fix it ↓

this is a properly emulsified sauce! →

A

B

recipe continues ▸▸

2. Keep the Sauce Warm

- Set the bowl in a larger bowl of warm water to keep warm. If you plan on using the sauce later than the time it takes to cook the eggs, place a piece of plastic wrap directly on its surface to keep a skin from forming.

3. Toast and Butter the Muffins

- Using a fork, split open the English muffins and lightly toast in a toaster. Generously butter them and divide among four serving plates, cut-side up.

4. Poach the Eggs

- Add the vinegar to a pot of boiling water and reduce the heat to a very low simmer.
- Crack the eggs into individual ramekins (coffee mugs work, too).
- Create a vortex in the water by swirling it with a spoon C. Place the edge of a ramekin in the water and allow the egg to drop in. Repeat by lowering a few more eggs into the water, or as many as will fit, leaving space around each egg. Don't make a vortex for each egg, just the initial one. Cook, gently releasing eggs from the bottom of the pan if necessary, until the whites are set but the yolks are still runny, 3 to 5 minutes. Using a slotted spoon, remove the eggs from the water D and place one on each toasted muffin. Repeat the process with any remaining eggs.

6. Plate, Garnish, and Serve

- Spoon a tablespoon or two of sauce over each egg. Sprinkle with chives, and a pinch or two of Old Bay. Serve with any extra sauce on the side.

SWAP IT

Switch things up by adding a little something extra under the eggs: a lightly fried piece of Canadian bacon for authentic eggs Benedict, a small mound of wilted spinach, or smoked salmon or lump crabmeat if you're feeling fancy.

split your muffins with a fork,
not a knife!
that's how they stay
nice and fluffy

Level Up

Homemade English Muffins

Makes 8 English muffins

1½ cups / 360g whole milk
½ stick (4 tablespoons / 56g) unsalted butter
¼ cup / 72g honey
⅔ cup / 146g warm (105°F to 110°F) water
2½ teaspoons / 10g active dry yeast
Two pinches of sugar
4 cups / 560g all-purpose flour, plus more for the work surface
1 tablespoon / 15g kosher salt
Neutral oil, for greasing the bowl
Semolina flour

SERVING

A few tablespoons of butter

My mantra: Homemade is better! And English muffins are no exception. Although they may seem like they are hard to make, they really aren't. It just takes time, because you need to let the dough sit in the fridge for at least 8 hours; that's how it develops flavor. It's noticeable if you don't. I like to use English muffins for sandwiches, especially breakfast sandwiches and as a base for poached eggs (page 189) or even better, a classic eggs Benedict. They are just good on their own smothered in butter, too. They taste so much fresher than store-bought.

TINI'S TIPS

"Proofing," or waiting for yeast to get bubbly in the water, lets you know if the yeast is active and working. If not, you'll need to buy fresh yeast.

If you don't have a circle cutter, use flour-dusted hands to lightly form each piece into a ball and press down to form a 3¼-inch round.

You can throw any leftovers in the freezer in a freezer-safe bag. Be sure to split them in half with a fork before freezing so they are ready to pop in the toaster straight from the freezer.

If your muffins haven't cooked through after 16 minutes on the stovetop, continue cooking them until they are done, or you may finish "baking" your muffins in the oven. After cooking for the recommended stovetop time, transfer the skillet to a 350°F oven and bake until the muffins are cooked through. The best way to check for doneness is with an instant-read thermometer.

1. Scald the Milk

- In a small saucepan over medium heat, warm the milk until small bubbles just start to form around the edges—it shouldn't bubble in the center. Remove the pan from the heat. Stir in the butter and honey, and continue to stir until the butter is melted. Pour the milk mixture into the bowl of a stand mixer and let cool until it's warm to the touch, 105°F to 110°F on an instant-read thermometer.

2. Proof the Yeast

- Meanwhile, pour the water into a small bowl and stir in the yeast and sugar. Let it stand until foamy (if you know your yeast is active you may skip the waiting—it just lets you know if the yeast is still alive!). When the milk mixture is cooled, stir in the proofed yeast.

3. Mix the Dough

- In the stand mixer bowl with the cooled milk mixture, add the flour and salt. Using the paddle attachment, mix on medium speed, scraping the sides of the bowl with a rubber spatula once or twice to ensure even mixing, until a very sticky and wet yet also elastic dough forms, 5 to 6 minutes.

4. Proof the Dough

- Oil a large bowl.
- Using the spatula, scrape the dough into the bowl and fold the edges in to create a tight ball (again this is a wet dough, so do what you can). Flip the ball over so the top is smooth **A**.
- Cover the bowl with plastic wrap and let stand for 30 minutes at room temperature, then refrigerate for 8 hours (or overnight). The dough should be doubled in volume after the full rise time **B**.

A

B

I like making EVERYTHING from scratch, including English muffins

recipe continues ▸▸

5. Shape the Muffins

- Generously dust a large baking sheet with semolina flour; set aside. Dust a work surface with both all-purpose and semolina flours, then scrape the cold proofed dough from the bowl onto the surface. Using floured hands (the dough will still be sticky), gently press the dough out into a ½-inch-thick square. You don't want to overwork the dough—just scrape it out and gently shape it. Don't be tempted to knead in more flour or form a ball. Using a 3¼-inch cutter, cut 8 rounds of dough **C** and gently transfer them to the semolina-dusted sheet. If necessary, re-form any scraps and cut. Sprinkle the tops of the rounds with semolina, too. Cover and let rise until puffy and soft, about 1 hour.

7. Brown and "Bake" the Muffins

- In a large (12-inch or larger), heavy cast-iron or oven-safe skillet over medium-low heat, sprinkle 1 tablespoon semolina and, using an offset spatula, very carefully transfer four of the muffins to the skillet **D**. Cover with a lid or aluminum foil and "bake," flipping halfway through the cooking time, until browned on both sides and cooked through, 16 minutes, or 8 minutes per side. Check the bottoms occasionally, because every stove is different. For the most even color, rotate the muffins in the skillet after a few minutes. The final temp on an instant-read thermometer inserted into the side of a muffin should read 200°F **E**; otherwise the muffins will be gummy. If you don't have a thermometer, cut open a muffin to check for doneness (you don't want any "wet" dough).
- Transfer the muffins to a plate and let cool. Wipe out any cooked flour from the pan and repeat the "baking" process with the 4 remaining muffins.
- To serve, use a fork to "split" the muffins to maintain the desired craggy texture, and toast **F**. I like to smear them with a good pat of butter before serving.

if you don't have an instant-read thermometer, buy one, you won't regret it

C

D

E

F

How to Make Fresh Juice

(WITHOUT A JUICER)

Makes 2 to 2½ cups, depending on the size and juiciness of your fruits

- 1 small pineapple
- 2 small oranges
- 1 small lemon
- 3 medium carrots, roughly chopped
- 1 (2-inch) piece fresh ginger, peeled and roughly chopped
- 1 Granny Smith apple, cored and roughly chopped
- 1 handful fresh mint leaves

Whenever I am feeling under the weather, I try to feed myself healthy things, and this juice is loaded with them! Fruit, a little vegetable, herbs, and ginger—actually a good bit of ginger, because it's so good for you. The beauty of this juice is you can make it however you want (try banana and berries)—this blend just happens to be one of my favorites. Because I try not to waste any ingredients, I use the leftover pulp for muffins. Sometimes I'll put it in a pot with some water to gently simmer. Then it becomes a natural air freshener, making my house smell fruity and fragrant.

TINI'S TIPS

A fine-mesh strainer is plenty fine enough to get a completely pulp-free juice, but if yours isn't very fine, line it with cheesecloth before straining the liquid.

A high-speed blender works best for making juice. If you have a smaller machine such as a Nutribullet, blend the fruits in smaller batches and combine all the strained juices into one pitcher or glass.

If you won't finish the juice in 3 days, freeze it in ice cube trays, then defrost as needed (or blend it into smoothies straight from the freezer).

If you want to drink your juice immediately, pour it over ice to chill it.

1. Prep the Fruits

- **PEEL THE PINEAPPLE:** Using a sharp chef's knife, slice the top and bottom off the pineapple so that it stands flat **A**. Run the knife along the outside of the pineapple in a curved motion to remove the skin **B**. If needed, use a paring knife to remove any of the dark eyes (these are what make your mouth itchy). Slice around the core, breaking the pineapple into four sections **C** **D**, then roughly chop.
- **PEEL THE CITRUS:** Slice the top and bottom off the oranges and lemon the same way, then run the knife around the outsides to remove the peel and all the white pith. Roughly chop.

2. Blend the Juice

- Put the pineapple, oranges, lemon, carrots, ginger, apple, and mint leaves in a high-speed blender, then blend on high speed until very smooth, about 1 minute. If the ingredients seem stuck, using the tamper stick, push down through the lid to get them moving. You may need to slow down the speed as well, and then increase it.

3. Strain the Juice and Chill

- Place a fine-mesh strainer over a large container, then strain the juice, pressing against the solids to extract as much juice as possible (you can also stir them to increase the flow of liquid through the strainer). Seal the container and store the juice in the refrigerator for up to 3 days. Give it a shake before enjoying.

A

B

C

D

Game Day Goods

Maryland Crab Dip

Serves 6 to 8 as a main / 8 to 10 as an appetizer

- 8 ounces cream cheese, softened
- ½ cup sour cream
- ¼ cup mayonnaise
- ¼ cup Tini's Homemade Hot Sauce (page 38) or store-bought (I love Old Bay hot sauce)
- Juice of ½ lemon (1 to 2 tablespoons)
- 1 tablespoon whole-grain mustard
- 1 teaspoon Old Bay Seasoning, plus more for sprinkling
- ½ teaspoon smoked paprika
- ¼ teaspoon onion powder
- 1 head of roasted garlic (page 23)
- Kosher salt and freshly ground black pepper
- 16 ounces fresh lump crabmeat
- 16 ounces Gruyère cheese, coarsely grated (about 4 cups)
- 12 ounces smoked Gouda cheese, coarsely grated (about 3 cups)
- 1 tablespoon fresh chives, for garnish
- Pretzel Crisps and/or carrot and celery sticks, for serving

If I say so myself, I make the best Maryland crab dip. I like to compare mine to one you'd find in an upscale restaurant in Maryland, versus a mass-chain restaurant on the Inner Harbor. (At the time of printing, Jimmy's Famous Seafood in Baltimore was selling my crab dip!). If you want to make yours as good, don't use that canned crab meat you find on the shelves next to canned tuna fish. Instead, look for pasteurized, refrigerated fresh lump crabmeat, preferably from Maryland. It's the only way to go. The delicate meat is gently folded into a cheesy mixture (I get a little fancy with the cheese and use smoked Gouda and Gruyère), then baked till it's creamy and bubbling. This dip is so rich and delicious you'll want to eat it by the spoonful—but most people dip into it with something other than a spoon, like Pretzel Crisps, which I like because they are sturdier than most chips or crackers. Carrot and celery sticks are a great option, too.

TINI'S TIPS

Don't overmix before baking. You want to preserve those chunks of crab. Can you tell I am serious about my crab?

Don't get fussy about pan size. You can bake it in a 7 × 10-inch pan or a 6-inch round casserole dish, or whatever you think may work; the dip will just be a little thicker or thinner. Adjust the baking time accordingly so the dip is warmed through and the cheese is melted.

1. Make the Dip

- Preheat the oven to 375°F. In a medium bowl, stir together the cream cheese, sour cream, mayonnaise, hot sauce, lemon juice, mustard, Old Bay, smoked paprika, and onion powder until well combined.
- Squeeze the cooled roasted garlic out of the skin into the dip and stir to combine. Taste and add salt and pepper as needed.
- Gently fold in the crab and about three quarters of the cheeses **A**.
- Transfer the dip to an 8 × 8-inch oven-safe dish or baking pan and sprinkle the rest of the cheese and a bit of Old Bay on top. Bake until the dip is bubbly and the cheese just starts to turn golden, about 20 minutes. Sprinkle with chives and serve warm with Pretzel Crisps and/or carrot and celery sticks.

heads up! this dip comes together really fast, but the roasted garlic, which adds to the layers of flavor, bakes for almost an hour in the oven

Buffalo Chicken Dip

Serves 8 to 10 as an appetizer

- 2 tablespoons ranch seasoning
- ¾ teaspoon kosher salt
- ¼ teaspoon onion powder
- ¼ teaspoon garlic powder
- ¼ teaspoon chili powder
- ¼ teaspoon smoked paprika
- Pinch or two of cayenne pepper
- 2 small boneless, skinless chicken breasts (about 12 ounces)
- 1 tablespoon vegetable oil, plus more for drizzling
- 8 ounces cream cheese, softened
- 8 ounces sharp cheddar cheese, grated (about 1½ cups)
- 8 ounces smoked Gouda cheese, grated (about 1½ cups)
- ½ cup Frank's RedHot, or your favorite hot sauce
- 1 head of roasted garlic (page 23)
- ¼ cup minced chives

SERVING

- Celery and carrot sticks
- Sturdy tortilla chips

This hot, spicy, cheesy, chicken-y dip, which famously has all the flavors of America's favorite chicken wing, is a game day essential in our house. Antoine, after all, is from Buffalo. One time I had a girl come up to me and say it was one of best Buffalo chicken dips she'd ever had—and she was born and raised there. Adding smoked Gouda and roasted garlic are my secret. They add depth of flavor, which is important even in something as simple as a dip, to keep it from being one-note.

TINI'S TIPS

I prefer to cook my own chicken so I can season it how I want. But you can use rotisserie chicken, or even leftovers. If you replace the chicken in the recipe with leftover chicken or rotisserie chicken, shred it, then toss it with the same spice mix you would toss with the raw chicken. Cook as directed.

If you can't find smoked Gouda, try smoked mozzarella.

1. Get Ready

- Preheat the oven to 400°F.

2. Roast the Chicken

- In a small bowl, stir together the ranch seasoning, ¼ teaspoon of the salt, the onion powder, garlic powder, chili powder, smoked paprika, and cayenne. Rub the chicken with the oil, then sprinkle the spice mix evenly over the chicken. Place on a rimmed baking sheet.
- Roast until a meat thermometer inserted into the thickest part registers 155°F and the juices run clear when a knife is inserted into the meat, 15 to 20 minutes. Remove from the oven and let cool, then using two forks, shred the chicken.
- Lower the oven temperature to 375°F.

3. Make the Dip

- In a large bowl, stir together the cream cheese, ¾ cup of the cheddar, ¾ cup of the Gouda, the hot sauce, the roasted garlic squeezed out from the papery skin, 2 tablespoons of the chives, and the remaining ½ teaspoon salt until well combined, then stir in the shredded chicken.

4. Bake and Serve

- Spread the mixture evenly into a 7 × 10-inch or equivalent size baking dish (an 8 × 8-inch baking pan will work) and sprinkle with the reserved cheeses. Bake until the mixture is warmed through and the cheese on top is melted, 18 to 20 minutes. Sprinkle with the remaining chives. Serve with celery, carrots, and tortilla chips for dipping.

Best Oven-Fried Buffalo Wings

Serves 4 as an appetizer (or 1 serving if it's for Antoine)

WINGS

- 1 tablespoon baking powder
- 1½ teaspoons kosher salt
- 1 teaspoon cayenne pepper
- 1 teaspoon chili powder
- 1 teaspoon smoked paprika
- 1 teaspoon onion powder
- 1 teaspoon garlic powder
- ½ teaspoon freshly ground black pepper
- 3 pounds bone-in chicken drumettes and wingettes (about 18 wings)

SAUCE

- 1 stick (8 tablespoons) unsalted butter
- ½ cup Buffalo hot sauce (I like Frank's!)
- 2 tablespoons packed light brown sugar
- 1 tablespoon Worcestershire sauce
- 1 teaspoon cayenne pepper (optional)
- Kosher salt

SERVING

- ¾ cup homemade Ranch Dressing (page 167) or store-bought and/or blue cheese dressing
- Handful of carrot and celery sticks

I think these wings could fool you into thinking they were deep fried. They get browned and crispy outside (thanks to the baking powder I put in the coating—it creates tiny air pockets), yet the meat stays juicy and moist. Then there's the sauce. It's so spicy and buttery that you won't even care how the wings were cooked. For game day, I especially like oven-frying them because I can cook more wings at once for a crowd. I'm sorry, Buffalo people: I serve my wings with ranch, not blue cheese. What team are you on? Blue cheese or ranch?

TINI'S TIPS

Roasting and baking are the same technique in that they are both cooking something in the oven. The difference is temperature. The term *roasting* is generally used for foods such as meats and vegetables cooked at 400°F and above, and *baking*, which usually refers to foods made from doughs and batters, is done at 375°F and below. Meats can be baked as well, but they are usually at a lower temperature or in a covered dish. Patting the wings dry, dredging them (see page 37) (baking powder is key), and roasting these wings at a very high temp somewhat mimics the end result of deep frying.

If you like a spicier wing, reduce the amount of butter the wings are tossed in.

1. Get Ready

- Preheat the oven 450°F. Fit a baking sheet with a wire rack.

2. Dry and Dredge the Wings

- In a large bowl, stir together the baking powder, salt, cayenne, chili powder, paprika, onion powder, garlic powder, and black pepper.
- Pat the wings dry with paper towels and add them to the bowl. Toss to coat.
- Transfer the wings to the prepared rack, allowing for a little space between each wing so they don't touch **A**.

3. Cook the Wings

- Roast the wings for 20 minutes **B**, then take them out of the oven and flip them. Cook until they are crispy and a deep golden brown, about 20 more minutes, or until an instant-read thermometer inserted in the biggest wing reads 165°F **C**. Depending on the size of the wings, they can take anywhere from 40 to 60 minutes to cook.

4. Make the Sauce (While the Wings Cook!)

- In a small saucepan over medium-high heat, combine the butter, hot sauce, brown sugar, Worcestershire sauce, cayenne (if using), and a pinch of salt. Cook, stirring occasionally, until the butter is melted and the sauce comes to a simmer, 5 to 7 minutes. Set aside.

5. Toss to Coat

- Put the cooked wings in a bowl and pour the sauce over them **D**. Using a spoon or a cheffy flip, toss the wings in the sauce, transfer them to a platter, and serve with ranch or blue cheese and veggie sticks.

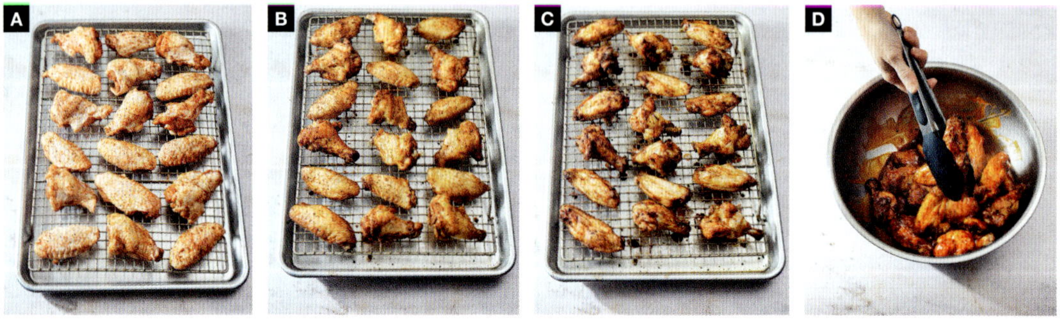

A
B
C
D

Game Day Chili

Makes about 2½ quarts

- 1 tablespoon plus 1 teaspoon kosher salt
- 2 teaspoons garlic powder
- 2 teaspoons onion powder
- 2 teaspoons chili powder
- 2 teaspoons smoked paprika
- ½ teaspoon ground cumin
- ½ teaspoon freshly ground black pepper
- ¼ teaspoon cayenne pepper, or to taste
- 8 slices thick-cut bacon, diced
- 1½ pounds 85% lean ground beef (see Tini's Tips)
- 3 tablespoons tomato paste
- 1 large red onion, diced
- 1 large red bell pepper, diced
- 1 small jalapeño, seeds removed and finely chopped
- 1 Italian long hot chile, seeds removed and finely chopped
- 3 large garlic cloves, finely grated
- 1 (14.5-ounce) can diced fire-roasted tomatoes
- 1 (15-ounce) can tomato sauce
- 1 cup beer, ideally a porter or stout (I like Guinness)
- 1 (15.5-ounce) can dark kidney beans, drained
- 1 (15.5-ounce) can pinto beans, drained
- 2 cups beef broth
- 1½ teaspoons unsweetened cocoa powder
- Sour cream, grated cheddar cheese, and a generous handful of cilantro leaves, for serving

During football season, chili is a must. If you are from Texas, though, look away: I use beans in my chili. I don't love soaking beans, though, but you can (see page 114). I think canned beans work just fine here. This chili is all about layering flavors. I roast the tomato paste in the pan, which caramelizes the sugars and deepens its taste. I also use fire-roasted canned tomatoes for a more intense tomato flavor. I always bloom my spices, and here there's no exception. The real flavor boss here? Bacon! It gives this chili a nice bit of fat for sautéing the veggies and contributes to the thick, hearty texture. And the almost hidden earthy flavor? Cocoa powder. And oh, I also add a beer! This all makes for a more complex, delicious outcome!

TINI'S TIPS

Most grocery stores (and definitely any butcher) will custom grind beef for you. Ask for a coarse grind, which will give you nice chunks of beef in the chili as opposed to finely ground, which can become pebbly and mealy.

You can replace the Italian long hot chile with a second jalapeño pepper if you prefer.

1. Make the Spice Mix

- In a small bowl, combine the 1 tablespoon salt and the garlic powder, onion powder, chili powder, smoked paprika, cumin, black pepper, and cayenne. Set aside.

2. Cook the Bacon

- Add the bacon to a large Dutch oven or pot and turn the heat to medium, allowing the fat to slowly render. Cook the bacon, stirring frequently, until it's crispy and the fat has fully rendered, about 15 minutes **A**. Using a slotted spoon, transfer the bacon to a medium bowl and set aside.

3. Bloom the Spices and Cook the Beef

- Raise the heat to medium high and add half the spice mix to the bacon fat. Stir constantly, cooking until fragrant, 30 seconds **B**.
- Add the ground beef, breaking up any large pieces with a wooden spoon, and cook until browned and cooked through, about 7 minutes. With a slotted spoon, transfer the beef to the bowl of bacon and set aside.

4. Cook the Veggies

- Reduce the heat to medium and add the tomato paste and the remaining spice mixture and stir, cooking until the tomato paste darkens and the spices are fragrant, 2 to 3 minutes. Add the onion, bell pepper, jalapeño, chile, garlic, and remaining 1 teaspoon salt. Stir to coat the veggies with the spices and tomato paste. Cook, stirring frequently, until the veggies have softened, 6 to 8 minutes.

5. Deglaze and Simmer

- Add the tomatoes, tomato sauce, and beer, then scrape the bottom of the pot with a wooden spoon to release any brown bits.
- Add the kidney beans, pinto beans, beef broth, cocoa powder, bacon, and ground beef and stir well to combine **C**. Bring the chili to a boil, then reduce the heat to low, partially cover, and gently simmer, until the chili has thickened and the flavors have melded, about 20 minutes **D**. Taste and season or add additional spices as needed.

6. Serve

- Ladle the chili into wide, shallow bowls, then top with a dollop of sour cream, a sprinkle of cheese, and cilantro leaves.

Loaded Sheet Pan Nachos

Serves 6

- 1 tablespoon vegetable oil
- 1½ pounds 85% lean ground beef
- 2 teaspoons chili powder
- 1 teaspoon garlic powder
- 1 teaspoon kosher salt
- 1 teaspoon ground cumin
- ½ teaspoon smoked paprika
- ½ teaspoon onion powder
- ¼ teaspoon freshly ground black pepper
- ¼ teaspoon crushed red pepper flakes
- 2 pinches dried oregano
- 1 (10-ounce) bag tortilla chips
- 8 ounces pepper Jack cheese, grated (about 2 cups)
- 8 ounces mild cheddar cheese, grated (about 2 cups)
- 1 cup Pico de Gallo (recipe follows)
- ½ cup Pickled Jalapeños (recipe follows)
- ⅓ cup Avocado Crema (recipe follows)
- ⅓ cup sour cream or Mexican crema
- ⅓ cup roughly chopped cilantro

I always order nachos when I eat out. They are a family favorite. When I make them at home, though, I can make them even better. I like them with *real* cheese, not processed cheese sauce. I go for a *big* cheese pull—I want cheese on every chip! At home they never get soggy, either, and of course I go for homemade everything—I pickle jalapeños, chop up a fresh, bright pico de gallo, and whip up an avocado crema. These get a chef's kiss from me every time. I like to serve my nachos straight from the sheet tray, but if you feel like doing extra dishes, you could use an offset spatula to transfer them to a serving platter. You do you: It's your game plan!

TINI'S TIPS

Use sturdy tortilla chips for this recipe—the flimsy ones can't handle all of the toppings.

Save time by making the components a day in advance (the pico de gallo, the pickled jalapeños, the avocado crema).

1. Cook the Beef

- Move a rack to the middle of the oven and preheat it to 400°F.
- In a large skillet over medium-high heat, add the oil and heat until it shimmers. Add the ground beef and cook, breaking up the meat with a wooden spoon, until just beginning to brown, about 3 minutes. Add the chili powder, garlic powder, salt, cumin, smoked paprika, onion powder, black pepper, red pepper flakes, and oregano and stir to coat. Cook until the meat is just cooked through, 3 to 4 minutes.

2. Assemble the Nachos

- Spread half of the tortilla chips over an 11 × 17-inch baking sheet, then sprinkle with half of each cheese and half of the ground beef. Top with the remaining chips, then the remaining cheese and beef.

3. Bake the Nachos

- Bake until the cheese is melted, about 5 minutes. Scatter the pico de gallo and pickled jalapeños over the top. Immediately dollop (or squirt) the top with the avocado crema and sour cream. Sprinkle with cilantro and serve hot.

PICO DE GALLO

Makes about 2½ cups

- 1 pound plum tomatoes (3 to 4 medium), seeded and finely diced
- ½ small white onion, finely chopped (about ½ cup)
- 1 small bunch of cilantro, leaves and stems, chopped (about ½ cup)
- 1 small serrano, ribs and seeds removed, finely chopped
- 3 tablespoons freshly squeezed lime juice, plus more to taste
- 1½ teaspoons kosher salt, plus more to taste

- In a medium bowl, combine the tomatoes, onion, cilantro, serrano, lime juice, and salt. Taste and adjust seasoning with more salt and lime juice if needed. Cover and refrigerate for up to 5 days.

PICKLED JALAPEÑOS

Makes one 32-ounce jar

- 1½ cups distilled white vinegar
- ¾ cup water
- ¼ cup sugar
- 1 tablespoon kosher salt
- 1 pound jalapeños, thinly sliced
- 3 garlic cloves, smashed and peeled (see page 23)
- 2 teaspoons whole black peppercorns

- In a small saucepan, combine the vinegar, water, sugar, and salt. Place over medium-high heat and bring to a boil, stirring until the sugar and salt are dissolved. Remove from the heat and add the jalapeños. Let stand for 15 minutes.
- Add the garlic and peppercorns to a 32-ounce sterilized heatproof jar. Transfer the jalapeños and pickling liquid to the jar (if you don't have enough liquid to cover the jalapeños completely, add a combination of more vinegar and water).
- Let the liquid cool completely, then seal the jar and refrigerate at least 4 hours (preferably overnight) before enjoying.

AVOCADO CREMA

Makes 1½ cups

2 ripe Hass avocados (each 8 ounces), pitted and peeled
½ cup Mexican crema or sour cream
½ teaspoon garlic powder
1½ teaspoons kosher salt, plus more to taste
2 tablespoons freshly squeezed lime juice, plus more to taste
⅛ teaspoon cayenne pepper

- Combine the avocado, crema, garlic powder, salt, lime juice, and cayenne in a high-speed blender or food processor. Process until silky and smooth, about 1 minute. Taste and adjust seasoning with more salt and lime juice if needed. Cover and refrigerate for up to 2 days (the color will dull slightly when not fresh, but it still tastes good).

when I'm feeling extra fancy, I thin out the crema, put it in a squeeze bottle, and squirt it over the nachos for a restaurant-style presentation

Holidays from Scratch

‣ And of course, I serve my famous mac and cheese (page **89**) at every holiday meal

Level Up

The Juiciest Roast Turkey

WITH RICH GRAVY

Serves 10 to 15

BRINE

- 2 to 6 quarts cold water
- 1 to 2 cups kosher salt
- ¼ cup honey
- ¼ cup packed dark brown sugar
- 2 navel oranges, cut into ½-inch slices
- 2 large yellow onions, quartered and peeled
- 12 large garlic cloves
- 4 fresh or dried bay leaves
- 4 sprigs rosemary
- 4 sprigs thyme
- 3 sprigs oregano
- 2 sprigs sage
- 2 tablespoons whole black peppercorns
- 1 (5-pound) bag of ice
- 1 whole fresh or thawed frozen turkey (13 to 15 pounds)

ROASTING

- 3 medium carrots, roughly chopped
- 2 celery stalks, roughly chopped
- 1 large yellow onion, roughly chopped
- ½ cup chicken stock or white wine
- 1 small yellow onion, halved
- 1 whole lemon, halved
- 1 head of garlic, halved crosswise
- 1 bunch of parsley
- 2 sprigs sage
- 2 sprigs thyme
- 1 sprig rosemary

Fall is *my* time of year—I love all the colors, warm feelings, flavors . . . and especially the holidays. This recipe may seem like a lot of work, and honestly, it is, but this is a turkey your family won't forget. I swear, this one breaks the rating scale. If you brine, rub, and inject, juice will pour out of your finished roasted turkey—the meat will literally drip with flavor. The process starts with a wet brine of citrus, herbs, and salt, which infuses the meat with extra flavor. Then I rub an herb butter all over the turkey for a savory, garlicky skin. I also use a flavor injector to get those juices all up into the meat. Don't skip any step. Purchase a thermometer and injector if you don't have them. The investment is worth it. I can't promise success without the right tools. If you overcook your turkey, which is easy to do without a thermometer, it'll likely be dry. And rest—never forget to rest the turkey! All those juices need to reabsorb into the turkey when it comes out of the oven. One bite of this finished bird and you'll forget that a turkey could ever be anything but moist and flavorful!

TINI'S TIPS

If you don't have a pot large enough to hold the turkey, you can always boil the brine in a pasta pot, then add everything to a brine bag (available online or in-stores around the holidays). A bag is easier to store in the fridge overnight.

As the turkey cooks, some spots might brown quicker than others (like the wing tips!), so use foil to cover or wrap pieces throughout the cooking process to protect them from burning.

While many stores sell fresh turkeys around the holidays, frozen are still a great, affordable option. It does take a couple of days to defrost one, though. I let my frozen turkey sit in the refrigerator for 2 to 3 days until it's fully defrosted. There really is no fast way to defrost a turkey because it's not recommended to leave frozen turkeys sitting out at room temperature for safety reasons, so just be sure you have your planning game on. To carve your turkey, make sure your knife is sharp for easy slicing. If you don't own a knife sharpener, buy one! Never use a dull knife, full stop.

1. Brine the Turkey

- In the largest pot you have, add 2 quarts (8 cups) of the water, 1 cup of the salt, the honey, brown sugar, orange slices, onions, garlic, bay leaves, rosemary, thyme, oregano, sage, and peppercorns **A**. Bring the liquid to a boil over high heat, then continue to boil until the salt dissolves, the mixture is fragrant, and the oranges start to break down, 2 to 5 minutes.
- Remove the pot from the heat, add 12 cups of the ice cubes, and stir to cool **B**. Let the mixture sit at room temperature until fully cooled, then slowly add the turkey to the pot, breast-side down. If the turkey isn't fully submerged, whisk ¼ cup of kosher salt into every quart of water necessary, and add the salty water 1 quart at a time until the turkey is fully covered. (You could also transfer the turkey and all the brine to a brining bag at this point **C**.) Refrigerate for at least 12 hours and up to 24 hours.

recipe and ingredients continue ▸▸

A

B

C

COMPOUND BUTTER

2 sticks (16 tablespoons) unsalted butter, softened

¼ cup extra-virgin olive oil

8 garlic cloves, finely grated

Zest from 1 lemon (about 2 teaspoons)

2 tablespoons freshly squeezed lemon juice

¼ cup finely chopped chives

1 tablespoon finely chopped rosemary

1 tablespoon finely chopped oregano

1 tablespoon finely chopped thyme

2 tablespoons kosher salt

1 teaspoon freshly ground pepper

INJECTION BUTTER

1 stick (8 tablespoons) unsalted butter, melted

½ teaspoon freshly ground black pepper

½ teaspoon onion powder

½ teaspoon garlic powder

½ teaspoon smoked paprika

GRAVY

Low-sodium chicken broth, as needed (optional)

6 tablespoons unsalted butter

½ cup all-purpose flour

1 tablespoon Worcestershire sauce, plus more to taste

Kosher salt and freshly ground black pepper

SERVING

Orange wedges, lemon halves, thyme sprigs, rosemary sprigs, bay leaves, and sage leaves

2. Prep the Turkey

- About 2 hours before you're ready to roast, remove the turkey from the brine and set it on a wire rack in a roasting pan. Pat it dry with paper towels and let sit at room temperature for about 2 hours, continually patting it dry as it condensates.
- Put the carrots, celery, chopped onion, and chicken stock in the roasting pan **D**. About 20 minutes before you're ready to roast, place a rack in the lower third of the oven and preheat to 330°F.

3. Make the Compound Butter

- In a medium bowl, add the butter, olive oil, garlic, lemon zest, lemon juice, chives, rosemary, oregano, thyme, salt, and pepper and stir to combine. Alternatively, add all ingredients to a blender (no need to chop the herbs; just strip from stems) and blend until smooth, about 2 minutes **E**. Set aside.

4. Make the Injection Butter

- In another medium bowl, combine the butter, pepper, onion powder, garlic powder, and smoked paprika and stir to combine **E**. Set aside.
- Using a meat injector, inject the turkey with the seasoned melted butter in 6 spots: twice in each breast, once in each leg, and once in each thigh **F**.
- Spread some of the compound butter all around the turkey, including underneath the skin at the breast **G**. Stuff the cavity with the halved onion, lemon halves, garlic, parsley, sage, thyme, and rosemary. Truss (see page 31) or at least tie the legs together with butcher's twine **H**.

5. Roast the Turkey and Rest

- Cook the turkey, basting it (spooning the juices from the bottom of the pan and pouring them over the bird) **I** and injecting it in several places with the juices and remaining butter as well, every 30 minutes, for 2½ to 3 hours, until the skin turns deep mahogany brown and a thermometer reads 160°F when inserted in the breast. Every time you take the turkey out to baste it, rotate the pan 180 degrees before putting it back in the oven, for even browning.
- Transfer the turkey to a cutting board **J**, then cover loosely with aluminum foil and let it rest for at least 20 minutes and up to 45 minutes before slicing.

6. Make the Gravy

- Set a fine-mesh strainer over a medium bowl, then strain the contents of the roasting pan. Discard the solids and measure out 4 cups of liquid. If you didn't get at least 4 cups of liquid from the turkey, supplement with low-sodium chicken broth until you have 4 cups.

SPECIAL EQUIPMENT

Brining bag or large bucket

Heavy metal roasting pan

Roasting rack

Meat injector (preferably stainless steel with a long, open-tip needle)

Butcher's twine

Instant-read thermometer

Baster (optional)

there are no shortcuts here, the effort is worth it

- Set the roasting pan over two burners set to medium high, then add the butter (you can also do this in a clean pot if your roasting pan is aluminum or not stovetop-friendly, scraping any brown bits from the bottom of the pan into the pot). Once the butter has melted, add the flour slowly, whisking constantly and scraping up any browned bits in the pan. Cook the flour for about 1 minute, until it is fully hydrated and a light golden color.
- Slowly pour the liquid back into the roasting pan, whisking constantly. Add the Worcestershire sauce, then bring the liquid to a simmer over medium-high heat. Reduce the heat to low and cook for 8 to 10 minutes, whisking frequently, until the gravy has thickened and darkened slightly in color, 8 to 10 minutes. Season to taste with salt and pepper, and more Worcestershire if needed. Transfer to a gravy boat or other serving vessel and keep warm.

7. Carve the Turkey

- After your turkey has rested, remove any butcher's twine. Using a large, *sharp* chef's knife (sharpness is key!), gently pull one of the legs away from the body and slice down through the joint **K**, following the curve of the bird as you slice downward, to separate the thigh and leg from the body. Repeat with the second leg.
- Next, separate the drumstick from the thigh by placing your knife on the joint between the two and cutting downward **L**.
- Now slice off the wings using one hand to gently pull the wing as you cut through the joint, separating the wing **M**. Repeat with the second wing.
- Lastly, slice off one whole side of the breast, as close to the bone as you can get, keeping the skin intact **N**. Put the breast, skin-side up / flat-side down, on the cutting board and slice into ½- to 1-inch pieces of meat **O**.
- Transfer the sliced breast to a platter and surround it with the drumsticks, thighs, and wings. Garnish with oranges, lemons, herb sprigs and leaves. Serve with the gravy on the side.

TEMP IS EVERYTHING

Chefs *always* have thermometers in their pockets, and you should, too, when cooking meat. It leaves the guesswork out. This simple tool lets you know if foods are cooked to the correct temperatures, not only for proper texture (no overcooked, dry meat!) but also for an important safety reason: to kill unwanted bacteria. If you're taking the temp of a turkey or beef roast, put the thermometer in the thickest part of the meat. Make sure you don't hit the bottom of the pan, which will give you a higher temperature. I use an instant-read digital thermometer. I have three because I'm always misplacing them. It's a worthwhile investment.

Braised Collards
WITH BACON

Serves 6

- 2 large bunches of collard greens
- Splash of distilled white vinegar
- 1 pound sliced bacon, diced
- ½ stick (4 tablespoons) unsalted butter
- 1 large red onion, finely chopped
- 5 garlic cloves, finely grated
- 1 red bell pepper, diced
- Kosher salt and freshly ground pepper
- 2 teaspoons smoked paprika
- 1 teaspoon crushed red pepper flakes
- ½ teaspoon dry ground mustard powder
- 4 cups homemade chicken stock (page 134) or store-bought
- 1 fully cooked smoked turkey leg
- 1 tablespoon cider vinegar

Antoine grew up with collards. They are a soul food staple his family always had at Thanksgiving, so it's something I've added to our holiday spread. We do eat them a lot more, though, than just on holidays. They're a great side to fried chicken (page 37), and I like them with mac and cheese (page 89), too. The broth, which is cooked for a long time, becomes so rich and flavorful from the bacon and turkey leg—it adds just the right amount of smokiness to the greens. It's slurp-worthy.

A TINI TIP

If you can't find a smoked turkey leg, smoked turkey wings or neck will give a good smoky flavor. You can also try a smoked pork ham hock as well.

1. De-stem and Chop Your Greens

- Fold a large leaf in half and, using a chef's knife, run it right along the stem, cutting through both halves and removing the stem **A**. Repeat this for all the leaves.
- Pile a couple of leaves flat on top of one another, roll them up, and slice ribbons about 2 inches wide **B**, similar to a chiffonade (see page 25), then coarsely chop.

2. Clean the Greens

- If your greens are already cleaned, you can skip this step. In a large bowl filled with cool water, add a splash of distilled white vinegar and the chopped greens. Massage the greens **C**, then rinse and repeat at least 3 times, or until they don't feel gritty anymore **D**. Drain.

3. Cook the Bacon and Vegetables

- To a large pot, add the bacon and turn the heat to medium high. Cook, stirring occasionally, until all the fat is rendered and the bacon starts to turn golden, about 12 minutes. Using a slotted spoon, transfer the bacon to a plate and set aside.
- Reduce the heat to medium. To the same pot with the rendered bacon fat, add the butter and onion and cook, stirring, until the onion becomes softened and translucent, 5 to 7 minutes. Add the garlic and bell pepper and continue to stir and cook until the garlic becomes fragrant, about 1 minute. Season with a few pinches each of salt and black pepper.

4. Braise the Greens

- Add the collard greens, smoked paprika, red pepper flakes, and ground mustard. Stir to coat. Pour in the chicken stock, then add the turkey leg. Return the bacon and any juices that have accumulated back into the pot as well.
- Bring the liquid to a boil, then reduce the heat to low and cover. Braise until the greens are soft and silky, the broth is flavorful, and the turkey meat is tender and falls off the bone, about 1 hour and 10 minutes.
- Remove the turkey leg from the greens and shred the meat using two forks. Discard the skin and bones, then return the shredded meat to the pot. Add the cider vinegar and season to taste with salt and black pepper. Serve warm.

A
B
C
D

Bourbon Candied Sweet Potatoes

Serves 6

4 large sweet potatoes (about 2½ pounds)

½ stick (4 tablespoons) unsalted butter, cut into cubes

¾ cup granulated sugar

¼ cup packed dark brown sugar

Juice of 1 large or 2 small oranges (about ⅓ cup)

½ teaspoon ground cinnamon

½ teaspoon kosher salt

¼ teaspoon freshly ground nutmeg

3 tablespoons bourbon

1 teaspoon pure vanilla extract

2 to 3 cups (6 to 9 ounces) large marshmallows, for topping (optional)

My holiday meals are never complete without these sweet potatoes. I always start with fresh ones. I did use canned yams once, but I like my potatoes to be a little al dente, not soft like baby food, which canned ones taste like to me. When you use fresh, you have complete control over their texture. I cook thin sweet potato rounds in a sweet, buttery sauce that has a hint of orange and is infused with bourbon and vanilla for a smooth finish. Topping with marshmallows is optional. They'll come out of the oven like puffy white-golden clouds, and then they'll start to melt into the dish, making the sauce extra sweet and wonderfully gooey!

TINI'S TIPS

Rolling citrus fruits, like oranges and lemons, back and forth under your palm on a hard surface before squeezing, helps release the juices so you can get as much out as possible.

A large skillet is best for this recipe, because you want the potatoes to cook in a single layer if possible (slightly overlapping is okay) for even cooking.

If you don't have dark brown sugar, feel free to use light brown sugar.

1. Prep the Potatoes

- Peel the potatoes and, using the pointy end of your peeler (or a paring knife), take off any small, dark indentations on the potatoes.
- Slice the potatoes into ¼-inch-thick rounds **A**.

2. Make the Sauce

- In a large, 12-inch (ovenproof if you are adding the marshmallows) skillet with a lid (or a Dutch oven will work) over medium heat, melt the butter. Add in the granulated and brown sugars and stir until well combined. Add the orange juice, cinnamon, salt, and nutmeg and stir again. Add the bourbon and vanilla and bring the mixture to a slight simmer.

3. Cook the Sweet Potatoes

- Lay the sweet potatoes in the skillet in a single layer if possible. If you're tight on space you can lay the small ones on top or overlap the potatoes slightly, like a holiday wreath **B**.
- Cover the skillet (this is important, or your potatoes won't cook through!) and continue to simmer, stirring occasionally and spreading them back out in an even layer each time, until they are fork-tender and the sauce has thickened some, like a thin caramel, about 25 minutes.

4. Bake the Marshmallows (optional)

- If you'd like to top your potatoes with marshmallows, preheat the oven to 375°F. If your skillet is not ovenproof, transfer your potatoes to an ovenproof serving dish (a 9 × 13-inch dish works; I have a pumpkin dish I use for Thanksgiving). Place the marshmallows evenly over the potatoes **C**.
- Bake, uncovered, until the marshmallows are puffed and golden **D**, 6 to 8 minutes. Serve immediately.

A

B

C

D

Roasted Garlic Parmesan Mashed Potatoes

Serves 6

- 3 pounds Yukon Gold potatoes
- 3 teaspoons kosher salt
- ½ cup heavy cream
- ½ cup evaporated or whole milk
- 1 stick (8 tablespoons) unsalted butter plus 1 tablespoon for garnish
- 1 sprig rosemary
- 1 bay leaf
- 1 head of roasted garlic (page 23) or 2 to 3 teaspoons roasted garlic powder (see Tini's Tips)
- ½ ounce Parmesan cheese, finely grated (about ¼ cup), plus more for garnish
- 1 teaspoon freshly ground black pepper
- 1 tablespoon chopped chives, for garnish

When you're the cook in my family, you are in charge of everything for Thanksgiving. I take the job seriously. I don't skimp on sides—and certainly not mashed potatoes, perhaps one of the most beloved comfort foods of all times. I use Yukon Gold for their buttery, rich taste, and add roasted garlic for a subtle hint of flavor. I want my potatoes to feel decadent, and I like to make them really smooth for Thanksgiving, so I push them through a ricer instead of mashing them. You can always make yours chunky if you prefer. I garnish the finished creamy potatoes with pats of butter, freshly grated Parmesan, and a sprinkle of fresh chives so they look like they belong in a magazine spread. Antoine always gives them a 10/10.

TINI'S TIPS

Be sure to cut all your potatoes the same size for even cooking.

If you don't have a potato ricer and want smooth, creamy potatoes, you can push your cooked potatoes through a fine-mesh strainer (use a rubber spatula to force them through, then scrape the pureed potatoes from the bottom of the strainer and continue until all the potatoes are pushed through). It'll get rid of any lumps.

If you don't feel like roasting garlic, you can use roasted garlic powder, which is what the name says, roasted garlic, and is available in the spice section of most grocery stores.

1. Prep and Cook the Potatoes

- Peel the potatoes and cut them into equal-size 2-inch chunks. Put them in a large pot, cover with at least 2 inches of water, and add 1 teaspoon of the salt. Bring to a boil, then reduce the heat to low and simmer until the potatoes are fork-tender (you can very easily pierce them with a fork), about 20 minutes. Drain and put the potatoes back into the warm pot, shaking the pot so any extra water evaporates.

2. Make the Cream

- In a small pot over medium heat, combine the heavy cream, milk, stick of butter, rosemary, and bay leaf. Squeeze the roasted garlic out of the skins into the pot (if a little skin slides in, that's okay, because you are going to strain it).
- Heat the mixture just until the butter is melted and you see small bubbles form in the milk/cream. Reduce the heat to low. Let the liquid gently cook for a minute or so. Remove from the heat and let the liquid infuse while you mash the potatoes.

3. Mash the Potatoes

- Using a potato ricer or masher, break up the potatoes. Then set a fine-mesh strainer over your potatoes and pour in the butter-and-cream mixture. Using the back of a spoon, push through any garlic you can. Continue to mash the potatoes until smooth. Stir in the Parmesan cheese, the remaining 2 teaspoons salt, and the pepper. Taste for seasoning and add more if needed.
- Transfer the mashed potatoes to a serving bowl and garnish with the remaining 1 tablespoon butter, a sprinkle of chives, and some Parmesan cheese.

Pumpkin Cheesecake Bars

Makes 24 diamond-shape bars (plus some extra smaller ones!)

CRUST

- 24 whole graham cracker sheets (3 cups crumbs from 13 ounces / 379g)
- ¼ cup / 45g packed light brown sugar
- 1½ teaspoons / 4g ground cinnamon
- ½ teaspoon freshly grated nutmeg
- ½ teaspoon kosher salt
- 1¼ sticks (10 tablespoons / 141g) unsalted butter, melted

FILLING

- 3 (8-ounce) packages / 678g cream cheese, softened
- 1 cup / 240g sour cream
- 1 cup / 200g granulated sugar
- 1 tablespoon / 8g ground cinnamon
- 2 teaspoons / 4g ground ginger
- ¾ teaspoon freshly grated nutmeg
- ½ teaspoon ground cloves
- ¼ teaspoon kosher salt
- ⅛ teaspoon ground allspice
- 5 large eggs, at room temperature
- 1¼ cups / 280g canned pumpkin puree
- 1 tablespoon / 15g pure vanilla extract

TOPPINGS (OPTIONAL)

- 2 cups Vanilla Whipped Cream, medium peaks (page 222)
- Ground cinnamon, for dusting

Anyone who knows me knows cheesecake and I have never gotten along. I overwhip it, I get water in the pan, it cracks. It took me many, many times to get it right. Instead of giving you a next-level cheesecake recipe, I wanted something that you can nail the first time. And if the top cracks (the goal is for cheesecake *not* to crack!), no one will know, because you top it with a luscious layer of whipped cream. These creamy, dreamy bars—a cross between a pumpkin pie and a cheesecake—have all the warming flavor of fall with a lightly sweetened, toasty graham cracker crust. They kind of taste like the best pumpkin pie you've ever had. And cutting them into diamonds makes them look a little fancy. They are the perfect holiday dessert—and they are so easy even I can't mess them up.

TINI'S TIPS

Three tips for preventing your cheesecake bar from cracking on top: (1) Don't overmix the batter (you're not trying to aerate the mixture like with cake batter); (2) don't be tempted to raise the oven temp—low and slow is the way to go; (3) let the bars cool completely before transferring to the refrigerator (a shock in temperature can cause the top to split).

You can swap in 2 tablespoons store-bought pumpkin spice mix for the warming spices in this recipe.

Cracking the eggs in a bowl before adding them through the feeding tube gives you a chance to fish out unwanted shell.

A 15-ounce can of pumpkin puree is 1¾ cups to 2 cups, so you'll have some left over. Use it in a smoothie or do like I do and give it to your dogs as a special treat.

1. Make the Crust

- Preheat the oven to 375°F. Line a 9 × 13-inch baking pan or dish with parchment paper, overhanging by 2 inches on the long sides.
- In a food processor, pulse the graham crackers until very finely ground (you'll have about 3 cups). Add the brown sugar, cinnamon, nutmeg, and salt and pulse to combine. Add the butter and blend until the mixture is evenly moistened.
- Transfer the crumb mixture to the prepared pan and, using an offset spatula, firmly and evenly press the graham cracker crust over the bottom of the pan.
- Bake on the center rack until firm, dry, and fragrant, 10 to 12 minutes. Let the crust cool completely on a wire rack.

2. Make the Filling

- Reduce the oven temperature to 325°F. Rinse and dry the food processor bowl, then add the cream cheese, sour cream, granulated sugar, cinnamon, ginger, nutmeg, cloves, salt, and allspice and run until smooth and creamy, 1 to 2 minutes. Add the eggs, one at a time through the feeding tube, pulsing to incorporate after each addition, scraping down the sides of the bowl as needed. Add the pumpkin and vanilla and pulse again until fully combined and no uneven streaks remain (finish mixing with a spatula by hand if needed). You can also use a stand or hand-mixer to mix the filling.
- Pour the filling over the cooled crust and, using an offset spatula, spread it into a smooth layer.

3. Bake the Bars

- Bake until the filling is puffed and fully set around the edges but still slightly loose in the center when gently jiggled, 40 to 45 minutes. Let fully cool to room temperature, then chill in the refrigerator until cold and fully set, at least 4 hours.

recipe continues ▸▸

4. Spread the Whipped Cream

- You can serve the bars as is (move ahead to the next step) or, if you're a whipped cream person, right before you are ready to serve, dollop the whipped cream over the top of the chilled cheesecake bars and, using an offset spatula, spread it in an even layer.

5. Cut and Serve the Bars

- Using the "handles" of the parchment paper, pull the bars from the pan and transfer the entire rectangle to a cutting board (leave the parchment underneath). Dust with cinnamon, if desired, and slice into diamonds, using toothpicks to help guide, if you'd like **A** **B**. An offset spatula works great if you're transferring individual bars to a serving platter.

TINI'S TIPS

Your cream should be very cold for the best whipping! Chilling your bowl and/or whisk makes whipping the cream easier.

Medium peaks are the best consistency for piping and holding their shape for whipped cream topping (see Whip for the Win, page 257).

VANILLA WHIPPED CREAM

Whisking cream by hand does take some work, but the sweet, creamy result is worth every ounce of energy expended.

Makes 2 cups

1 cup cold heavy cream

2 to 4 tablespoons powdered sugar, depending on your desired sweetness

1 teaspoon pure vanilla paste or vanilla extract

¼ teaspoon ground cinnamon (optional)

1. Whisk the Cream

- Pour the heavy cream into a medium metal bowl and whisk until soft peaks form (see Tini's Tips), a long time, about 5 minutes. This could take longer depending on how fast you whisk (or better, use an electric mixer!).

2. Sweeten and Flavor Your Cream

- Hold a fine-mesh strainer over the heavy cream and spoon in the sugar. Shake the sieve to get rid of the clumps in the sugar and add it all to the cream.
- Add the vanilla and cinnamon (if using).

3. Whisk More

- Continue to whisk your cream until it thickens to the consistency you want. I like mine a little looser than stiff peaks. Refrigerate until ready to use. Whipped cream can be made up to 24 hours in advance.

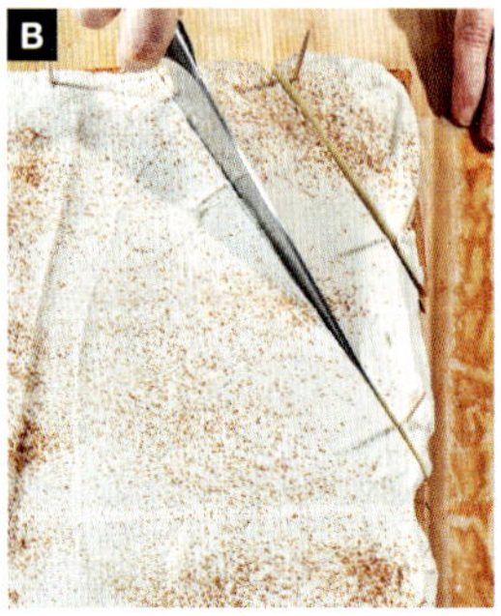

Level Up

A Perfect Prime Rib

Serves 8 to 10

8 pound boneless prime rib roast

DRY BRINE

- 3 tablespoons kosher salt
- 1 tablespoon freshly ground black pepper
- 1 tablespoon roasted garlic powder

HERB BUTTER

- 2 sprigs rosemary
- 1 stick (8 tablespoons) unsalted butter, softened
- 2 garlic cloves, chopped
- 1 tablespoon coarsely chopped chives, plus more for garnish
- 1 tablespoon Dijon mustard
- ½ teaspoon kosher salt
- ½ teaspoon freshly ground black pepper

SERVING

Horseradish Sauce (page 226)

SPECIAL EQUIPMENT

Butcher's twine, instant-read thermometer

Prime rib is a big, expensive piece of meat—to be clear, this roast could cost upward of $160 or more. Because of that, it can be a little scary to cook. You certainly don't want to mess it up, especially if it's for a holiday dinner (you know how that can go!). I have cooked these large roasts many times and nailed the process. To get the juiciest, most flavorful meat, follow my directions, take the tips, and go in there with confidence. Rubbing the roast with a dry brine, a mixture of salt and seasonings, in addition to adding flavor, helps make the meat tender by concentrating the meat's own moisture content, but this takes time, so don't rush it. If you are making this for Christmas dinner, I recommend starting the dry brine process Christmas Eve morning. The fatty crust becomes caramelized with a wonderfully garlicky-herb flavor (starting the roast at a very high heat helps make this happen). Making a prime rib is an investment of time and money, for sure, but it feels fancy, and festive, and when you start slicing the roast and see the pretty pink meat (yes, it's supposed to be pink!) and the juices start seeping out, you'll know you've nailed it, too. I like to serve my beef with a creamy, tangy horseradish sauce. If you prefer a red wine reduction, see page 50.

TINI'S TIPS

When buying a big cut of meat like this, it's a good idea to talk to a butcher. Even at chain supermarkets, a butcher is usually available for questions. They can guide you on your purchase.

A prime rib can also be called a standing rib roast (long curved bones are left intact), or a bone-in rib roast. I always opt for a boneless roast.

There are three grades of beef: prime, choice, and select. Prime has the most fat marbling (remember, fat equals flavor). Buy whatever you can afford.

Why tie a roast? It helps keep it together for more even cooking (the outer meat can start to pull away otherwise), and makes it look better for the final presentation!

If you don't have a food processor or blender, using a knife, mince the herbs and garlic and, using a spatula, mix them into the softened butter.

One thing you can't do without when making this meat is a thermometer.

1. Trim the Meat

- Using a sharp knife, trim any excess fat off the fat cap, the thick white layer of fat on the meat, leaving a ½-inch layer.

2. Dry Brine the Meat

- In a small bowl, stir together the salt, pepper, and roasted garlic powder.
- Fit a rimmed baking sheet or a baking pan with a baking rack (use whatever will fit in your fridge). Place the roast on the rack and pat the seasoning mixture all over it **A**.
- Put the meat, uncovered, in the fridge for 12 to 24 hours to brine.

3. Bring the Meat to Room Temp

- Take the meat out of the fridge about 2 hours before roasting.

recipe continues ▸▸

4. Make the Herb Butter

- Remove the leaves from the rosemary stems and put them in a food processor or blender.
- Add the butter, garlic, chives, mustard, salt, and pepper and process until the rosemary and garlic are minced and the butter is smooth.

5. Prep the Meat for Roasting

- Place a rack in the center of the oven and preheat to 425°F.
- Smear the butter all over the meat **B** and, using butcher's twine, tie up the beef (single ties about 2 inches apart work great **C**.

6. Roast the Meat

- Put your meat in the oven and cook for 15 minutes to sear the outside.
- Reduce the heat to 330°F and roast until an instant-read thermometer, when inserted into the center of the roast, reads 125°F for medium rare (my rec!). Depending on the size of your roast, this should take another 15 to 25 minutes per pound for medium rare, so 1½ to almost 3 hours for an 8-pound roast. After 1½ hours, start checking the temperature of the meat to get an idea of how fast it's cooking; if it reads 125°F, take it out. If not, as your roast gets closer to 125°F, check it more frequently. You'll get a feel for how fast the roast is cooking. This is where you really don't want to mess up. Checking the temp often is important. The roast rises 5 to 10 degrees when it rests, so your final temp will be 130°F to 135°F. For rare, take your meat out at 115°F for a final temp after resting of 120°F to 125°F.

7. Rest and Carve the Meat

- Remove the meat from the oven and cover it with foil. Let it rest for 20 minutes so all the juices get reabsorbed into the meat.
- To serve, snip off the twine then thinly slice the beef. Serve with dollops of horseradish sauce and sprinkle with chives.

PRIME RIB COOKING TIMES

RARE: 15 minutes per pound

MEDIUM RARE: 20 to 25 minutes per pound

MEDIUM: 25 to 30 minutes per pound

MEDIUM WELL: 30 to 35 minutes per pound

HORSERADISH SAUCE

Makes about 1¼ cups

1 cup sour cream
3 tablespoons mayonnaise
2 tablespoons store-bought jarred horseradish
2 teaspoons Dijon mustard
1 garlic clove, grated
1 tablespoon fresh chives
½ teaspoon kosher salt
¼ teaspoon freshly ground black pepper

- In a small bowl, stir together the sour cream, mayonnaise, horseradish, Dijon, garlic, chives, salt, and pepper until thoroughly combined. The sauce can be made up to 1 day in advance.

I'll say it again: buy a thermometer (or two), so you don't mess this up!

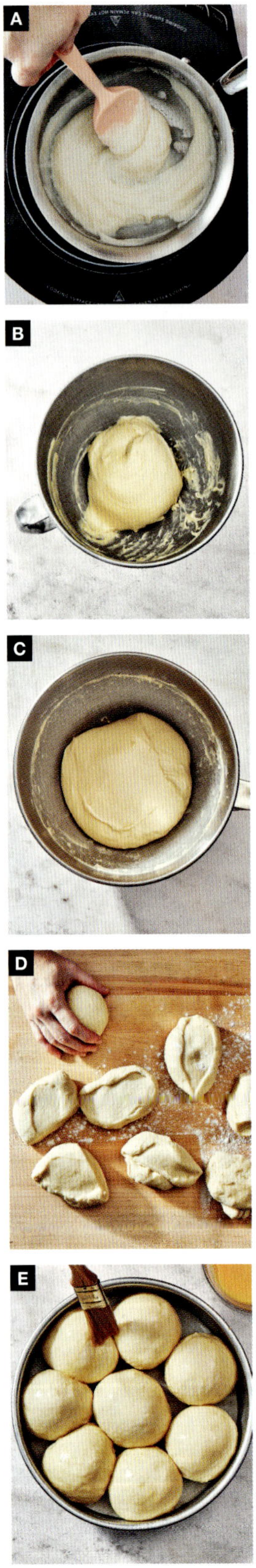
A
B
C
D
E

Fluffy Milk Bread Buns

Makes 8 rolls

TANGZHONG

¼ cup / 60g whole milk

2 tablespoons / 30g water

2 tablespoons /18g bread flour

DOUGH

2½ cups / 360g bread flour, plus more for the work surface

½ cup / 120g whole milk

6 tablespoons / 84g unsalted butter, melted, plus more for greasing the pan

¼ cup / 50g sugar

1 egg

2 tablespoons dried milk powder

1 tablespoon active dry yeast

¾ teaspoon kosher salt

EGG WASH

1 egg

1 tablespoon water

These rolls are soft, pillowy, and the tiniest bit sweet. I crave them on the regular. They are the perfect side dish for any holiday meal. The shiny, perfectly rounded golden tops make these rolls look very professional, too. Cooking milk and flour before adding it to a dough comes from an Asian technique called *tangzhong* (pronounced tang-jong), which locks moisture into the flour (flour can absorb up to twice as much warm liquid versus cooler liquid) and helps the dough rise more and stay softer longer. The milk powder adds extra milk solids (proteins and sugar), which helps the rolls brown in the most beautiful way.

A TINI TIP

Bread flour has a higher protein content than all-purpose flour, which helps the gluten develop, allowing these rolls to rise and become fluffy; if you use all-purpose flour, your outcome will be different.

1. Make the Tangzhong (also called starter)

- In a small saucepan over medium-high heat, stir together the milk, water, and flour. Cook, stirring constantly, until it thickens to a paste, kind of like mashed potatoes, about 5 minutes **A**. Remove the pan from the heat and let the mixture cool.

2. Make the Dough

- In the bowl of a stand mixer, combine the flour, milk, butter, sugar, egg, milk powder, yeast, salt, and tangzhong. Using a dough hook, mix on low speed until a shaggy mass forms. Increase the speed to medium high and mix until the dough becomes shiny and smooth, about 10 minutes total **B**.

3. Let the Dough Rise

- Cover the bowl with plastic wrap and set it aside to rise in a warm place until the dough has gotten puffy, not quite doubled in size, about 1 hour **C**.

4. Form the Rolls

- Grease a 9-inch round baking pan with butter.
- Sprinkle your work surface with flour, then divide the dough into 8 pieces. Take one of the dough pieces and form a ball by pinching the dough, then folding the edges under. Place the dough ball on your work surface under a cupped hand and use the pressure of your palm to roll the dough ball back and forth between your thumb and your pinky finger to create a smooth ball **D**. Put the ball in the prepared pan.
- Repeat with the remaining pieces of dough and fill the pan, with one in the center. It's okay for the rolls to be close in the pan.

5. Shape and Rise Again

- Lightly cover the rolls with plastic wrap and let them rise until doubled in size, about 30 minutes. Meanwhile, preheat your oven to 350°F.

6. Egg Wash and Bake

- In a small bowl, whisk together the egg and water until fully combined. Brush the tops of the buns with the egg wash **E**.
- Bake until golden and cooked through, 20 to 25 minutes. Enjoy warm.

Any-Greens Gratin

Serves 4 to 6

- 2 tablespoons unsalted butter, plus more for greasing the dish
- 1 tablespoon extra-virgin olive oil
- 1 medium red onion, thinly sliced
- 3 garlic cloves, thinly sliced
- 1 teaspoon kosher salt, plus more to taste
- ¼ teaspoon freshly ground black pepper, plus more to taste
- 1 canned chipotle chile in adobo, minced
- ¼ teaspoon dried thyme
- 10 packed cups roughly chopped leafy greens, tough stems removed (from 2 to 3 large bunches)
- 8 ounces smoked Gruyère cheese, grated (about 2 cups)
- 4 ounces Parmesan cheese, finely grated (about 1 cup)
- 4 teaspoons cornstarch
- 2 cups half-and-half
- ⅛ teaspoon cayenne pepper

If you know me, you know I *do not like* bread crumbs as a topping. I repeat: I DO NOT like bread crumbs. I don't want them on my mac and cheese and I do not want them on my gratins, which I know is what gives the traditional French dish its signature brown, crispy crust. Because there is no golden topping, maybe I should've called these creamed greens, oh well. I also add a little chipotle and cayenne, giving them my own twist. Plus, the top does brown nicely, even without the topping. No matter what you call them, they feel special enough for the holidays.

TINI'S TIPS

Any leafy green, from spinach and collards to Swiss chard and kale, can be used in this recipe.

A shallow, ovenproof dish works best for a gratin.

1. Get Ready

- Place a rack in the upper third of the oven and preheat to 375°F. Grease a shallow 2-quart baking dish generously with butter. Line a rimmed baking sheet with aluminum foil. Set aside.

2. Cook the Vegetables

- In a large saucepan or Dutch oven over medium-high heat, combine the butter and olive oil. When the butter is melted, add the onion and garlic and season with the salt and black pepper. Cook, stirring occasionally, until deeply browned and beginning to caramelize, 12 to 14 minutes. Add the chipotle chile and thyme and cook until fragrant, 1 to 2 minutes.
- **WILT THE GREENS:** Add the greens to the pan, a few handfuls at a time, and cook, stirring, until collapsed and dark green, about 8 minutes total (feel free to add a splash of water to the greens and cover the pan to help them break down quicker). Season with a pinch or two of salt and pepper, then transfer the mixture to the prepared baking dish and spread into an even layer.

3. Make the Cream Sauce

- In a medium bowl, toss both cheeses with the cornstarch.
- In a medium saucepan, bring the half-and-half to a simmer, then remove the pan from the heat and stir in the cayenne pepper and cheeses until melted. Pour the sauce over the greens in the baking dish. Place the dish on the prepared baking sheet.

4. Bake the Gratin

- Bake on the upper third rack until the sauce is bubbling around the edges and the cheese is golden brown in spots, 30 to 35 minutes. Let stand at least 15 minutes before serving.

SWAP IT

Any cheese that melts well can be used here. Try regular Gruyère, Gouda, sharp cheddar, or even plain ol' mozzarella.

Crispy Hasselback Potatoes

Serves 4

POTATOES

- 4 medium russet potatoes (about 2 pounds)
- ½ cup extra-virgin olive oil, plus more for drizzling
- Kosher salt and freshly ground black pepper
- 4 to 5 sprigs thyme

GARLIC-CHIVE SOUR CREAM

- ½ cup sour cream
- 1 small garlic clove, grated
- 2 tablespoons minced chives, plus more for serving
- Kosher salt and freshly ground black pepper

if you want to be fancy, dollop caviar on top!

Crispy outside and tender inside, these potatoes have a lot going for them. They are so flavorful from basting in oil it's almost like you get baked potato chips in a baked potato. They are much prettier than a baked potato, though—the thin, fanned-out slices look really cool and feel kind of fancy. You can serve them as a side or alone using whatever toppings you like on baked potatoes. Serving these with steak (page 50) and spooning a red wine reduction over them is pretty darn good. Another killer topping is my herby garlic butter from my boardwalk fries (page 173). If you do this, don't forget to sprinkle them with Parmesan.

A TINI TIP

If you don't have chopsticks to guide your cutting, you can use the flat wooden handle of a rubber spatula or even a pen or pencil.

1. Roast the Potatoes

- Place a rimmed baking sheet on a rack in the upper third of the oven and preheat to 400°F.
- Cut about ¼ inch from one long side of each potato so that it sits flat on a cutting board. Lay two chopsticks lengthwise down the sides of the potato, then, using a sharp chef's knife, cut the potato crosswise into very thin slices (about 1/16 inch), slicing until you hit the chopsticks (don't slice all the way through) **A**.
- Rub the potatoes all over with the olive oil and season with salt and pepper, getting some oil and seasoning between the layers as well.
- Carefully remove the preheated baking sheet from the oven and drizzle it lightly with olive oil. Place the potatoes, flat-side down, on the baking sheet. Roast for 30 minutes.
- **BASTE THE POTATOES:** Drizzle 2 tablespoons olive oil over each potato **B**, then season again with salt and pepper. Tuck a few sprigs of thyme in between some of the potato slices **C**. Continue roasting, occasionally spooning any accumulated oils in the pan (about every 10 minutes or so), over the tops of the potatoes (it's easiest to spoon the oils when you slightly tilt the pan to collect the oil in a corner), until the insides are very tender and the outside edges of the potato fans are crisp and lightly browned, 45 to 55 minutes more.

2. Make the Garlic-Chive Sour Cream

- In a small bowl, stir together the sour cream, garlic, and chives; season to taste with salt and pepper.
- Serve the hot potatoes dolloped with the garlic-chive sour cream. Sprinkle more chives over the top for serving.

SWAP IT

Flavored compound butters are also great to serve on these potatoes. Combine 4 tablespoons softened salted butter with any of the following combos (add more salt as needed):

- 1 teaspoon grated lemon zest + 1 teaspoon minced rosemary
- 1 teaspoon orange zest + 2 tablespoons minced parsley
- 1 mashed roasted garlic clove + 2 minced sun-dried tomatoes

Chocolate Mousse

WITH BAILEYS AND HOMEMADE WHIPPED CREAM

Serves 6

- 2½ ounces / 70g dark (70% or more) chocolate chips
- 2½ ounces / 70g semisweet (35% to 60%) chocolate chips
- 5 tablespoons / 70g unsalted butter
- ¼ cup / 58g Baileys Irish Cream
- 3 large eggs, separated (see Tini's Tips)
- 2 tablespoons / 18g powdered sugar
- ½ cup / 118g heavy cream
- 1 teaspoon /5g pure vanilla extract
- 1½ cups Vanilla Whipped Cream (page 222), for serving
- Chocolate sprinkles, for garnish (optional)

Heads up! You'll need a few bowls to make this dessert, but it's worth it!

Growing up, whenever my family had a special occasion, we always brought chocolate mousse. My mom made a microwave version that was very fudgy and pudding-like. My version is fluffier and lighter, yet still rich, silky, and creamy. It feels like a fancier pudding. I love chocolate, so I use a mix of dark and semisweet chocolates. Dark chocolate, usually 68 to 70 percent cocoa solids or more (that's the percentage you may see on the package), gives the mousse a deeper, balanced, less sweet flavor, and it seriously satisfies any chocolate craving. Adding a splash of Baileys gives this decadent dessert a boozy, celebratory kick!

TINI'S TIPS

No need to get fancy when separating eggs. I simply use my hands: Crack a cold egg into your palm held over a bowl and let the whites slide through your fingers into the bowl **A**. Transfer the yolk to a second container **B**.

Cold eggs separate easier than warm ones.

If you don't have a stand mixer, you can whisk the eggs and cream by hand—it'll just give your arms a nice little workout.

1. Melt the Chocolate and Butter

- In a microwave-safe bowl, combine the dark chocolate chips, semisweet chocolate chips, and butter. Microwave on high until the butter is melted and the chocolate is soft or melted, 60 to 90 seconds. Remove from the microwave and stir well until fully incorporated and smooth.
- Stir in the Baileys and set aside.

2. Whisk, Whisk, Whisk!

- In the bowl of a stand mixer with a whisk attachment, whisk the egg whites on medium speed until foamy, about 1 minute. Add the powdered sugar and continue to whisk on medium until stiff peaks form, about 3 minutes **C**. Transfer the whipped egg whites to a clean bowl.
- In the same stand mixer bowl you whipped the whites in, whisk the egg yolks on medium-high until the yolks are pale and increase in volume, 6 to 8 minutes. Transfer the pale yolks to a separate clean bowl and set aside. Rinse and dry the bowl.
- In the clean stand mixer bowl, whisk the heavy cream and vanilla on medium until stiff peaks form, about 3 minutes **D**.

3. Fold and Combine

- Using a rubber spatula, fold the pale egg yolks into the whipped cream. Fold no more than 10 times **E**.
- Gently fold the chocolate mixture into the egg yolk/cream mixture, again no more than 10 times **F**.
- Fold a quarter of the egg white mixture into the chocolate mixture **G**.
- Fold the chocolate mixture into the remaining egg white mixture until it is incorporated but not so much that the mixture loses its fluffiness.

4. Chill and Serve

- Divide the mousse evenly among 6 (3-ounce) serving containers **H** and chill for at least 6 hours or overnight. Right before serving, top with a dollop of whipped cream and chocolate sprinkles (if using).

A

B

C

D

E

F

G

H

Baking 101

Banana Bread

Makes one 9 × 5-inch loaf

- 1 stick (8 tablespoons / 227g) unsalted butter, melted
- ½ cup / 100g packed light brown sugar
- ½ cup / 100g granulated sugar
- 2 to 3 ripe bananas, mashed (1¼ cups)
- 2 large eggs
- ⅓ cup / 75g vanilla whole milk yogurt
- 2 teaspoons pure vanilla extract
- ½ teaspoon toasted sesame oil
- 2 cups / 280g all-purpose flour
- 1 teaspoon baking soda
- 1 teaspoon ground cinnamon
- ½ teaspoon kosher salt

Whenever I forget to eat my bananas, I make this bread. It's my take on a classic banana bread with my secret ingredient—toasted sesame oil, which enhances the vanilla flavor (if you want to know who taught me this, check out page 244). Eat this bread whenever you want. It's not just for breakfast, but I *do* like to make French toast (page 178) with it!

TINI'S TIPS

Bananas for baking are at their best when they are brown or are just turning brown, because that's when they are at their sweetest, plus they are easier to mash.

As with all quick breads, don't overmix this batter, because it can overwork the gluten, which might result in a dense bread.

1. Get ready

- Preheat the oven to 350°F. Grease a 9 × 5-inch loaf pan with butter or baking spray, then line it with parchment, leaving a 2-inch overhang on the two long sides **A**.

2. Make the Batter

- In the bowl of a stand mixer fitted with a paddle attachment, beat the butter, brown sugar, and granulated sugar on low speed until the sugars and butter are thoroughly combined, about 3 minutes. (You can also make this without a mixer. Instead, use a whisk to mix everything together.)
- Add the bananas and mix on medium until combined.
- **ADD THE WET INGREDIENTS:** Add the eggs, yogurt, vanilla, and sesame oil. On low speed, mix until everything is combined **B**.
- **ADD THE DRY INGREDIENTS:** Add the flour, baking soda, cinnamon, and salt. Mix (using a spoon or rubber spatula if mixing by hand) until just combined and all the dry ingredients are moistened **C**.

3. Bake the Bread

- Scrape the batter into the prepared pan **D** and bake until a toothpick inserted into the center of the bread comes out clean, 60 to 70 minutes. Remove the bread from the oven and let it cool in the pan for 10 to 15 minutes, then turn it out onto a baking rack to cool completely before slicing and serving.

Chewy Lemon Cookie Bars

Makes 18 bars

BARS

- 1½ sticks (12 tablespoons / 170g) unsalted butter, melted, plus more for greasing the pan
- 2 cups / 280g all-purpose flour
- 1½ teaspoons / 6g kosher salt
- ¼ teaspoon baking soda
- ¼ teaspoon baking powder
- 1 cup / 200g packed light brown sugar
- ¾ cup / 150g granulated sugar
- 1 tablespoon / 6g grated lemon zest
- 2 large eggs
- 2 tablespoons / 28g freshly squeezed lemon juice

GLAZE

- 1 cup / 113g powdered sugar
- ¼ teaspoon grated lemon zest plus ¼ cup / 56g freshly squeezed lemon juice from about 2 lemons
- Pinch of kosher salt

Whether it's for a savory dish or a sweet(ish) dessert, lemon is one of my all-time favorite flavors. I love it so much even my (and Antoine's) wedding cake was lemon. This is a simple no-machine-necessary dessert. And why a cookie bar and not just cookies? Because it's a time-saver. No need to form individual cookies, and the high ratio of sugar and fat to flour still creates a really nice chewy cookie-like texture. The lemon juice and zest keep these bars from getting too sweet, and because you can build layers of flavor with desserts, too, brown sugar adds an interesting element of complexity.

> **A TINI TIP**
>
> Leaving an overhang of parchment paper on two sides of the pan allows you to easily lift the cooled bars out for cutting.

1. Get Ready

- Put a rack in the center of the oven and preheat to 350°F. Grease a 9 × 13-inch cake pan with butter. Line the pan with parchment paper overhanging by 2 inches on the long sides of the pan.

2. Mix the Dry Ingredients

- In a medium bowl, whisk together the flour, salt, baking soda, and baking powder.

3. Make the Batter

- In a large bowl, combine the brown and granulated sugars and lemon zest. Rub the zest and sugars together between your fingers to release the oils from the zest.
- Pour in the butter and, using a rubber spatula, stir well until the mixture looks shiny, not gritty, about 45 seconds.
- One at a time, stir in the eggs until fully combined with the mixture. Stir in the lemon juice.
- Add the dry ingredients and stir and fold to combine, scraping the sides to incorporate everything until no dry ingredients are visible.

4. Bake the Bars

- Using a rubber spatula, scrape the batter into the prepared pan, smoothing the top with the spatula. Bake until golden brown and a cake tester inserted in the center comes out clean, 25 to 30 minutes.

5. Cool the Bars

- Let the bars cool in the pan for 20 minutes, then carefully run a paring knife around the edges and, using the parchment overhang, gently lift the bars out of the pan. Let the bars cool completely on a wire rack.

6. Glaze and Cut

- In a small bowl, whisk together the powdered sugar, lemon zest and juice, and salt to create a pourable glaze. Spread the glaze over the bars and let set for at least 30 minutes. Cut into 18 squares and serve.

Antoine and I love lemon desserts, even our wedding cake was lemon

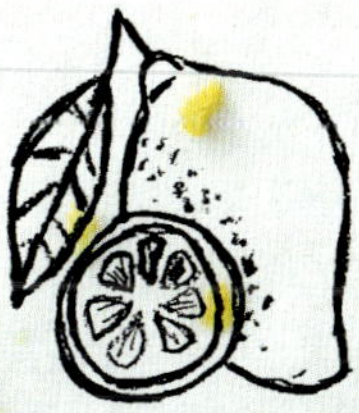

Peanut Butter Swirl Brownies

Makes 16 brownies

- 1 stick (8 tablespoons / 113g) unsalted butter, plus more for greasing the pan
- ¾ cup (about 4.5 ounces / 127g) bittersweet or semisweet chocolate chips
- 1 cup / 200g sugar
- 3 large eggs, at room temperature
- 1 teaspoon / 5g pure vanilla extract
- ½ teaspoon kosher salt
- ½ cup plus 2 tablespoons / 87g all-purpose flour
- ¼ cup / 63g creamy natural peanut butter (See Tini's Tips)

I am not a fan of nuts in desserts *at all!* In fact, nuts in any baked good make me mad. Peanut butter (only creamy, though) is another story. When mixed with chocolate it's a pretty great combination, and when swirled into these slightly cakey brownies, the nut butter makes some deliciously soft, gooey spots. The swirls make them look a little fancy, too (although they are super easy to make!).

TINI'S TIPS

Sub in sunflower butter for anyone with a nut allergy.

Natural peanut butter, the kind you have to stir, is easier to swirl in.

1. Get Ready

- Preheat the oven to 350°F. Brush an 8 × 8-inch baking pan with butter, then line it with parchment paper, leaving a 2-inch overhang on the long sides. Set aside.

2. Melt the Chocolate in a Double Boiler

- In a medium saucepan, bring 1 inch of water to a simmer over medium heat. Place the butter and chocolate chips in a large bowl and set it over the saucepan (don't let the bottom of the bowl touch the water—it could scorch the chocolate). Heat, stirring, until smooth and melted, 3 to 5 minutes (this can also be done in the microwave on high in 30-second increments, stirring after each).
- Remove the bowl from the heat.

3. Mix the Batter

- To the bowl with the melted chocolate, add the sugar and whisk vigorously until smooth and no longer grainy, about 30 seconds. Add the eggs, vanilla, and salt and whisk until thick and shiny, about 1 minute.
- Add the flour and fold with a rubber spatula until fully incorporated.
- Scrape the batter into the prepared pan and spread to the edges using an offset spatula **A**. Dollop the peanut butter over the batter **B** and, using the tip of a knife, swirl it into the batter **C**.

4. Bake, Cool, and Cut

- Bake until the top is crackly and a toothpick inserted into the center comes out with moist crumbs attached, about 25 minutes (the center may seem jiggly from the peanut butter). Let cool completely on a wire rack, then lift the brownies from the pan using the parchment overhang and cut into 16 squares.

SWAP IT

Want these brownies even more chocolaty? Stir another ½ cup of chocolate chips into the batter. Peanut butter lover? Swap those extra chocolate chips with peanut butter chips.

A

B

C

Brown Butter Chocolate Chunk Cookies

Makes about 24 cookies

- 2 sticks (16 tablespoons / 227g) unsalted butter
- 1¼ cups / 225g packed dark brown sugar
- ¼ cup / 50g granulated sugar
- 1 large egg plus 1 large egg yolk
- 2 tablespoons / 30g plain whole milk Greek yogurt
- 1 tablespoon / 15g pure vanilla extract
- ¼ teaspoon toasted sesame oil
- 2½ cups / 350g all-purpose flour
- 1 teaspoon / 5g baking soda
- ½ teaspoon kosher salt
- ¼ teaspoon ground cinnamon (optional)
- 1½ cups / 220g dark chocolate chunks

for more warming, holiday vibes, add the [illegible]

I am a cookie enthusiast. (I love *all* kinds!) I like chewy ones, thin and crispy ones—I even love the sugar cookies at Walmart with the thick frosting. When it comes to chocolate chip cookies, I go with a classic—very soft and lots of chocolate (chunks in this case). I brown the butter for this version, which makes it feel a little special, adding a deeper flavor to the dough. And there's my special ingredient, which I learned from Reenie Karim, so it's actually *her* special ingredient: toasted sesame oil. Just a few drops enhance the vanilla and the nuttiness of the brown butter.

A TINI TIP

Use a stainless or light-colored pan when making brown butter so you can see the change in color.

1. Make the Brown Butter

- In a large, light-colored skillet or small pot over medium heat, melt the butter **A**. Once it's melted, swirl the pan occasionally, until the butter is golden and beginning to smell nutty, 5 to 7 minutes **B**. When you see the milk solids settling to the bottom of the pan and starting to turn dark, remove the pan from the heat and set aside to cool **C**.

2. Make the Dough

- In the bowl of a stand mixer fitted with a paddle attachment, mix the brown sugar, granulated sugar, egg plus egg yolk, Greek yogurt, vanilla, and sesame oil on medium speed until combined, about 1 minute (or you can whisk by hand).
- Add the cooled brown butter, scraping in all the browned bits, and mix again until thoroughly combined.
- Add the flour, baking soda, salt, and cinnamon (if using). Mix on low (or use a wooden spoon) until no dry ingredients are visible.
- Sprinkle in the chocolate chunks and mix again.

3. Form the Cookies and Chill

- Using a tablespoon measure, scoop up a rounded spoonful and form a ball about the size of a walnut (about 42g each) and place on a large plate or container that will fit in your fridge. Repeat this with all the dough to make 24 cookies (the dough balls can be close together; they just need to chill). Place the dough balls in your fridge and chill for 30 minutes. If you plan on baking them later, store them in an airtight container.

4. Bake the Cookies

- When you're ready to bake the cookies, arrange two oven racks in the upper and lower thirds of the oven and preheat to 350°F. Line two baking sheets with parchment paper.
- Place the chilled dough balls about 2 inches apart on the prepared baking sheets. (If they don't all fit, work in batches.)
- Bake until just set, 10 minutes. You won't see much change in color; this timing will yield a soft yet tiny-bit-chewy cookie.
- Remove from the oven and let the cookies cool on the pan for at least 5 minutes before transferring them to a wire rack to cool completely. Repeat the baking process with any remaining dough balls if they didn't all fit on the baking sheets.

A

B

C

← this is what brown butter is supposed to look like. don't go any darker than this. if it's black, it's burnt.

A Very Berry Crisp

Serves 6 to 8

Baking spray or softened butter for greasing the pan

FILLING

- 4½ cups / 630g fresh or frozen mixed berries such as blackberries, blueberries, and raspberries
- ½ cup / 100g granulated sugar
- 3 tablespoons / 26g all-purpose flour
- 1½ teaspoons freshly squeezed lemon juice
- 1½ teaspoons orange juice
- 1½ teaspoons / 8g pure vanilla extract
- ¾ teaspoon ground cinnamon
- ¼ teaspoon kosher salt

TOPPING

- ¾ cup / 150g packed light brown sugar
- ¾ cup / 75g old-fashioned rolled oats
- ½ cup / 70g all-purpose flour
- 1 teaspoon / 2g ground cinnamon
- ½ teaspoon baking powder
- 1½ teaspoons grated lemon zest
- 1½ teaspoons orange zest
- ¼ teaspoon kosher salt
- Pinch of ground nutmeg
- 5 tablespoons / 70g cold unsalted butter, cut into small cubes

SERVING

No-Churn Vanilla Bean Ice Cream (page 257) or store-bought

I am a cinnamon girl and add it to everything I can, even my berry crisp. Along with some orange zest and nutmeg, the spices make the juicy berries and golden, crunchy oats taste cozy and warm. You might even think this crisp tastes holiday-ish, which makes sense because I don't just make crisps in summer, when berries are fresh. I love using frozen berries (also much easier on your budget!) and make this berry dessert year-round. Serving it with a big scoop of vanilla ice cream on top is a must.

1. Get Ready

- Preheat the oven to 375°F. Generously grease an 8 × 8-inch baking dish with baking spray or butter.

2. Make the Filling

- In a large bowl, stir together the berries, granulated sugar, flour, lemon juice, orange juice, vanilla, cinnamon, and salt until thoroughly combined.
- Pour the mixture evenly into the prepared baking dish.

3. Make the Topping

- In a medium bowl, whisk together the brown sugar, oats, flour, cinnamon, baking powder, lemon zest, orange zest, salt, and nutmeg.
- Scatter the butter cubes on top of the mixture. Using your fingers, a pastry blender, or two knives, work the butter into the dry mixture until it is well combined and no longer dry. Sprinkle over the berry mixture.

4. Bake the Crisp

- Bake until the berries are bubbling and the topping is golden brown, 30 to 40 minutes. Serve warm, topped with vanilla ice cream.

Bourbon Peach Cobbler

Serves 8 to 10

FILLING

- 2 tablespoons / 28g unsalted butter
- 8 peaches (2½ to 3 pounds / 1.13kg to 1.4kg)
- ½ cup / 135g packed light brown sugar
- 3 tablespoons bourbon
- 1 tablespoon / 9g all-purpose flour
- 2 teaspoons / 10g pure vanilla extract
- 2 teaspoons / 4g ground cinnamon
- ⅛ teaspoon ground nutmeg
- Pinch of ground cloves
- Pinch of kosher salt

TOPPING

- 1 cup / 140g all-purpose flour
- ¾ cup / 150g granulated sugar
- 1 teaspoon / 4g baking powder
- ½ teaspoon kosher salt
- 1 stick (½ cup / 113g) unsalted butter, melted
- 1 egg, at room temperature
- ½ teaspoon pure vanilla extract

SERVING

No-Churn Maple Ice Cream (page 257) or your favorite ice cream

When I was growing up, there was a family grocery store nearby that sold fried chicken with all the sides, including my favorites, mac and cheese and mashed potatoes. For dessert, apple cobbler was always on the menu. That childhood memory inspired me to bake up my own cobbler. To me, peaches and bourbon are a natural combo, so I started there. The fruit, mixed with sugar and spices, turns all sweet and soft when baked under dollops of a golden, buttery crust that isn't quite a biscuit, but not too cakey either. It's light, sweet, and sure to satisfy any cobbler cravings. As with most warm fruit desserts, ice cream is a must.

1. Get Ready

- Preheat the oven to 375°F.
- Put the butter in a 9 × 13-inch dish or pan and put it in the oven to melt, about 5 minutes. Remove the dish from the oven, tilt the pan around to coat the bottom and sides with the butter, and set aside.

2. Blanch the Peaches

- Bring a pot of water to a boil. Fill a large bowl with ice and water.
- Cut a small x in the flower side (which is the bottom or non-stem side) of each peach **A**. Add the peaches to the boiling water and cook briefly, just until the skin starts to peel back from the flesh, 1 to 2 minutes **B**. Transfer the peaches to the ice bath and let them cool to the touch **C**.
- Remove the peaches from the ice bath and peel **D**. Cut them into ¼-inch-thick slices and place them in a large bowl. Add the brown sugar, bourbon, flour, vanilla, cinnamon, nutmeg, cloves, and salt and stir to combine. Spoon into the prepared pan in an even layer and bake for 15 minutes.

3. Make the Topping

- In a medium bowl, stir together the flour, granulated sugar, baking powder, and salt until combined. Add the butter, egg, and vanilla and stir until smooth.
- Remove the peaches from the oven. Drop spoonfuls of the batter evenly over the peaches (there can be a few bare spots since the topping spreads).

4. Bake and Serve

- Bake until the peaches are bubbly and the topping is golden brown and bounces back when pressed with your finger, 15 to 20 minutes. Serve warm with ice cream.

don't even think about serving this cobbler without ice cream!

A
B
C
D

5 Level Up

GG's Favorite Apple Pie

Makes one 9-inch pie

CRUST

- 2½ cups / 350g all-purpose flour, plus more for rolling
- 1 tablespoon granulated sugar
- 1 teaspoon kosher salt
- 2 sticks (16 tablespoons / 227g) cold unsalted butter, cubed
- 7 to 8 tablespoons ice-cold water

FILLING

- 3 pounds / 1.4kg Granny Smith apples (7 to 8 medium), peeled, halved, cored, and cut into ¼-inch-thick wedges (about 6 cups)
- ½ cup / 100g granulated sugar
- ½ cup / 100g packed light brown sugar
- ¼ cup / 35g all-purpose flour
- 4 teaspoons freshly squeezed lemon juice or cider vinegar
- 2 teaspoons / 4g ground cinnamon
- 1 teaspoon / 5g pure vanilla extract
- ¾ teaspoon kosher salt
- ¼ teaspoon freshly grated nutmeg
- 2 tablespoons / 28g unsalted butter, cut into small cubes

EGG WASH

- 1 large egg
- 1 tablespoon water
- Granulated sugar, for sprinkling

SERVING

No-Churn Vanilla Bean Ice Cream (page 257)

GG was my grandmother, and she wasn't the happiest old lady. She didn't give many compliments, but she *did* love my mom's pie. This recipe, which originated from my mom, is a great example of how recipes change through generations. I've added my own tweaks to this family recipe, as people do. Instead of Crisco in the crust, I use all butter, and I thicken up the filling with some flour, whereas my mom prefers a runnier filling. Food is personal, and you should feel free to make things your own, too. Switch up the filling, swap out spices, experiment with different crusts. Cooking is an expression of creativity, and recipes are definitely a way I express mine.

TINI'S TIPS

Take a shortcut by making the pie dough in the food processor. Start by pulsing together the flour, sugar, and salt to combine, then add the butter and pulse about 10 times, just until the butter is the size of peas. From there, drizzle in the water and continue to pulse until the mixture is crumbly and holds together when pressed between your fingertips. This technique keeps the butter cold, since you aren't using the heat of your hands, which will create an even flakier crust.

If you don't have a rolling pin, use a wine bottle!

1. Make the Crust

- **CUT THE FAT INTO THE FLOUR:** In a large bowl, combine the flour, granulated sugar, and salt. Add the butter and, using two forks (or a pastry cutter if you have one), toss the butter with the flour to coat the cubes. Next, press down on the butter repeatedly to form smaller pieces, about the size of flattened peas **A**. Drizzle the water over the mixture and toss with the forks, pressing the fat into the flour and evenly incorporating the liquid until a shaggy dough comes together.
- Transfer the dough to a clean work surface and knead it a few times to bring it together **B**. Divide the dough in half, wrap each half in plastic, and press into a flat disk. Refrigerate until firm, at least 2 hours and up to 2 days.

2. Make the Filling

- **MACERATE THE FRUIT:** In a large bowl, toss the apples with the granulated and brown sugars, flour, lemon juice, cinnamon, vanilla, salt, and nutmeg until well coated. Let stand at room temperature for 30 minutes, tossing occasionally, until the fruit has released some of its juices.

3. Roll Out the Crust

- Place a rack in the lower third of the oven and preheat to 400°F. Place a foil-lined baking sheet on the rack to heat while you roll out the crusts.

recipe continues ▸▸

- Transfer 1 crust to a lightly floured work surface. Using a rolling pin, roll it into a 12-inch round **C**, lifting and rotating the dough and adding another dusting of flour as needed to keep it from sticking. Lift the dough and place it over a 9-inch pie plate, gently pressing it into the edges **D**. Using a pair of scissors, trim the excess dough from around the rim, leaving a 1-inch overhang.
- Roll out the second crust to a 12-inch round.

4. Assemble the Pie

- Spoon the apples into the crust **E**, then drizzle any accumulated juices over the top and dot with the butter. Lay the second pie crust over the top of the fruit **F**, then fold the top crust under the bottom overhang, crimping to seal **G**.
- In a small bowl, whisk the egg with the water. Brush evenly over the top crust, then sprinkle generously with more sugar. Using a small paring knife, cut a few 1-inch slits in the center of the dough (this will help trapped steam escape during baking).
- Carefully remove the baking sheet from the oven and set the pie on it.

5. Bake the Pie and Serve

- Return the baking sheet to the oven and bake until the crust is golden brown on top and the filling bubbles slightly, 55 to 65 minutes (if the top is browning too quickly, tent the top loosely with foil).
- Let the pie cool for at least 4 hours, or even overnight, on the baking sheet before slicing and serving with vanilla ice cream.

SWAP IT

You can make a lattice topping using the same top crust. Once the crust is rolled out, use a pizza wheel or sharp knife to cut the dough into 1½-inch-long strips. Lay half of them going one way across the top of the pie, then lift half of them and lay the other strips going the other way, weaving them together. This creates natural air pockets, so there is no need to cut slits in the top crust.

Other simple ways to crimp the pie dough: Use the tines of a fork to make indents all around the edge, or work your way around the edge with an upside-down spoon, making scalloped markings all around.

Level Up

Antoine's Strawberry Birthday Cake

Serves 10 to 12

CAKE

- 2 tablespoons unsalted butter, melted, plus 2 sticks (16 tablespoons) / 227g unsalted butter, softened
- 2½ cups / 350g all-purpose flour
- 2 cups / 400g granulated sugar
- 1½ teaspoons / 5g kosher salt
- 1½ teaspoons / 6g baking powder
- ½ teaspoon / 4g baking soda
- 4 large eggs, at room temperature
- ¾ cup / 160g sour cream, at room temperature
- 1 tablespoon / 15g vanilla bean paste or extract

FROSTING

- 2 (8-ounce) packages / 452g cream cheese, softened
- 2 sticks (16 tablespoons) / 227g unsalted butter, softened
- 2½ cups / 270g powdered sugar
- 2 teaspoons / 10g vanilla bean paste or extract
- Kosher salt
- 6 to 8 tablespoons / about 48g freeze-dried strawberry powder (see Tini's Tips)

FILLING AND TOPPING

- 1 pound fresh strawberries

Making food for others is my love language, so when it's my husband's birthday, I like to surprise him with a cake he'll love (although he always tells me *not* to do too much!). Antoine loves fruit, so I've loaded this cake, dedicated to him, with strawberries. There are sliced berries between each of the four layers, along with a smooth cream cheese frosting that is flavored with freeze-dried strawberry powder. Using powder instead of a puree or jam gives the frosting a concentrated flavor when the amount of puree or jam needed to give the same amount of flavor could make a frosting break or become runny. The cake layers themselves are light and vanilla-y—exactly what you want a birthday cake to be.

TINI'S TIPS

It may sound extra, but I grease my pans, then put in parchment and grease that, too. The first round helps the parchment "stick" and not curl up in the pan. Greasing the parchment is not always 100 percent necessary, but it ensures that the cake does not stick. If you prefer, you may use baking spray instead of butter for greasing.

If your cakes form a "dome" when baking, use a serrated knife to trim the tops so that they lie flat—it will make layering and frosting much easier.

If you can't find freeze-dried strawberry powder in the store, it is easily available online, or you can finely grind 1.7 ounces freeze-dried strawberries in a blender, food processor, or a spice/coffee grinder to yield 6 to 8 tablespoons of powder.

For easy cake assembly, make the cakes the day before serving, wrap them in plastic, and chill overnight. Cold cakes are easier to cut. The frosting may also be made the day before. Stir well before using.

reverse creaming (adding the butter directly to the dry ingredients) makes the cake extra tender

1. Get Ready

- Place a rack in the middle of the oven and preheat to 350°F. Brush the bottom and sides of two 8-inch round cake pans generously with the melted butter. Line the bottoms with parchment rounds and brush the parchment with butter, too. Set aside.

2. Make the Cake Batter

- REVERSE CREAM: In the bowl of a stand mixer fitted with the paddle attachment, combine the flour, granulated sugar, salt, baking powder, and baking soda. With the mixer on low speed, add the 2 sticks of softened butter, a few tablespoons at a time, and mix until the batter is crumbly and the butter is evenly distributed, about 3 minutes.
- Add the eggs, sour cream, and vanilla to the bowl and mix on low until combined, scraping down the sides of the bowl as you go. Increase the speed to medium and beat until light and fluffy, about 3 minutes.

3. Bake the Cakes

- Divide the batter between the prepared cake pans, spreading it to the edges. Bake, rotating the pans halfway through, until golden brown on top and a toothpick inserted into the center comes out clean, about 35 minutes.
- Let the cakes cool for 20 minutes, then invert them onto a wire rack to cool completely. Remove and discard the parchment paper.

4. Make the Frosting

- In a clean stand mixer bowl with a clean paddle attachment, beat the cream cheese, butter, powdered sugar, vanilla, and a pinch of salt on medium speed until smooth and fluffy, 2 to 3 minutes. Add the strawberry powder and mix until fully incorporated.

5. Hull and Slice the Berries

- Set aside 8 to 10 of the prettiest strawberries, then hull the remaining berries (trim the tops) and cut them into ¼-inch-thick slices.

recipe continues ▸▸

6. Assemble the Cake

- Level the cakes if needed **A** (see Tini's Tips). Place one cake on a cutting board. Using a serrated knife, slice the cake in half horizontally. Repeat with the second cake to create four layers.
- Place one cake layer, cut-side up, on a cake plate or serving platter **B**. Spoon a generous ½ cup of frosting on top, and using an offset spatula, spread it to the edges **C**. Top with an even layer of sliced strawberries **D**. Place another cake layer on top **E**, then add another generous ½ cup of frosting and another layer of sliced strawberries. Repeat with another cake layer, generous ½ cup of frosting and more sliced strawberries. Place the final cake layer on top, cut-side down **F**. Press down gently to secure the layers together.
- Using an offset spatula, spread the remaining frosting evenly over the top and sides of the cake to cover **G**. Top with the reserved strawberries **H**. Refrigerate until you are ready to serve.

SWAP IT

Other fruits can be used instead of both the fresh and freeze-dried strawberries—try blueberries, mango, raspberries, pineapple, or whatever else looks good.

Between the layers, you can add a bit of strawberry compote (page 186) instead of fresh strawberries.

Love you Antoine ♡

STAINLESS

No-Churn Vanilla Bean Ice Cream

Makes about 1 quart

- 2 cups heavy cream
- 14 ounces sweetened condensed milk
- 1 tablespoon vanilla bean paste
- Kosher salt

I am in love with this ice cream because it's so easy to make. It's basically three ingredients you whip and freeze. A stand or electric mixer is very helpful for making this, but you can whip it by hand, too (I won't lie, though, a mixer is SO much easier). I learned from someone who owns an ice cream shop in L.A. how important it is to freeze your bowl first. It keeps the fat in the cream cold, which makes it trap air more effectively when whipping and prevents graininess for a smoother ice cream. Use this vanilla recipe as your base, and once you get the hang of making it, add your own mix-ins.

A TINI TIP

I like to see the vanilla bean specks in my ice cream, so I use vanilla bean paste. You can easily sub in the same amount of vanilla extract.

1. Get Ready

- Chill the bowl and whisk attachment of your stand mixer (or a medium bowl if you are whisking by hand), at least 10 minutes. (Use your freezer if they can fit.)
- Line an entire 9 × 5-inch loaf pan with one large piece of parchment paper; the edges should just reach, or extend over, the top of all four sides of the pan **A**.

2. Whisk

- Pour the cream into the chilled bowl and attach to the stand mixer along with the chilled whisk attachment. Whisk the cream on medium-high speed until it just begins to thicken and soft peaks form (one that falls over easily, see below), 3 to 4 minutes (if you do this by hand, it will just take longer) **B**.

3. Sweeten the Mixture

- Add the condensed milk, vanilla, and a small pinch of salt and whisk on medium until everything is combined and the mixture once again forms soft peaks, 2 to 3 minutes.

4. Freeze the Ice Cream

- Using a rubber spatula, transfer the mixture to the prepared pan and evenly smooth the top **C**.
- Cover with plastic wrap and freeze the mixture until it's firm to the touch, 4 to 6 hours.

SWAP IT

For maple syrup ice cream, add ½ cup maple syrup at the same time you add the condensed milk.

Before the mixture goes into the pan, fold in crushed Oreos for homemade cookies and cream ice cream, pieces of raw chocolate chip cookie dough (page 244), or any other candy or cookie you like.

check out those vanilla bean specks

A

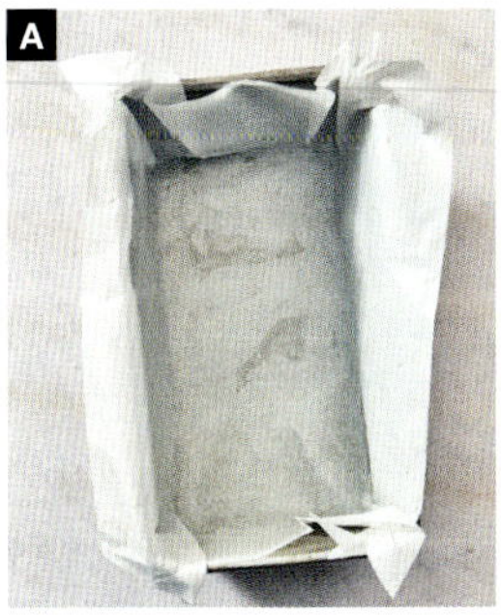

B

C

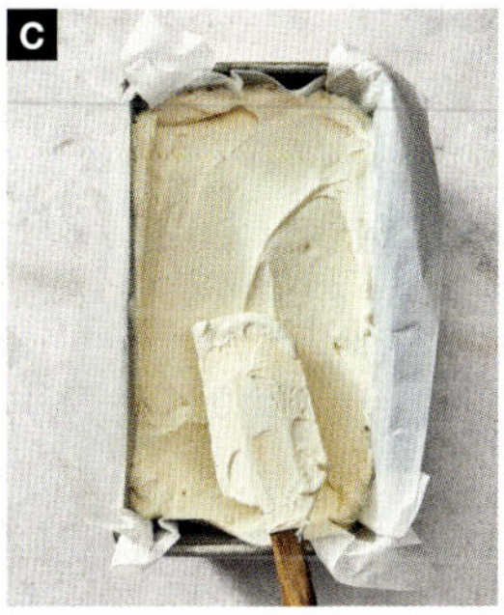

WHIP FOR THE WIN

Whipping is a common baking term, and you'll see many of my recipes use this technique to incorporate air into things like heavy cream or egg whites, which creates peaks. One that falls over slightly is called a soft peak, one that just stands up and falls a tiny bit is a medium peak. A firm peak stands straight up, but this can start to curdle and clump. Medium peaks are the best consistency for piping and holding their shape for whipped cream topping.

Level Up

Homemade Brioche Buns

Makes 6 buns

- ½ cup whole milk / 120g, warm (like bathwater, 100°F to 115°F)
- 1 tablespoon / 9g active dry yeast
- 1 tablespoon / 20g sugar
- 2½ cups / 350g all-purpose flour, plus more for the work surface
- 1 teaspoon / 3g kosher salt
- 2 large eggs, at room temperature, plus 1 egg for the wash
- ½ stick (4 tablespoons / 56g) unsalted butter, softened and cut into small pieces
- Neutral oil, for greasing the bowl
- 1 tablespoon water
- Sesame seeds, for sprinkling

Before I was known for my mac and cheese (page 89), I was known online as the "peanut butter and jelly girl" for making a completely homemade PB&J. I made every part: the bread, peanut butter, and jam. I'd make everything myself if I had the time (and energy!). For those times when I do, brioche buns are worth every ounce of effort. They turn out so beautifully golden and round, fluffy, and light—anyone who doesn't see you make them may find it hard to believe they are homemade.

TINI'S TIPS

Proofing the yeast—whisking it into the warm milk and letting it stand to see if it bubbles or foams—lets you know if your yeast is active (the yeast feeds on the sugars in the milk). If it doesn't foam, you'll have to get some new yeast!

You can easily make the dough without a mixer. Knead in the butter pieces, a few at a time, then continue to knead to build the gluten, 10 to 15 minutes. When you press the dough ball with your finger and the dough springs back, you'll know it's ready for the next step.

1. Proof the Yeast

- In the bowl of a stand mixer, pour in the milk and whisk in the yeast and sugar. Let stand for 5 minutes, until very foamy.

2. Make the Dough

- Add the flour and salt and stir to combine. Crack 2 eggs into the bowl. Attach the bowl to the mixer fitted with a dough hook and combine on medium speed.
- Add the butter, a couple of pieces at a time, until it's incorporated. The dough will be sticky, then, as the mixer kneads it, it will become smooth and form a ball, pulling away from the sides of the bowl, 8 to 10 minutes.

3. Proof the Dough

- Oil a large bowl then add the dough, turning to coat **A**. Cover with plastic wrap and set in a warm place, such as on a radiator or under a lightbulb, to rise until doubled in size, about 1½ hours **B**.

4. Shape and Rise Again

- Sprinkle your work surface with flour, then divide the dough into 6 pieces.
- Take one of the dough pieces and form a ball by pinching it and then folding the edges under. Place the dough ball on your work surface under a cupped hand and use the pressure of your palm to roll the dough ball back and forth between your thumb and your pinky finger to create a smooth ball **C**.
- Place the ball on a parchment-lined baking sheet and press gently to form a 3-inch round.
- Repeat with the remaining pieces of dough, evenly spacing them at least 2 inches apart on the baking sheet.
- Lightly cover the baking sheet with plastic wrap and let rise in a warm spot again until doubled in size, about 30 minutes.

5. Finish and Bake

- Meanwhile, preheat the oven to 350°F.
- In a small bowl, whisk the remaining 1 egg with the water and brush the tops of the buns. Sprinkle with sesame seeds. Bake until golden and cooked through, 20 to 25 minutes. Let cool before serving.

SWAP IT

Make it everything-style: Replace the sesame seeds with your own everything bagel mix (combine 1 tablespoon each poppy seeds, sesame seeds, granulated garlic, granulated onion, and flaky sea salt).

*don't skip the egg wash,
that's what makes these buns
so shiny and pretty*

Acknowledgments

Thank you to everyone who helped me produce this cookbook and make it what it is.

My supporters for requesting this book and encouraging me to write it, and especially for using my recipes for feeding your family and for your holiday celebrations. It means the world.

And extra love and thanks to my family: Arya, Baby L, Antoine, my mom and dad, my brothers This and Tage, and Leia and Chef.

A shout-out to my team at UTA: Katie Baral, Brandi Bowles, Jordyn Palos, Malcolm Roberson, and Max Stubblefield.

Thanks to everyone on my creative team: Jenn Sit, Stephanie Huntwork, Elaine Hennig, Rebecca Ffrench, Caitlin Bensel, Sara Baurley, Torie Cox, Kelly Peacock, and Christine Keely, and Katie Jacoby for doing my hair and makeup.

And my culinary team: Sarah Carey, Camilla Ffrench, Fríða Kristinsdóttir, Laura Manzano, Hannah Packman, Allison Radecki, Eric Salazar, and Riley Wofford.

Thank you to Chef Gordon Ramsay, Chef Richard Blais, and Chef Nyesha Arrington for being my mentors and culinary inspiration.

Index

Note: Page references in *italics* indicate photographs.

C

T

V

W

CLARKSON POTTER/PUBLISHERS
An imprint of the Crown Publishing Group
A division of Penguin Random House LLC
1745 Broadway
New York, NY 10019
clarksonpotter.com
penguinrandomhouse.com

Library of Congress Cataloging-in-Publication Data

Names: Younger, Tini author | Bensel, Caitlin photographer
Title: Today we are cooking: recipes that teach you to think like a chef / Tini Younger; photographs by Caitlin Bensel.
Description: First edition. | New York : Clarkson Potter/Publishers, [2026] | Includes index.
Identifiers: LCCN 2025050921 (print) | LCCN 2025050922 (ebook) | ISBN 9798217035410 hardcover | ISBN 9798217035427 ebook
Subjects: LCSH: Comfort food | LCGFT: Cookbooks
Classification: LCC TX714 .Y695 2026 (print) | LCC TX714 (ebook) | DDC 641.5—dc23/eng/20260409
LC record available at https://lccn.loc.gov/2025050921
LC ebook record available at https://lccn.loc.gov/2025050922

ISBN 979-8-217-03541-0
Signed edition ISBN 979-8-217-03720-9
Ebook ISBN 979-8-217-03542-7

Editor: Jennifer Sit
Editorial assistant: Elaine Hennig
Designer: Stephanie Huntwork
Production designer: Jan Derevjanik
Production editor: Abby Oladipo
Production: Jessica Heim
Compositor: Merri Ann Morrell
Food stylist: Torie Cox
Food stylist assistant: Kelly Peacock
Prop stylist: Christine Keely
Photo assistant: Sara Baurley
Editorial collaborator: Rebecca Miller Ffrench
Copyeditor: Alison Kerr Miller
Proofreaders: Jude Grant, Penelope Haynes, Sarah Rutledge, Sigi Nacson, and Eldes Tran
Indexer: Elizabeth Parson
Publicists: David Hawk and Natalie Yera-Campbell
Marketer: Stephanie Davis

Manufactured in China

10 9 8 7 6 5 4 3 2 1

First Edition

The authorized representative in the EU for product safety and compliance is Penguin Random House Ireland, Morrison Chambers, 32 Nassau Street, Dublin D02 YH68, Ireland, https://eu-contact.penguin.ie.